Second Edition

APPROACHES TO
CRIMINAL
JUSTICE
TRAINING

By
John Fay

Carl Vinson Institute of Government
The University of Georgia

Approaches to Criminal Justice Training, Second Edition

Editor: Emily Honigberg
Design and production: Reid McCallister
Typesetting: Debra Peters, Anne Huddleston
Proofreading: Dorothy Paul, Charlotte Eberhard

Library of Congress Cataloging-in-Publication Data
Fay, John
   Approaches to criminal justice training.

   Bibliography: p.
   Includes index.
   1. Criminal justice, Administration of—Study and teaching—Handbooks, manuals, etc. 2. Criminal justice personnel—Training of—Handbooks, manuals, etc. 3. Lesson planning—Handbooks, manuals, etc. I. Title.
HV6024.F38 1988   364'.07   88-5448
ISBN 0-89854-128-X

Foreword

When *Approaches to Criminal Justice Training* was first published in 1979, criminal justice professionals were strongly advocating that substantial improvements be made in preparing people to perform jobs in the criminal justice system, particularly in law enforcement and corrections. We have seen considerable progress since then, including new academies, updated courses, and new personnel in the instructor ranks. Still, improvement in how training is conducted has been slow in coming.

Today, the reality of civil liability litigation reinforces—and indeed makes more urgent—the need to address the weak links in criminal justice training. As does the first edition, this book provides practical suggestions, based on sound theory, for improving teaching effectiveness. The author describes instructional approaches and tells how to translate real criminal justice job tasks into meaningful "hands-on" instruction. This second edition goes further, however, adding three new chapters on curriculum development, testing, and civil liability for negligent training.

The curriculum development chapter presents the mechanics of creating a curriculum and how job task analysis can assist in that process. The curriculum as a control tool for management is also discussed. The new chapter on testing, complementary to the one on practical exercises, examines the various techniques for measuring acquired knowledge and skill through written examinations. Finally, the civil liability chapter identifies the major teaching pitfalls that lead to lawsuits and provides some good methods for preventing and defending against them.

The author of this publication is John Fay, former police officer, investigator, instructor, and training administrator. Mr. Fay has served as director of the National Crime Prevention Institute and as chief of training standards for the Georgia Peace Officer Standards and Training Council. In 1980, he left law enforcement to seek a second career in the corporate world, where he is presently manager of security for the world's third largest oil company.

The Vinson Institute is pleased to publish this new second edition, written especially to meet the needs of criminal justice instructor-training programs.

May 1988
Melvin B. Hill, Jr.
Director
Carl Vinson Institute of Government

Contents

PART I

INSTRUCTION
THEORIES, METHODS, AND TECHNIQUES

HOW DOES LEARNING REALLY OCCUR?

Traditional Ideas about Learning • Scientific Theories of Learning
• A Contemporary Theory of Learning • Conclusion

We may not be conscious of it, but each of us has his or her own pet theories about teaching and how people learn. We like to think that our personal teaching styles firmly rest on tried and true principles; at the same time we tend to be blind to their defects.

TRADITIONAL IDEAS ABOUT LEARNING

Many criminal justice instructors make the mistake of taking learning for granted; that is, they assume that learning occurs when tradition-al methods are applied. Because such methods are so much a part of our up-bringing, it seems blasphemous to question them. Let's look at some of the more common traditional theories.

•Rewards and Punishments Theory

This theory contends that humans have a natural tendency to engage in activities they find enjoyable. People will repeat behavior that has rewarding consequences and will avoid behavior that has unpleasant consequences. Of course, an instructor and his students may fre-quently hold differing ideas about what is and is not a reward.[1]

In recent years it has become fashionable to employ rewards, but teaching still tends to be punishment-oriented. Satisfactory student performance, considered normal, rarely rates the instructor's atten-tion. On the other hand, a student mistake often evokes criticism. An instructor may try to justify criticism offered for the good of the learner. Most people, however, develop negative feelings when they are criticized, and negative feelings obstruct learning.

Using rewards and punishments together can produce learning results, but not always the desired ones. A student may learn blind obedience to authority, or he may develop such an intense dislike of a teacher that his learning progress is severely inhibited. At least one study has found that teachers who are autocratic and domineering have difficulty in leading their students toward desired goals.[2] Repeated application of rewards and punishments also makes the instructor, instead of the student, the central figure in the learning process. Those who embrace the theory of rewards and punishments presume that learning only takes place when rewards and punishments are administered.

Although rewards and punishments can be effective methods of controlling students, the goal of teaching goes beyond classroom control. What really matters is the later behavior of students, particularly as that behavior relates to job performance. Conformity to standards in the training environment does not guarantee conformity to standards in a job environment.

Another problem with the rewards and punishments method is that students respond in different and sometimes unpredictable ways. Reproof for one student may be easily accepted, but for another student it may be intolerable. The teacher may need to vary his approach according to variances in student personalities —a tricky task, for students quickly sense when rewards and punishments are not evenly meted out.

If this theory is marred by so many flaws, why is it so popular? One reason is that sometimes it works, even though the character of the learning is more in the nature of conformity and is typically transient. A more subtle reason is that instructors cling to this theory to avoid facing the complexity of the learning process, demanding as it does the application of numerous concepts and techniques. How much easier it is to believe in simple solutions to complicated learning problems!

●Nothing Is Forgotten Theory

Some teachers seem to have a naive faith in the permanence of learning. An instructor may be surprised when he discovers that a student has forgotten something taught to him last week or last month. Although it is true that humans learn facts, they do so by fitting those facts into their previous experiences.[3] The student will remember information that relates to his experience; the rest is quickly forgotten.

There is nothing surprising about the forgetting that occurs after formal classroom learning. The average student is able to retain useless bits of information for a short period of time in order to pass a test, but after the test the useless information leaves the student's memory. What usually happens is that a student will learn a piece of information not once but several times and also forget it several times. If the student has not discovered how to apply the information for valuable, self-satisfying purposes, he will probably not retain it.

Even when put into practice, information may be lost under some conditions. There must be consistent assurance that what was learned has functional value. An on-the job skill developed through formal training, for example, can deteriorate if the skill seems to have little value to the job. An illustration in point is the supervisor who advises the recent graduate to forget what he has learned in the academy because now he is going to see "how it really is in the field."

●Learning through Repetition Theory

"The things learned best are the things repeated most often," is a central concept of the theory that repetition is a good way to get students to learn. However, experiments have shown that when repetition is used to teach, a sharp decline in remembering occurs immediately after the practice. An explanation for this quick loss of information is that it is not being used in some functional way.

Why is long-term retention not achieved by repeated drill? The answer is that information needs to be presented in ways that encourage students to associate it with past experiences. A sense of self-involvement with the information allows the students to establish personal associations. Information that is personally important and usable takes on more significance than information acquired through mere practice and drill.

While there may be some validity to the notion that information learned through repetition will be retained, this holds true only to the extent that the information has some kind of personal value.

We all tend to remember information acquired long ago which has no practical value to our everyday living. We are able to recall the information, useless as it may be, because somehow it *seems* important. It may be an old telephone number or some lines of poetry, not valuable in the ordinary sense but personally significant nonetheless.

●Teaching by Telling Theory

There is a popular assumption that knowledge exists apart from learning, and somehow the knowledge has to be brought inside the individual. This theory embraces the idea that the brain is like a water vessel waiting to be filled. Instruction is the process of filling the vessel with facts. The more facts that are poured in, the more the student has learned. This idea is often fostered when we discover that a student has actually gained new knowledge from attending a lecture or reading a book. However, such learning experiences do not merely result from what was said during the lecture or what was printed in a book. Learning depends on a number of factors, such as student interest, student involvement, instructional method, student practice, and relevancy of the information to the student as a person.

Teaching by telling is in fact one of the more difficult methods for establishing long-term retention. Our everyday experiences should prove to us that there is very little change in human behavior when people are merely told something. Teenagers, for example, are more likely to be influenced by what their friends do than what their parents say.

●The Theory First Theory

Proponents of this approach say that learning should move from the general to the particular. A person should understand the theory of what he is about to do before he actually tries it. Only after the learner has mastered broad concepts and principles is he allowed to practice specific skills. In this learning through deduction approach, theoretical principles can modify actual experience, but the experience can have no effect on the principles.

Instructors who work from this premise are likely to be subject matter specialists who stand apart from the mainstream of experience. They believe that the purpose of education or training is to "qualify" people. The process of qualification takes on a dimension of its own quite apart from the job itself. The training process is likely to be concerned more with philosophy and form than with practical outcomes. Less emphasis is given to developing ordinary job abilities.

Research has shown, however, that learning is more effective when the student is permitted to derive or develop his own conclusion from real-life situations. In other words, experience should precede the development of theory. When experience is used to develop theory, the student forms generalizations. The ability to apply what has been learned in a previous situation is commonly called "transfer of learning."[4]

●Learning Transfers Automatically Theory

A fundamental objective of training is to prepare a person to perform a particular job. The criminal justice trainer intends that what he teaches in the classroom will transfer to activities performed by the learner when he is on the job; he expects that students are changed by their training experiences in such a way that their later behavior on the job will be productive and intelligent.

The assumption that skills and knowledge learned through training should transfer to the job environment becomes twisted into the assumption that it happens automatically. Unfortunately, it does not.

The failure to transfer to real-life situations information that is taught in the classroom results partly because instructors are unaware that students need help in making mental connections between real life and training. Consider the police academy instructor who had just concluded a training session on ethics when he was invited to eat lunch with the students at a nearby restaurant. While dining, the instructor discovered that the students always ate at that particular restaurant because meals were half-price for police students. The instructor was particularly distressed because a good portion of his class presentation that day had emphasized the impropriety of police officers accepting price reductions.

Another drawback of the automatic transfer of learning theory is that it gives a false sense of security. Instructors and their supervisors are lulled into a feeling that course content and instructional methods need not be examined for validity.

●Learning Should Be Made Difficult

Many training practitioners today believe that training is and should be a kind of toughening process. There is an assumption that the brain can be strengthened by vigorous and difficult exercise. The more difficult, unpleasant, and stressful the training, the more rewarding it will be in the long run. A trainer who believes that learning should be stressful is likely to favor drill and repetition as instructional methods because they "discipline" the mind.

People are sometimes disturbed when it appears that students are having fun. Training is, after all, a serious business with no room for enjoyment. This is one reason why training institutions are sometimes criticized for providing activities that are apparently enjoyed by the students. Many persons, instructors included, will say that training needs more discipline, more hard work, and a return to the fundamentals.

Psychologist and educator William James tested the assumption that mental exercise helped the mind perform better. He and his students memorized sections of poetry, establishing base times for achievement and later memorizing other sections. The results of the experiment led James to conclude that practice in memorizing did not improve the memory.[5]

●Learning Should Be Fun

This is a mirror image of the theory just described. The idea that learning should be pleasant springs from a belief that training experiences are essentially good experiences. Trainers often become personally involved in the development of training programs; because they have put so much time and effort into them, they feel that students should enjoy instruction. The "learning must be fun" concept is one that derives considerable support from people who like to teach and want to share their pleasure with others.

Certainly, a valuable instructor quality is an enthusiasm for teaching. Is it desirable, however, that all aspects of the learning process be pleasurable? What about the natural student frustrations that occur during the application of problem-solving instructional methods? What about the disappointment of receiving a lower-than-expected grade? All training experiences cannot be enjoyable. In fact, moderate frustration is considered by many to be a necessary and desirable aspect of teaching complex skills. Shielding students from unpleasantness is likely to inhibit learning.

Advocates of this theory employ instructional strategies that rule out student failures. Diverting a student from failure, however, can detract from effective learning. That we learn from our mistakes is an inescapable truth. A student cannot do this if he is never allowed to make mistakes.

Normal anxiety is present in most learning situations, and a student naturally experiences puzzlement and tension when confronted with a problem that calls for the application of a new skill or the acquisition of new knowledge. It is, for all practical purposes, impossible to separate internal discomfort from the learning process. For learning to take place, there must have been some behavioral change in the learner. Most people resist change, and the normal anxiety that accompanies resistance acts as an incentive to learn. Once the learner is caught up in the learning process, he enjoys a feeling of accomplishment in discovering how to cope with a new situation.

When training is made entirely pleasurable, learning becomes less effective. Successful learning never does run smoothly. Even the superior student will occasionally experience frustration in his encounters with new ideas.

SCIENTIFIC THEORIES OF LEARNING

From these brief discussions of traditional theories of learning, it should be clear that they remain attractive because they are psychologically comforting and reassuring, even when they are apparently unsuccessful. Evidence of the importance placed by many instructors on these popular learning theories is indicated by fears that are aroused when attempts are made to implement methods based on newer ideas. Traditional theories have become so ingrained with some people that any attempt to change established methods for something more efficient is seen as an unwarranted attack upon cherished values.

With the rise of modern technology has come a healthy skepticism of traditional beliefs. Educators and trainers are becoming a little more tolerant of teaching concepts and strategies that do not fit the common molds. There is also a greater willingness to permit scientific investigations of human behavior. The remainder of this chapter deals with the development of learning concepts based on scientific research.

●Classical Conditioning

During the early years of the twentieth century, behavioral scientists began to examine the relationships between human beings and their environment in order to discover the process by which learning occurs. Researchers have found that a certain response can be expected when a human being is subjected to a certain stimulus. They have also found that when a second and nonrelevant stimulus is introduced coincidentally with the first stimulus, the expected response can be evoked by the second stimulus without the presence of the first.[6] As an example, it is expected that a human being will twitch when subjected to a mild electrical shock. If, at the time the shock is administered, a light is flashed, the individual is conditioned to relate the flashing light to the electrical shock. After a while, the flashing of the light alone will cause the individual to twitch even though there has been no shock.

Experiments conducted by Pavlov, a Russian scientist, are considered the "classical" models of conditioning research. A moderate amount of classical conditioning research has been carried out in America, but for the most part there has been little direct application of the theory to classroom teaching.

●Instrumental Conditioning

An approach that is quite different from classical conditioning is termed instrumental conditioning. This theory follows the simple premise that humans tend to repeat behavior that is satisfying to them and to avoid behavior that is not satisfying. Behavior can be influenced by subjecting a person to stimuli that have satisfying effects whenever he shows a desirable response. For example, giving praise to a child who has exhibited desirable behavior will encourage the child to repeat the behavior because of the satisfying effects such behavior produces.

B. F. Skinner found that it is not necessary to reward or reinforce every desirable response in order to achieve results. He discovered that people will satisfactorily respond more often and more consistently if they are reinforced according to an irregular pattern. Partial and unpredictable reinforcement seems to lead to more and better responses than does reinforcement all of the time.

Unlike classical conditioning, instrumental conditioning has extensive application in the classroom. A wide range of student behavior can be influenced by expressions of teacher interest and approval. Although teacher rewards may appear only occasionally, individual students will put forth a great deal of effort.

The ability of a trainer to reinforce desirable student behavior is influenced by the number of students in the class. Reinforcement works best on a person-to-person basis. A large number of students makes it difficult, if not impossible, to apply reinforcement. A high ratio of instructors to students is therefore desirable if the benefits of positive reinforcement are to be realized.

One answer to the problem of providing reinforcement on a person-to-person basis is the so-called "teaching machine" developed by Skinner.[7] Using a properly constructed program, a machine of this type will reinforce correct responses and ensure that a student has learned all necessary principles before moving on to any higher step in the program.

What we are talking about, of course, is programmed learning. A variation of this approach is the programmed textbook. The possibilities of programmed instruction continue to be developed through the use of the computer. Actual teaching methods, however, are still far removed from the intriguing and innovative developments taking place in the research setting. While there is little doubt that theories based on conditioning and reinforcement will extend some types of learning for some types of students, they do not enhance all learning processes under many conditions for many people.

●Gestalt Psychology

The term "Gestalt" is a German word for "shape" or "form." Gestalt psychology holds that learning occurs through insight.[8] The idea is that a learner will approach a learning situation while in possession of certain skills and attitudes acquired from previous experiences. He interprets the learning situation not as a specific or isolated case, but in terms of how the learning situation blends with the whole pattern of experiences that has meaning for him personally.

Learning, according to Gestalt psychology, is a process through which problems are solved by discovery. A discovery is facilitated by previous experiences. By arranging and rearranging past experiences in relation to current experiences, a person is able to make sense of the world around him. For example, a child who is attempting to derive meaning from a new word will try to understand the word in its relationship to the rest of the sentence in which it is used. He knows the meanings of the other words through his past experience with those words. He naturally tries to relate the new word to the larger idea contained in the sentence. For a while he may make no progress at all, and then suddenly, like a bolt out of the blue, the child recognizes the meaning of the unfamiliar word. Suddenly, everything makes sense. This is an example of learning through insight.

Because the Gestalt theory considers insight, which is useful in learning situations that require problem-solving skills, the Gestalt approach is potentially more useful for teaching than theories limited to classical or instrumental conditioning.

●Field Theory

The central idea of the field theory is that every individual exists in a "field of forces." The behavior of a person at any given time is the product of forces operating simultaneously upon him. According to the field theory, a person is subjected at any given time to *internal* forces such as attitudes, feelings, emotions, expectations, and needs. Simultaneously, a wide variety of *external* forces also acts upon the individual. The interaction of internal forces with external forces will determine a person's responses or changes in behavior.[9]

Field theory and Gestalt psychology are very similar. Both theories are concerned with the whole aspect of human learning and with the structure of a situation as it is perceived by the individual. This should be of interest to the trainer who must necessarily deal with learning as a whole and who needs to formulate teaching strategies that stimulate learning. One of the major contributions of field theory might be found in the proposition that trainers can structure and restructure teaching activities to create a rich variety of learning climates.

●Problem Solving

The problem-solving theory is less of a theory and more of a practical approach to learning. The problem-solving approach is concerned with practical outcomes that improve a student's ability to solve problems in the real-life environment outside the classroom.[10] Problem solving is therefore inherently critical of the idea that students will automatically transfer abstract concepts learned in the traditional classroom to the everyday problems of life.

A leading exponent of problem solving in education was John Dewey. Approaches to learning developed by Dewey are based on an understanding of the student within the context of a total situation. If information is to be used productively, it must be translated into the learner's method of attempting to solve a problem. If the information cannot be translated into something the student can understand, the information is simply useless and wasted. The translatability of information is dependent upon how meaningful the information is to the student.

A difficulty with many instructional programs is that trainers rather arbitrarily decide what information should be taught and how it should be taught, without any regard for what the information and method of teaching will mean to the learner. As a consequence, learners will often refuse to open their minds or will not willingly respond to instructional methods that to them appear ineffective. The problem-solving approach avoids these kinds of obstacles because the teaching method and the learning derived from the method are seen by the student as having functional value and transferability to real-life situations.

●The Phenomenological Theory

This theory places great emphasis on perception. Educators who believe in this theory will say that an individual behaves in accordance with the way in which he views himself and the world around him. Each individual tends to live in a private world that constitutes reality for him. A student therefore sees the need to learn only in respect to his own and very unique private world. Commenting on this, the renowned psychotherapist Carl Rogers said ". . . as changes occur in the perception of self and in the perception of reality, changes occur in behavior."[11]

A phenomenologist is likely to be critical of training institutions that persist in directing students into activities which fail to provide them with opportunities for meeting their own learning needs as they perceive them. Students will show great ingenuity in avoiding learning activities that have no personal self-enhancement. The traditionally oriented training institution has countered such student disenchantment by requiring the conventional system of grading. As noted earlier, however, a student who is forced to learn information that is apparently useless to him will usually forget the information as soon as a passing grade has been assured.

If learning is in fact facilitated by making use of the varied experiences that students bring to the training situation, there are a number of actions that a school can take. First, the school can provide opportunities for each student to identify with the job he is being trained to perform and, by extension, the role he will take as a responsible and contributing member of society-at-large. Second, a training institution can provide a student with sufficient chances to succeed. Success should be based on positive and productive achievement of established student learning goals. Third, a training program should take advantage of the natural human motivation to develop efficiently and adequately. In other words, a school should help students identify with life and society, provide opportunities for positive accomplishment, and harness the drive for learning that people naturally possess. These recommendations may seem overly ambitious, but there is some support for the idea that significant improvements can be made.

A CONTEMPORARY THEORY OF LEARNING

Traditional and scientific learning theories have some things in common. First, they are generally derived from experience with teaching children. Second, they are based on the premise that the purpose of teaching is to transmit knowledge which will be used by the learner in the future rather than immediately and will be valid for the learner's lifetime. From the various traditional and scientific learning theories a technology emerged called pedagogy. The term is rooted in the Greek stems *paid* (meaning child) and *agogos* (meaning leading). Pedagogy literally translates as "child leading" or the process of teaching children.[12]

Inherent to a pedagogical approach is the notion that the learner, presupposed to be a young person in compulsory attendance, should be provided with knowledge useful for a lifetime and which is not necessarily required in the *immediate* future. A problem with this approach is that many learners are not children, and the learning required by adults is very likely to evolve several times in the span of one human generation. Life in the fast lane of the twentieth century is change and more change, at an ever-quickening pace.

The insufficiency of pedagogy is being remedied by a fairly recent technology called andragogy, which means "man leading" or the art and science of helping adults learn.[13] The word is not new; it was used in Germany as early as 1833.[14] What is new, beginning in the early 1970s, is the development of the theory of andragogy and its practical applications.

Andragogy differs markedly from pedagogy and operates from four main assumptions.[15]

●Self-Concept

This assumption is that as a person grows older he moves from a state of dependency on others to a state of increasing self-directedness. The point at which the individual achieves a self-concept of independence is the point at which childhood is psychologically cast aside. The individual has a self-image of being in control of his fate and will resist attempts by others to curtail that control.

We can observe that persons who enter a criminal justice training program are essentially self-directing. They know who they are, they know what they want, and they are in training because they made personal decisions that brought them there. In short, they are adults and any attempts to put them in a position of being treated as children while they are in training is certain to interfere with their learning.

●Experience

This assumption is that in the process of growing older a person collects a growing pool of personal experiences which serves as a resource for learning. At the same time, this pool of life experiences provides the person with an expanding base to which he can relate and compare new learnings. The technology of andragogy places less emphasis on traditional teaching techniques (such as lecture) and greater emphasis on experiential techniques (such as applying experience in practical exercise or field training exercises).

●Readiness to Learn

This assumption is that as a person grows older his readiness to learn undergoes a fundamental change. No longer is the readiness to learn a function of parental demands and academic pressure, but a function of what the person perceives as a requirement for achieving in life. Andragogy holds that an adult wants to learn in order to succeed in the various roles he or she plays—as worker, spouse, parent, hobbyist, and the like.

The implication of this assumption is that a professional training program can be totally out of sync with a student's readiness to learn. For example, if a trainee needs to perform a specific function to gain employment, the theory of how to perform is of little value to the student; however, the actual performance is of great value.

●Orientation to Learning

This assumption is that a child is conditioned to regard learning as something that will be applied later in life. An adult sees learning as an answer to a problem that exists right now. The problem may be to qualify for a job, obtain a promotion, or switch to another career. The adult regards learning as a problem-solving and goal-directed activity.

With children and the pedagogical approach there is no sense of immediacy, but with adults and andragogy there is. Because the adult wants to use tomorrow what he learns today, the teaching approach must convey knowledge and skills that are meaningful and useful.

CONCLUSION

This chapter has examined various learning theories along three major lines—traditional, scientific, and contemporary. Each of us follows or believes one or more theories about the process of learning, and our teaching activities reveal the type of learning principles we follow. In many cases, ideas that seem like common sense to us may in fact interfere with the effectiveness of our teaching. Because people have a natural tendency to prefer traditional teaching beliefs, no matter how inaccurate they may be, there continues to be a reluctance to try new ideas.

This chapter offers no profound conclusions as to a theory that will adequately explain the tremendously complex process known as learning. As diverse as these theories seem, there is a common bond among them. All learning theories, to be adequate, must address certain broad observations. These observations are

1. man has a continuing drive to become competent;
2. competence is principally the result of learning;
3. the development of competence depends on learning that is directly relevant to the real-life environment; and
4. becoming competent is a continuous, life-long process.

NOTES

1. Several excellent examples of rewards (and nonrewards) and their importance to students and teachers are described in *Personality and Psychotherapy* by John Dollard and Neal E. Miller, McGraw Hill Book Co., Inc. 1950, pp. 25-46.
2. Stuart C. Tiedeman, "A Study of Pupil Teacher Relationships," *Journal of Educational Research* 35 (1942), pp. 231-48.
3. Karl C. Garrison, Albert J. Kengston, and Arthur S. McDonald, *Educational Psychology* (New York: Meredith Publishing Co., 1964), p. 37.
4. Ibid., p. 197.
5. William James, *The Principles of Psychology* (New York: Holt, Rinehart and Winston, 1890), p. 667.
6. James C. Coleman, *Abnormal Psychology and Modern Life* (Glenview, Ill.: Scott, Foresman and Co., 1972), p. 57.
7. B.F. Skinner, "Teaching Machines," *Science* 128 (1953), pp. 969-77.

8. Kurt Lewin, "Field Theory and Learning," in *The Psychology of Learning*, pp. 215-42.

9. Floyd L. Ruch, *Psychology and Life* (Chicago: Scott, Foresman and Co., 1958), p. 319.

10. Dollard and Miller, mentioned earlier, set up a problem-solving experiment in which a six-year-old girl was told that her favorite candy was hidden in a library. Through trial and error she found it. On successive attempts to find more candy she was able to significantly reduce her performance time. See *Social Learning and Imitation* (New Haven: Yale University Press, 1941), pp. 14-16.

11. From an address by Carl R. Rogers delivered at the 1947 annual meeting of the American Psychological Association.

12. Malcolm C. Knowles, *The Modern Practice of Adult Education* (New York: Association Press, 1977), p. 37.

13. Ibid., p. 38.

14. K. Patricia Cross, *Adults as Learners* (San Francisco: Jossey-Bass, Inc. 1981), p. 222.

15. Malcolm C. Knowles, *The Adult Learner: A Neglected Species* (Houston: Gulf Publishing Company, 1973), pp. 45-48.

2

FUNDAMENTALS OF INSTRUCTION

The Nature of Learning • Instruction as a Three-Stage Process • Recognizing Predetermined Student Characteristics • Using Motivation Techniques • Providing Classroom Experience • Summary

An instructor who is unwilling to acquire an understanding of the learning process will find it exceedingly difficult to put into action teaching procedures that result in successful student learning. To develop even a minimally effective repertoire of teaching abilities, an instructor must have a firm grasp of proven learning principles. If students are no better equipped to do something at the end of a lesson than they were prior to it, an admission must be made that learning has not resulted.[1] The instructor must accept final responsibility for student learning, and if learning does not occur, then the instructor is well advised to look first to himself and his methods for the cause. Problems in the conduct of training can usually be traced back to defects in an instructor's grasp of fundamentals.

THE NATURE OF LEARNING

The nature of learning is not and will probably never be entirely comprehended. Because it is not possible to directly observe the working operations of the mind, we are limited to making observations of visible human behavior. Our judgment of whether learning has occurred must be predicated upon our observation of learner actions. Learner actions are manifested in a process frequently referred to as performance, or more specifically, student performance.

Performance reflects a large number of student actions, i.e., changes in behavior that are brought about through practice. When a change in behavior is observed to be relatively permanent we can claim that learning has taken place. When a change is not permanent, successful learning cannot be claimed.

●Stimulus, Response, and Feedback

If we are to judge the success of teaching on the basis of student performance, what elements of the performance process are we able to observe and measure?

There are three principle elements: stimulus, response, and feedback.[2] A *stimulus* is an event which precedes or triggers a response. It is the stimulation that causes a student to react in some form of visible behavior. Stimuli can range from very simple events (such as a question, an instruction, a flashing light, or a tone) to complex events (like a map, a diagram, or a problem).

The *response* is the observable activity of the student. Because a response is observable, it is also measurable. A particular desired response is usually anticipated from a particular stimulus. The extent of variance of the actual response from the desired response is measured. Accuracy, speed, and completeness are some of the standards by which an act is measured.

A response may also become a stimulus for another response. For example, a police trainee who has arrested a suspect in a role-play situation might make a "rights" warning (a response to the stimulus event constituted by the arrest itself). The rights warning is a stimulus to the role-playing suspect, who responds by asking for a lawyer, which in turn is a stimulus to the student to react in some expected manner.

Feedback, the third element present in performance learning, has powerful connotations and will be discussed here and in other parts of the book. Feedback is a consequence of performance and can take several forms. It can be a reward, punishment, correction, congratulation, incentive, or combinations of these forms. Receiving a grade on an examination is feedback; if the grade is high the feedback is a reward, if low it is a punishment. Incorrect responses on the examination guide the student to the correct answers, while correct responses should congratulate him and provide incentives for improved performance. Feedback is present whenever students perform—during classroom discussions, critiques, practical exercises, and even individual learning sessions.

●Knowledge, Skills, and Attitudes

Learning refers to behavioral changes that occur as a result of a person's interaction with his environment. Learning can be observed in three types of behavioral change: the manner of thinking, the manner of physical action, and the manner of emotional reaction. These three types of behavioral changes that represent learning are generally called knowledge, skills, and attitudes.

Knowledge can be designated as an awareness of facts, principles, meanings, concepts, ideas, and relationships. The terms "cognitive" and "cognition" are frequently associated with knowledge. The pattern of an individual's thinking, performing, and responding emotionally are conditioned by the knowledge he possesses. The probability that a person will call the police when he sees a robbery in progress is dependent upon whether he (1) knows the act is a crime which requires police attention, (2) cares enough to make the call, or (3) even knows how to call. Knowledge is therefore supportive of behavior. A conscious act can occur only if the individual knows what he is expected to do and has a willingness to do it.

Skills refer to both physical and mental abilities. Manipulating the hands, running, and jumping are physical kinds of skills. Mental skills include problem solving, analysis, critical thinking, judgments, and synthesis of ideas. More often than not, a single job skill requires both physical and mental activity. The switchman in a railroad yard must know when the tracks are to be switched, which is a mental skill, and he must be able to manipulate the switch, which is a physical skill. Because training is usually created to fill an absence of on-the-job skills, there is a built-in emphasis in training programs upon the development of job-related skills. Unlike educational programs, which are typically knowledge-oriented, training is concerned with the teaching of skills.

A third outcome of student learning is the development of *attitudes*. Knowledge and skills may make it possible for students to act in a certain way, but attitude influences whether the student will decide to act. What is an attitude? We know it is not something that can be touched, tasted, or smelled. Nor can it be handled, taken apart, or rearranged. One of the main reasons we have difficulty with attitudes is that we don't really know what they are. Like the forces of gravity, an attitude cannot be observed directly. The existence of an attitude is inferred from visible human behavior.[3] What a person says or does indicates his attitude.

The instructor's main concern with an attitude is its effect on desired student behavior. For example, a student's feelings about the legal requirement to respect a criminal's rights may influence his ability to apply the concept. If the student's attitude prevents him from applying the appropriate concept, he is said to have a "negative" attitude. "Negative" attitudes obstruct, and that is why the instructor is concerned.

It is usually not difficult for the instructor to detect unfavorable attitudes. They reveal themselves in the interference they cause to learning. Occasionally an instructor will misinterpret a human behavior as being evidence of a "negative" attitude. Long hair, short dresses, and love beads are examples of behavior signals that might be misread because they conflict with an instructor's attitude. The real significance of an attitude, however, is in how it contributes to or detracts from the performance of an intended student behavior. Student attitudes that are irrelevant to the attainment of established learning goals should be treated with neutrality.

What is difficult to define is a "positive" attitude. How is it displayed? Does the student possess a "positive" attitude when he smiles, says hello, is pleasant and polite? Maybe he does and maybe he doesn't. It all depends on the instructional objective. If it is the instructor's objective to teach students to appreciate poetry, what are the behavior signals that indicate achievement of the objective? Sighing? Reciting poetry?

The problem with teaching to achieve an attitude is the abstract nature of attitudes. How does the poetry teacher really know if his students have developed an attitude of appreciation for poetry? When teaching a skill or transferring knowledge, the instructor has a handle to grab because the objectives of training can be formulated in specific, concrete terms. If the skill is manipulative, the instructor requires the student to show it. If the skill is mental (covert), the instructor requires the student to make an audible or visible (overt) response. The desired student behaviors associated with the learning of skills and knowledge can be made visible in forms that are capable of being evaluated and measured by the instructor. Such is not the case with the teaching of attitudes. This is not to say that attitudes cannot be taught. How successfully they are taught depends upon the ability of the instructor to precisely describe his teaching objective and to assess student behaviors that reflect attainment of the intended attitude.

INSTRUCTION AS A THREE-STAGE PROCESS

Broadly viewed, instruction is a three-stage operation. It includes

1. presentation by the instructor;
2. application by the student; and
3. evaluation.

Many approaches exist for an instructor to present information and engage students in application activities. Presentation and application can occur separately or conjointly. The instructor can present information that enables students to perform a skill and then permit them to apply the information in a practical exercise, or the instructor can use an approach that alternates presentation and practice in small increments.

Evaluation that occurs apart from presentation and application is usually in the nature of the examination—that is, measurements are made and grades assigned. Evaluation that is continuous throughout the presentation and application stages is essentially informal. It is directed toward enhancing student learning as opposed to measuring it. The informal method of evaluation plays a large and valuable part in the instructional process.

The three stages of instruction are discussed in the following pages. Examining the instructional process in terms of its parts risks an incorrect impression that instruction is and should be carried out in distinct, discrete stages. A key word here is "process." By its nature, the instructional process flows and blends so that its parts cannot be fully understood unless examined in relation with one another.

●Presentation

In the first stage of the process, the student gains the concept of the subject. He can do this by completing a study assignment, by listening to an explanation, by participating in a conference, or by watching a demonstration. For most subjects, presentation consists of a combination of these activities. In a general sense, the activities require study by the student with a certain amount of telling and showing by the instructor.

The so-called "principles" of a subject or skill are addressed during the instructor's presentation. These principles constitute the major teaching points that must be learned if the student is to apply the principles in a later practical activity. The instructor's objective in this regard is to assist the student in reaching an understanding of the critical features of the subject or skill.

The key to learning is experience. Student understanding will be assisted when the instructor provides examples for students to use in forming clear and useful concepts that have meaning in terms of firsthand student experiences. Building on the past experiences of students, the instructor adds new ideas to arrive at new concepts. By using fairly common human experiences that exemplify major teaching points, he/she helps students form understandings that have some degree of personal familiarity.

When preparing lesson material for presentation, the instructor should be judicious in selecting principles or teaching points. The number of principles should not exceed what the students are able to master. If a principle is not to be applied during training, nor expected to have substantial importance on the job, there is little to be gained by requiring students to learn it. It is far better to select the more critical principles, teaching them thoroughly, than to lightly touch upon a large number of principles, many of which are certain to be forgotten when not put to use.

Learning and retention are facilitated when information is presented in *a context that is meaningful* to the student.[4] If you were asked to memorize a list of randomly selected words that had no apparent sequence or connection, you would probably find it somewhat difficult to do.[5] But if these same words fit together in a logical and understandable pattern, you would have less difficulty remembering them.

An instructor understands that knowledge recently acquired or recently applied remains fresh in the mind of the learner. He reiterates and reemphasizes important information throughout his lesson and makes a point-by-point review at the lesson's conclusion. He also recognizes that students sometimes forget because certain information previously or concurrently learned interferes with similar information being taught.

The presentation stage of the instructional process needs to include techniques and media that excite the several human senses. The student who experiences a lively, stimulating presentation will learn more than a student who experiences a dull, monotonous presentation. Interest and excitement can be added to a presentation through skillful use of role playing, displays, mock-ups, slides, transparencies, filmstrips, charts, graphs, posters, television, and other aids to training.

The more interesting the training materials, the more probable it is that the students will retain information. The instructor, however, must not lose sight of his responsibility to teach. In striving to make training material interesting, the instructor may become more concerned with entertaining students than with providing meaningful information.

● Application

The student needs to be given an opportunity to apply new concepts gained by him during the presentation stage. It is during the second stage, called the application stage, that learning is most productive. A successful student performance in the application stage is a critical moment in the learning process. In planning for instruction during the application stage, the instructor should always keep in mind that it is not so much what he does or says that is important, but rather what he causes his students to do on their own.

In an application activity, the student should be expected to apply the concepts or skills covered in the instructor's presentation. Learning attained during the initial stage of the instructional process is transferred through the medium of a practical application. This transfer should be deliberately and meticulously planned. The instructor makes certain that the student understands the application in terms of what he learned previously and how the application will prepare him to function in on-the-job situations following graduation. The activity itself must necessarily provide an opportunity for the student to exercise ingenuity. It should also build upon each student's confidence in his natural ability to perform.

The ultimate verdict on the success of an application activity is reached only after the student has been given an opportunity to exercise his abilities in a genuine work situation. Judgment is based on how well the student is able to use in the job environment what he has learned in the training environment. Too often, unfortunately, students spend considerable time learning and practicing new skills and then fail to apply the skills to job needs. The instructor who wishes to enlarge the probability of successful job performance by his students will provide an application activity that permits each student to learn and practice a skill so well that it becomes almost habitual for him to perform it. The instructor will also take into consideration the difficulties some students will have in recognizing situations that require real-life application of skills learned in training. Because a training environment cannot always duplicate actual work conditions, the instructor must employ instructional methods that lead students to use learned abilities under a wide variety of conditions. In planning and constructing an application activity, the instructor considers the nature of the skills to be learned and how those skills can be practiced in a logical sequence that will help the student to function effectively in many different practical situations.

An important factor in the conduct of an application activity is the length of time devoted to practice. The nature of the skill itself will usually determine how much time is needed for practice. Some skills consist of one or two steps in a sequence. Other skills might require the student to learn a large number of closely related steps, each of which is built upon a preceding step. The instructor determines if an application activity should be long or short; continuous or intermittent; or some other combination which takes into account the type of learning that is desired. The instructor needs also to know at what point in the practical activity a student will begin to suffer from too much practice. Over-practice tends to increase the error rate and decrease student motivation. An experienced instructor is usually able to develop a number of different application activities that provide relatively short periods of practice interspersed with periods of rest or critique.

●**Evaluation**

Evaluation can be thought of in two ways: as a formal and systematic process of measuring learning effectiveness after instruction has concluded, or as an informal process that occurs concurrently with the presentation and application stages. Our present concern is with the latter form of evaluation.

Evaluation that occurs as part and parcel of instruction is intended to keep students informed of their progress and to prevent them from developing incorrect habits.[6] In learning simple tasks, a student frequently discovers his own mistakes. In learning more complex skills, however, the student may be incapable of recognizing his errors. The student may realize that something is wrong, but he may not know what to do about it. For example, the novice golfer knows he is doing something wrong when he observes his tee shot slice off into the rough, but he may not know how to correct the problem.

An essential function of the instructor is to inform each student as to the quality of his performance. This principle is the heart of reinforcement. At the time of making a mistake, or as quickly as possible following a mistake, the student should be informed of his error and be told or shown the proper way to perform. This helps prevent a learner from repeating a mistake that might become automatic through repetition. A mistake that has been allowed to go uncorrected is sometimes impossible to rectify. A student will always find it more difficult to unlearn a mistake than to learn correctly in the first place.

Informal evaluation occurs when the instructor detects student errors and makes on-the-spot corrections. The instructor monitors student performances and intervenes as necessary to make corrections and provide guidance. Instructor guidance in this regard is often characterized by a repeat demonstration to correct performance. This enables the erring student to compare his performance with the instructor's performance.

Evaluation can also consist of posing questions to the class or to individual students when a key idea or skill has been explained or demonstrated. The answers received will reveal to the instructor the nature and extent of student comprehension. The instructor's purpose is not to assign a grade of some sort but to discover and eliminate fuzzy thinking or substandard actions. Students, particularly beginners, need a constructive critic. Criticisms made through the medium of formal grades are less valuable to learning than practical suggestions. This does not imply that there is no place for formal evaluation in training, but it does suggest that the instructional process must include continuous informal evaluation to identify individual student strengths and weaknesses. With the identification of strengths comes the opportunity to reinforce correct performance through encouragement. With the identification of weaknesses comes the opportunity to make constructive criticisms and eliminate incorrect performance.

Instruction has to be arranged so that evaluation is concurrent with the presentation and application stages of instruction. A formal examination at the end of an instructional unit or phase of training serves a separate and important purpose, but it does not provide powerful reinforcement because of the time lag between student response and student awareness of the correctness of response. It is true that administrative considerations often preclude reinforcement that is concurrent with each individual response. When a formal examination is the only option available, the instructor should provide the results of the examination to students as soon as possible.[7] Otherwise, there is a risk that a student will forget many of the responses he made as part of the examination.

Indeed, students generally learn faster when learning activities include or are quickly followed by information concerning the adequacy of responses. The extent of student progress is conditioned by the timing of evaluation. If students are to progress, they need to be more or less continuously aware of their progress. To achieve that awareness, students must be called upon to demonstrate their acquisition of knowledge, preferably by applying it in practical work situations.

RECOGNIZING PREDETERMINED STUDENT CHARACTERISTICS

Two important factors affecting learning are already determined before actual instruction begins. They are the readiness of the student —the skills and abilities he brings with him to the course—and each student's past experiences. An instructor who understands these factors can put them to work in the learning process.

Material that is clearly and explicitly related to something the student already understands can be more readily learned and better retained than material that is introduced in an unfamiliar form within a context that has little personal meaning to the student. Despite this unassailable logic, it is quite usual for an instructor to present material, particularly introductory material to beginning students, in terms that have meaning to himself alone. Information is delivered in a pattern that is perfectly clear to the instructor but has little clarity and meaning for students. This is a fairly common example of teaching that fails to produce learning.

●Readiness

We often assume that a student has been through a filtering selection process or has had prior training or experience that equips him with the basic capabilities to successfully complete the course of instruction. We operate from a premise that every student already possesses certain entering abilities.[8] Because the premise is frequently false, we discover during the course that much of what is taught is beyond the comprehension of the student because he has no foundational skills or knowledge to build upon. When learning does not manifest itself as intended and designed, instructors and training managers are prone to rationalize that the student lacks sufficient motivation. But the student may be lacking less in motivation than in a baseline of information. At the other extreme, student readiness may be too far advanced for the beginning point of instruction. The result is wasted time and a definite loss of student confidence in the content of the course.

The design and execution of an instructional program is influenced by the entry level abilities of students. More than this, the changing skills of students during the course and their skills at the conclusion of it have an influence upon course design and execution. For instruction to be effective, it must identify student characteristics, establishing them as prerequisites when necessary. This applies equally to entry, interim, and terminal phases of the course. Instructional materials, teaching strategies, and scheduling are established with student readiness in mind.

●Past Experience

New experiences are most often interpreted on the basis of past experiences.[9] A person seeing a television for the first time may call it a picture that talks and moves, because the describer interprets the new object in terms of things learned in the past. An instructor can explain many new things by making comparisons drawn from past events.

Student experiences will, of course, vary widely. An instructor should recognize that not every student will attach to an explanation exactly the same meaning as every other student. Illustrations or teaching points must be selected and presented carefully so that all students will obtain the desired meaning. Instructors can draw from common experiences and use pertinent examples to amplify important teaching points. This principle is most often appropriate during the introductory stage of teaching. Students who have learned information or acquired skills from previous units of instruction can be reminded of what they learned previously and be told how previously taught material relates to new material.

USING MOTIVATION TECHNIQUES

For a student to be taught, he must want to learn. To develop in the student a desire to learn, and to sustain that desire, the instructor employs instructional methods that cause students to pay attention during the presentation. A number of techniques can assist in motivating students to learn. (See Chapter 13 for a discussion of motivation and need.)

Encourage Each Student to Feel Personally Responsible for Learning. Before instruction is presented, the student needs to be made to realize that he holds a personal responsibility for learning. It is not enough that a student be physically present; he must also be mentally prepared to learn. The instructor should encourage each student to apply himself in the learning process. When a student is made to feel responsible for learning, he senses an imperative to learn more.

Give Valid Reasons for Learning Information. It cannot be assumed that adult students will recognize the importance of learning certain information presented in a training program. Often important things seem unrelated to an actual work situation. This is particularly true when the student hears of these things for the first time while in a training situation. Instruction must therefore include convincing reasons for learning information and an explanation of how the information is applied on the job.

Early in the Program, Give Students Work They Can Complete Successfully. Early success in training has the effect of motivating students. A person's success encourages him to make greater effort and achieve additional success. Satisfaction arising out of success leads to a desire for more success.

Give Positive Reinforcement for Good Work; Avoid Punishment. A student desires, and has the right to expect, credit for work well done—it is his reward. Always start with favorable comments and then lead to suggestions for improvement. The anticipation of reward is a powerful incentive. The opposite of reward, punishment, is a less than desirable form of student motivation. Punishment can breed a refusal to learn the subject matter with which the punishment was associated. When the incentive is positive or rewarding, there is a stronger likelihood that learning will occur.

Provide a Description of Course Objectives. Learning is more successful when the student knows exactly what he is to learn and what is expected of him. At the outset of each period of instruction, the instructor should explicitly describe objectives that the student is required to achieve.

Encourage Competition. Competition, when it is friendly, will stimulate learning. Competition between two or more groups or teams can achieve a high degree of learning if the intensity of the competition does not get in the way of learning goals. When possible, group competition is preferable to individual competition. A preferable form of individual competition is to require a student to compete against his own past record.

Build on the Natural Enthusiasm of Students and Promote Enthusiasm Where None Exists. Learning is faster when it provides *enjoyment*. For example, your first attempt to ride a bicycle was probably made easier because it was something you wanted to do. At the time you likely felt that learning to ride a bicycle was the most important ability a person can have. Your mastery of bicycle riding surely required a shorter initial learning time because bicycle riding was fun. Another memory from your childhood may relate to the learning of a skill that didn't have much appeal to your personal needs. It may have been mowing the lawn, solving problems in arithmetic, or some other activity that was not fun for you or didn't seem too important at the time. Unless you were required to exert a deliberate effort to learn, it is certain your initial tries resulted in little progress and that the learning rate was slow. A person who lacks the desire to learn is not likely to learn very quickly or very much.

Create Learning Situations That Correspond with Student Purposes and Needs. A student brings his personal purposes with him to the training situation. The instructor can learn about student needs through regularly scheduled counseling sessions. Some student purposes may be unique while others are common. The extent of an individual student's learning is shaped considerably by his purposes. What an instructor plans to teach is sometimes less important than what a student intends to learn.

The social needs of a learner usually lie just beneath the surface of a student's purpose and are a driving force toward achievement. Recognition, self-esteem, and acceptance are social needs that compel people to strive for personal accomplishment.[10] Training objectives that parallel student needs are powerful learning motivators.

PROVIDING CLASSROOM EXPERIENCE

Learning is based on experience; it cannot exceed the experience from which it springs. Shallow, limited experience will result in shallow, limited learning. Instructional activities that are extensive, varied, and challenging, and that involve the "whole student" are more likely to produce greater, more enduring student learning.

Emphasis on "learning by doing" carries the implication that there are other ways to learn.[11] The fact is that there are no other ways of learning except through experience. All learning is derived from experience in one form or another. In creating a learning situation the issue is not whether "learning by doing" should be attempted, but whether the learning situation produces the desired learning outcome.

Learning involves a great deal more than just revealing to a student an idea or skill. It cannot be assumed that a student will apply what has been revealed to him in a textbook, or that he will correctly perform a skill he saw someone else perform. A student needs to participate, but just any kind of participative activity is not sufficient. The student must engage in a learning activity that is appropriate to the job for which he or she is being prepared.

Learning activities that relate closely to conditions as they exist in real life will engender a higher quality of student comprehension and performance. Insofar as is practicable, material used in a learning activity should be identical to material that will be used when the student is on the job. The use or application of materials in training should be as realistic as the activity will allow.

A cautionary point needs to be made regarding material presented in training. During the introductory stage of instruction, realism should not be allowed to overshadow learning. The fact that the trainee may someday have to administer emergency medical treatment in a life or death situation does not mean that preliminary instruction should be presented under identical conditions. Realistic situations in many cases should be introduced only after the student has mastered basic principles and techniques. Instruction during the introductory or presentation stage can be perked up with "Here is what this means to you," or "You can use this knowledge when you are on the job."

●Multidimensional Effects

Experiential learning is a multidimensional process. Obviously, the student who is being taught to drive an automobile will be developing mental ability in addition to the psychomotor or physical abilities involved in steering, accelerating, braking, and so forth. The student driver is required to understand that a red octagonal sign containing the word "STOP" means that the driver of an automobile must bring the automobile to a stop at a particular point immediately preceding the sign. The student is in effect acquiring important knowledge. Attitudes can also be developed during a learning activity. The student driver who sees a stop sign and responds by obeying the sign has demonstrated an attitude. A learning activity that places a student behind the wheel of an automobile is an example of an experience involving more than the application of certain physical skills. It is an experience that provides also for the demonstration of essential knowledge and attitudes. In this regard, learning is multidimensional in character.

The full potential of a teaching situation cannot be realized if the instructor perceives a learning objective as the development of skills only. Learning is not a compartmentalized process in which physical skills are learned separately from knowledge and attitudes. The student who is placed in a learning activity that is designed only to develop physical dexterity will not be able to turn off his mind or stifle his emotional feelings.

An instructor may be primarily concerned with student acquisition of a skill, or a knowledge, or an attitude, but the totality of the learning experience will shape the student's doing, thinking, and feeling behaviors. The student who attends a course in radio repair may be required to perform a specific repair operation. In the process of making the repair, the student also makes new generalizations. He is certain to learn something else about radio repair in general that he did not know prior to performing the specific repair operation. His complete learning experience has given him new information and insights even though the instructor's planned learning objective was mainly directed toward a student's manipulative dexterity in making a specific kind of radio repair.

Unintended learning frequently results from instructional experiences. Every student who enters a training program brings with him preconceived feelings; for many students these feelings will change as the result of interaction with the total training environment. A student may learn to cooperate or to not cooperate. He may learn how to get along with other people or to get by with minimum social contact. The student may learn something about leadership and the dynamics of a student group. Ideas and attitudes will be developed, positive and negative, depending on what the student personally experiences. In many cases, personal relationships among students will evolve into long-term friendships. Such friendships can, in fact, produce higher levels of job performance as the product of on-the-job cooperation. This form of incidental learning, which is usually not intended, plays a part in the complete development of a student.

SUMMARY   An understanding of the learning processes is essential if an instructor is to develop successful teaching procedures. When teaching is successful, the behavior or performance of the students will change. Such changes in performance can be measured by observing the three elements of the performance process: stimulus, response, and feedback. They will reveal changes in knowledge, skills, and attitudes —all indicators of student performance.

Instruction can be viewed as a process that includes three elements: presentation, application, and evaluation. In the simplest terms, the instructor tells and shows (presentation); the students try it themselves (application); and the instructor monitors, providing continuous feedback to the students (evaluation). Every teaching method contains one or more of the three constituents of the instructional process.

In order to facilitate learning, the instructor needs to be aware of predetermined student characteristics, such as readiness and past experience. The students' desire to learn is of paramount importance, and the instructor can employ various techniques to motivate students to learn.

How much the student learns, how much he retains, and how much he uses later on the job will depend to a great extent on the quality of the classroom experience. Great care must be taken to provide instructional activities that are meaningful and appropriate and that provide for student participation. Often learning activity will have multidimensional effects, sometimes resulting in learning beyond the intentions of the instructor.

NOTES

1. *Techniques of Military Instruction* (Washington, D.C.: Department of the Army, 1967), p. 8.
2. Donald F. Haggard et al., *An Experimental Program of Instruction on the Management of Training* (Alexandria, Va.: Human Resources Research Organization, 1970), p. 261.
3. *How to Prepare and Conduct Military Training* (Washington, D.C.: Department of the Army, 1975), p. 98.
4. Haggard et al., *Experimental Program of Instruction on the Management of Training*, p. 219.
5. Floyd L. Ruch, *Psychology and Life* (Chicago, Ill.: Scott, Foresman and Co., 1958), p. 330.
6. K. Patricia Cross, *Accent on Learning* (San Francisco: Jossey-Bass, Inc., 1976), p. 82.
7. Haggard et al., *Experimental Program of Instruction on the Management of Training*, p. 218.
8. James C. Coleman, *Abnormal Psychology and Modern Life* (Glenview, Ill.: Scott, Foresman and Co., 1972), pp. 100-101.
9. Allen Z. Gammage, *Police Training in the United States* (Springfield, Ill.: Charles C. Thomas, 1963), p. 200.
10. Ruch, *Psychology and Life,* p. 326.
11. *Principles and Techniques of Instruction* (Washington, D.C.: Department of the Air Force, 1974), pp. 2-5.

3

INSTRUCTIONAL APPROACHES

The Conference Method • Demonstrations • Question Techniques • The Case Study Method • The Critique • Lecture as a Teaching Method • Team Teaching • Peer Teaching • The Field Trip • Role Playing • Panels • Brainstorming

It is an important responsibility of the instructor to create learning situations that sufficiently stimulate the senses so that desired student responses are produced. Practical exercises, training aids, demonstrations, and other diversified teaching techniques contribute to effective learning by appealing to a variety of human sensory organs.

Learning is essentially an active process. It is not passive absorption of information. Students need to be kept active—both mentally and physically—in the acquisition of new knowledge, skills, and appreciations that permit them to do something they could not do before. This chapter describes various instructional approaches the instructor might use in order to provide stimulating and effective learning experiences in a training course.

THE CONFERENCE METHOD

Trainers and educators of adults have come to realize that discussion is an important means of reinforcing formal instruction and stimulating extra learning. Adult students respond positively to an opportunity for careful discussion of ideas with sufficient opportunity for refutation.

The conference technique involves group discussion that is dependent upon an instructor's control of the discussion process so that discussion is always directed toward specific goals. The method can use a single meeting or a series of meetings in which the instructor or discussion leader guides the group in examining topics relevant to the achievement of established learning goals.

•Advantages

Classroom discussions of pertinent issues reward the adult's need for active participation. Well-conducted classroom discussions are helpful also in conquering natural student resistance to new ideas. The instructor who relies upon a persuasive lecture to convince students of new ideas is less likely to succeed than one who permits the students to discuss those ideas in an open but organized fashion.

Classroom participation is a good substitute for traditional devices used by instructors to motivate younger persons. Diplomas and the usual rewards of training hold less value to adults than to younger persons. Reading assignments and required research cannot always be enforced with adult students. Although motivation of many adults is very high to begin with, even the less-motivated adult students become self-motivating when given a chance to participate in discussions.

The conference method can be useful in helping students to achieve new perspectives and solutions to problems. The interaction of group members provides all students with an increased awareness of diverse viewpoints that may exist with respect to an issue. It is also likely that students, by being provided with an opportunity to discuss issues that may be important to them, will acquire favorable or positive attitudes toward the training and the content of the instruction presented.

Group interaction tends to generate greater interest and involvement and will usually result in a higher level of understanding of a problem. Ideas and possible resolutions to stated issues emerge during conference from the sharing of experiences and thoughts of group members. Also, the student-centered nature of the conference method may result in an increased commitment by individual students toward solving problems.

•How a Conference Works

The conference is certainly the most commonly used small group instructional method. There are essentially two types of conferences —directed and nondirected—and it is important to distinguish between them.

The nondirected conference provides an uninhibited discussion usually centered upon a well-defined problem. The discussion agenda is very flexible, permitting discussions to flow from student experiences. The instructor need exercise control only in so far as ensuring that student comments are applicable to the stated problem.

The directed conference is used for training purposes more frequently than the nondirected conference.[1] Since training has specific goals, usually involving some expected change in student behaviors, it follows logically that the training conference would be directed toward established learning objectives. The instructor or leader usually follows a fixed agenda, making certain that particular learning points are covered in the discussions. Sometimes the conference method can be structured so that the instructor maneuvers the students toward a predetermined conclusion. The important thing, however, is that the conclusion be reached through active participation by the students.

The conference method is not intended to present theories and hypotheses. A conference deals with existing problems that need examination. Group discussions should, in addition to addressing an issue, attempt to discover answers. For the conference method to be effective, or even appropriate, it is essential that group members have some background or experience pertinent to the issue.

●Planning the Conference

The conference leader. The conference method is a premeditated, cognitive process directed by a leader. Since discussions are intended to lead toward the achievement of established training objectives, the discussion leader's skill is critical in guiding and controlling students along productive routes.

Subject matter experts are not always available to teach a particular subject, and it is possible to train relatively unsophisticated instructors to be conference leaders. A potential problem, however, in using inexperienced persons to lead conference groups is the risk of superficiality. Since it can be expected that students themselves lack expertise in the topic to be discussed, there is a possibility that key issues in the discussion will not be completely covered. A conference leader with expertise can give students greater insight to underlying issues. Obviously, a conference leader who is unable to articulate and to stir students toward meaningful discussions of the critical issues will be unsuccessful in achieving the established learning objectives, no matter how promising the instructional method may be.

When the conference leader is not a subject matter specialist, it is useful for him/her to learn as much as possible about the issue or topic content. Reading authoritative references, viewing films, or discussing the topic with specialists is helpful.

The conference method can be enhanced substantially through small investments in planning and preparation. A discussion guide made in advance helps a conference leader formulate thought-provoking comments. Handbooks or guides can be provided in advance of a scheduled conference so that the newly trained conference leader will have complete instructions for directing the conference. The training manager might even prepare a detailed outline that will include all teaching points to be covered during a conference. Even the actual words and actions for the opening and closing discussions and for important points in the conference agenda can be included.

The discussion plan. Any type of discussion plan should be used as a guide, not an inflexible script. Great flexibility is essential to productive discussions. It is suggested that a discussion plan include introductory remarks; the learning objectives of the conference; a logical sequence to be followed in the conference; the major issue points to be covered; questions to be posed and general parameters of answers expected; training aids, student handouts, and other materials to be used during the conference; conclusions that might be reached as a result of the conference; and concluding remarks.

A discussion plan should include some consideration of effective utilization of time and of introducing new material. The plan should anticipate problems that are likely to arise during conference and should contain ideas for provoking discussions if student interest and participation fall off.

●Leading the Conference

During the conference itself, the leader should—

1. Announce to the students that he does not represent himself to be the only authority on the subject under discussion. The conference leader should make it clear that he cannot answer all questions or offer solutions to all problems that are presented in the discussions. Students should be made to understand that the conference leader's main function is to stimulate student discussion and to keep the group "on track." The conference leader acts as a chairman who helps the group summarize its collective thinking and arrive at conclusions.

2. Seek chances to give every student a chance to express his or her opinion. Every member can contribute to the discussions by speaking freely and by giving the group the benefit of personal viewpoints and experiences.

3. Avoid the appearance of stressing an idea that may be personal to him. Any decisions that are reached should be decisions that represent the collective thoughts of the group and not the thoughts of the instructor. Being the expert or final authority inhibits a free flow of comments and detracts from the main purpose of the conference method. Instructor control should always be present—but in a subtle, flexible, and non-authoritarian form.

4. Prevent too many people from talking at one time. Several persons talking simultaneously is distracting and inhibits students who are less aggressive in seeking attention. It is, of course, important that free exchange of ideas take place. The conference leader must find ways to have those ideas expressed in an organized fashion. It is also important that no single group member dominate the session with prolonged remarks.

5. Summarize main ideas before moving on to new ideas. Shorten, lengthen, or refocus in relation to established learning objectives.

6. Present a final summary of the conference. Re-state the important issues covered and include strong emphasis on the feasibility of implementing group decisions or recommendations.

●**Limitations of the Conference Method**

Learning through the conference method is cognitive in nature. The emphasis in the conference method is upon gaining new insights into a particular real-life problem rather than coming to grips with the problem in a direct fashion. A criticism of the conference method is that it provides no opportunity for students to practice "hands-on" skills. It fails to bring the student into actual or simulated situations involving real-life behavior. This limitation can be overcome by linking the conference method with one or more instructional approaches that require direct application of ideas or solutions arrived at through earlier student discussions. Role playing, for example, can intensify and personalize insights developed through the conference. Insights or attitudes formed during discussions can serve as a foundation for wider and more intense student learning later in the training program.

Since classroom discussion cannot involve large numbers of people simultaneously, the use of discussion is inherently limited to small groups. Large numbers of students are difficult to stimulate and almost impossible to control. And, more important, a discussion that does not encourage each and every student to become involved is unfair and ineffective.

DEMONSTRATIONS

A primary purpose of training is to prepare a person to do a particular job. Therefore, instructional emphasis in training must be placed upon "doing" activities for students. "Doing" activities require the instructor to show as well as tell students. Providing some form of demonstration gives the students understanding of what they are expected to learn. For a demonstration to be effective, the instructor must understand the purpose for the demonstration and the forms that the demonstration may take.

The demonstration is not a separate teaching method but is actually used in combination with several other methods. A demonstration is usually accompanied by an explanation that employs either the lecture or the conference method, or both. Usually the explanation will begin prior to the demonstration and continue during the demonstration. When the demonstration is used to teach skills it should be followed by practical work on the part of the student. To a certain extent, a demonstration depends for its success upon the use of other instructional methods.

●Advantages

The demonstration as a method of instruction has very definite advantages. Whether or not these advantages are realized depends upon instructor planning and preparation.

The demonstration can be used to develop student understanding of basic principles. For example, in teaching a student how to clean and maintain a typewriter, the instructor may demonstrate functions of the typewriter by using an enlarged cut-away model, a training film, or other visual media that will reveal the movements and relationships of its several component parts.

A demonstration can be very effective in promoting manipulative skills that need to be performed with dexterity. Such skills, which are psychomotor in nature, can be improved through accurate, controlled, and repeated practice. The demonstration serves to establish for the student a visual image of how these manipulative skills should be performed.

A demonstration can teach how to apply skills and knowledge in the solution of problems. Demonstration helps the student to understand the way in which a particular task is performed. Minimum standards and procedures that are expected on the job can be explained in this kind of demonstration. When skillfully performed, a demonstration of problem solving creates interest and an appreciation of standards of performance required in real-life job situations.

●Methods

A *skit* or a *prepared exhibit* can be effective in demonstrating the operation of procedures in an office or some other activity involving human interrelationships. Procedures shown in this manner realistically and specifically show each student what he should do in his job.

The *field demonstration* is used mainly in connection with on-the-job activities. Field demonstrations are usually carried out by a field training officer or supervisor assigned specifically to assist the student in learning in an actual work environment. While field demonstrations are very effective, they should not involve the student in activities that require an understanding of complex skills outside the job he is being prepared to perform. (See "The Field Trip," page 56.)

Films or *video* presentations are a popular form of demonstration for illustrating the operation of equipment, activities of persons, or a combination of equipment and persons in portrayed situations.

Another form of demonstration is *instructor role playing.* An instructor or his assistant may act out operations or procedures. Role playing helps develop student appreciations and attitudes. It may be designed to show the wrong way as well as the correct way. To be effective the demonstration should be carefully planned, repeatedly rehearsed, and smoothly presented.

●**Preparation**

Attention to detail is very important in preparing a demonstration. A rehearsal of the demonstration will help identify problems that were not immediately apparent during planning. Rehearsals help to check procedures and guarantee that every piece of equipment is on hand and functioning properly. Blunders in operation are particularly distracting.

The *physical layout* for any kind of demonstration also requires special attention. The arrangement of equipment, tools, and related materials must be planned for the set up. If students are to perform the skills portrayed in the demonstration, the instructor must (1) have on hand tools or equipment needed for the demonstration and for student practice and (2) have the items arranged in an order that will facilitate a smooth demonstration. Although these details may seem insignificant, a failure to address them can result in an amateurish demonstration and personal embarrassment to the instructor.

A demonstration has value only to the extent that all students can see and hear it. Consideration should be given to the size of the class, the size and quantity of the equipment to be used, and the length of the demonstration. If equipment noise makes it impossible for students to hear, the oral portion of the demonstration can wait until the noise has subsided. When equipment is large and bulky, the equipment may block the light source, thereby making it difficult for students to see the demonstration.

Teaching aids. *Student handouts* that focus student attention on important facets of the demonstration can be very useful. Lesson plans or other written guidance materials should be available at the demonstration area to ensure that the technique involved in the performance of the skill or operation is correctly followed. This is in keeping with the need to reduce an operation to separate steps that can be shown in a logical sequence to the students. A lesson plan is, of course, written for the benefit of the instructor, but it may also be useful for the students to have some form of written guidance that will alert them to important points in any of the steps that comprise the demonstration.

When equipment, particularly complex equipment, is being demonstrated, it is useful to have *additional training aids* on hand. The aids might depict subcomponent operations or how the equipment interfaces with other equipment.

Difficult technological concepts can be translated into simpler comprehensible units through the use of supplementary aids. For example, a *chart* or *diagram* can be used when teaching a student how to load and unload a camera and make adjustments to it. A *cut-away model* of the camera can show the positioning of parts concealed by a covering or housing. Even the common *chalkboard* can be a useful training aid. When a demonstration consists of several steps, each step can be listed on the chalkboard. This helps the student remember the steps in their proper sequence.

●Conducting the Demonstration

A demonstration is effective because it appeals to several human senses, particularly to that of sight. Therefore it must be skillfully presented. How skillfully this is done depends to a very large extent upon the ability of the instructor to plan and implement a demonstration that will achieve a specific and intended training purpose.

The specific purpose of the demonstration should be foremost in the instructor's mind and clear to the students. Since the demonstration will usually involve several distinct phases of a larger operation, it is important for students to recognize and understand the total concept involved. If students are to learn more than one method of performing a skill or operation, a separate and distinct demonstration should be given for each method.

A demonstration that sets out to show the right way of doing a thing should be perfect in every important detail. If a demonstration is to be performed by the instructor alone, he should be able to show and to explain at the same time.[2] At the outset, the instructor should tell exactly what he is going to do and what important points the student should look for. Explanations should be timed so that only short pauses occur between remarks. Awkward gaps during an explanation sometimes lead the students to believe that the instructor is not in possession of all the needed information. After the demonstration, the instructor should explain why it was performed in a particular manner.

The use of assistants will help to eliminate delays in setting up and operating equipment required for demonstrations.

The demonstration should be broken down into separate steps. The instructor must keep in mind that even the best students can remember only a few images at a time. Therefore, the number of steps demonstrated at one time should be limited. Each step must be demonstrated slowly so that the students will grasp it thoroughly. Each step should be performed by the students before going on to the next step. It may be necessary to repeat a step several times to ensure student understanding. Demonstration should be repeated as often as necessary to ensure that all students have seen and understood it.

If a demonstration contains a particularly difficult step, the instructor should inform the students of that fact before beginning. The instructor should request their close attention to the difficult step. If something should go wrong, the instructor has prepared the student for that fact and may even capitalize on it. He can point out the difficulties that the students themselves may experience when required to perform that particular task either in the training situation or on the job at a later time.

Common mistakes in presentation that distract student attention should be avoided. One such mistake occurs when the instructor speaks toward the equipment or tool rather than toward the students. Another mistake can occur when one instructor is demonstrating a step while another is speaking. It is not unusual for students to focus attention on the instructor who is speaking and to miss entirely the other instructor who is demonstrating the steps of the operation being explained.

Frequent follow-up checks help to ascertain if all students understand the demonstrations. At the conclusion of each major step, the instructor asks questions to check student understanding. A skillful use of good instructional questioning techniques has a high degree of application in demonstrations.

Questions posed by students at planned intervals can be helpful, especially when the intervals occur between major steps of the operation. Although it is very desirable for students to be curious, they should be discouraged from interrupting a demonstration in progress. Questions asked and answered at natural stopping points will not distract from visual images.

Safety precautions, rules, regulations, and laws that relate to a demonstration should be emphasized and reiterated before, during, and after a demonstration.

At the completion of a demonstration it is useful to supply some written materials that will summarize the important points of the demonstration. This summary should include an enumeration of all steps performed in their order of demonstration. A written summary helps prepare the student for any later demonstration or application of a skill that is built upon the demonstration just conducted. When properly prepared, a written summary can also be of use to the student later, in performing on-the-job duties. A summary, for example, that explains to a student the procedural steps to follow in the reporting of an accident can be a valuable job aid.

QUESTION TECHNIQUES

The question-and-answer technique is perhaps the most important, surefire, and productive way of developing student interest in training. This technique encourages active student participation—an essential component in the learning process.

●Advantages

Questioning stimulates learning because the average student will pay closer attention and will think more intensely about a subject if he believes that questions will be asked. Questioning also manifests the instructor's determination to hold each student accountable for learning.

Questions used in the classroom situation need not emanate from the instructor only. Encouraging students to pose questions is a valid teaching technique. In fact, students tend to be very interested in responding to questions from fellow students. Further, a student feels he is contributing to the instruction when he asks questions and responds freely to questions posed by other students as well as the instructor.

Questions permit the instructor to adjust his instruction to the student's ability to learn.[3] A single class of students will include varying levels of experience and learning rates. To accommodate these differences, questions can be posed to simplify or clarify information; they can also be used to expand upon a concept so that superior students will have some challenge to their imaginations.

The use of questioning helps reveal student misunderstandings or noncomprehensions. When students consistently fail to respond to questions, the instructor receives a tip-off that he has failed to teach the students the information in question. The instructor then has an opportunity, while still in the presentation stage of instruction, to re-teach the points not understood.

Responses to questions often indicate individual student interests and attitudes toward the instructional unit or even toward the entire training course. Student attitudes are important to the instructor because they reveal personal motivation.

A student comes to the learning situation with his own unique set of experiences. The questioning technique allows individual experiences to be brought out in classroom discussion. Participation stimulates interest, adds variety, and can provide new and meaningful facets to a presentation.

Retention of important teaching points is made easier with the frequent recall provided by questions. The very fact that a question has been asked on a particular point emphasizes that point to the student. A response to a question also serves to reinforce the idea contained in the question.

Questioning in the classroom is one of the best methods for determining that students have, in fact, understood the information presented. Student answers, when evaluated by the instructor, can reveal where teaching has failed or succeeded.

●Preparation

The question-and-answer technique requires careful preparation. Questions that are intended to be used in a presentation should be written into a lesson plan. Improvised or spontaneous questions can detract from learning. The instructor who formulates and poses a question on the spur of the moment risks weakly or incorrectly emphasizing the teaching point covered by the question. Therefore, questions should be planned in advance, well constructed, and phrased in a logical way that will blend with the flow of ideas being presented.

The background and experience of the class influences the use and nature of questions. But an apparent lack of collective experience on the part of a class should not discourage the use of questions. A skilled instructor can obtain some level of student participation regardless of the collective character of a class.

Every question should have a specific purpose, and that purpose should be understood and planned by the instructor. A question may be used to emphasize a major point, stimulate a new thought, or simply cause students to pay attention. A question may have as its purpose a check on whether or not students have attained understanding of an important teaching point. An identical or similar question given at a later time in the instructional process may have as its purpose student recall of important information.

Questions should be phrased in terms and words that students can readily understand. Lengthy questions requiring clarification should not be used. Questions that are simple, direct, and easily understood serve their purposes best. Poorly expressed questions will discourage active participation and confuse the class.

A question should avoid covering two points at one time. When a question requires several responses, the responses ought to be distributed among several students. Such questions, although effective in promoting analytical skills, are generally too complicated to be effective in the normal classroom situation. It is usually more effective to prepare a separate question for each separate point.

What about questions that can be answered with a simple yes or no? While generally not very helpful, they can be made to work if the student is required to support a yes or no with detailed reasoning.

What about questions that suggest a correct answer? They are hardly productive and deserve no place in an instructor's repertoire.

What about questions that are designed to trip up a student by encouraging a wrong answer? If the purpose is to embarrass, asking such questions borders on the unethical; if the purpose is to emphasize or demonstrate an important point, this type of question has merit.

●Presentation

Each question should be worded to require a definite answer. Vague and indefinite questions invite vague and indefinite answers. A poorly articulated response causes confusion unless clarified. Those who were unsure when the question was delivered are certain to be lost, and those who know the answer are left wondering. It may be that the responding student was putting up a bluff, or he may have had genuine difficulty expressing his answer. In any event, a garbled answer cannot be allowed to pass. If necessary, the responding student should be asked to clarify his answer or elaborate upon it. In this way the instructor can ensure that the student has understood the teaching point involved. In many cases it is best to delay final evaluation of a response until other students have had a chance to answer. Even though a student may be uncertain of his knowledge, he should be encouraged to respond to a question to the best of his ability. The instructor should not accept "I don't know" without some effort to draw a response of some type.

Only after a teaching point has been thoroughly explored with a variety of pertinent questions and the instructor is reasonably sure that the class understands it, should he permit classroom discussion to move on to another teaching point.

Response to questions is an indicator of comprehension. If responses are limited or poor, adjustments to the presentation can sometimes be made on the spot. The teaching point might be covered again in its entirety, or only partly addressed. The instructor might discover that his presentation could stand improvement in respect to certain teaching points or that his questioning technique was faulty. He learns these things by feedback from his class—through the questions put to him and through the answers he elicits.

The instructor should prepare students for questions that are about to be asked. Questions should be expressed in a natural, interested, and conversational tone and should be audible to the entire class.

Each question should be addressed to the entire class before designating a particular student to answer it. This will hold the attention of the whole group. A student is motivated to think about the question and to form a tentative answer if he thinks he may be called on next. Between asking the question and calling on the student the instructor should pause briefly. This will give students time to prepare to answer the question if called upon.

Questions should be evenly distributed among the entire class so that maximum participation can be achieved. There is no advantage in calling on students in any set order, or reserving difficult questions for the most alert or apparently superior students.

●Questions from Students

Students need to know at the outset of the instructional period that questions are welcome from them and that questions will be asked of them, The presentation of complex ideas has to include a large allowance for the give and take of queries and replies. Questions flow more easily when students feel they are free to fire away when a point is unclear. It helps considerably if the instructor moves deliberately through difficult material, pausing frequently to permit student inquiry.

When a student asks a question, it may be stimulating to the entire class if the question is relayed to another student instead of being answered by the instructor. This technique helps obtain maximum participation by all class members.

If an instructor cannot answer a student question, he should say so. The experienced instructor will never attempt to bluff an answer but will say the answer will be researched and provided to the class at a later time. And, of course, the instructor should keep his promise by obtaining the answer and delivering it to the class.

●Summary

Good questioning techniques will increase student interest, stimulate student thinking, adjust the level of instruction to the ability of the class, provide opportunities for expression of student attitudes, introduce student experiences to classroom discussions, emphasize main teaching points, and test effectiveness of the instructor and his methods.

THE CASE STUDY METHOD

The case study method is founded upon the proposition that a student who solves problems in the training environment increases his capacity to solve similar problems after completion of training. By confronting realistic cases in the classroom, the student not only acquires new perceptions of typical on-the-job problems but also gains practice in the application of problem-solving principles. The case study method has been widely used in the study of law, personnel management, business, and industry. It has many advantages that mesh with training program objectives.

●Advantages

The case study method is definitely student centered. It causes the student to be the central point of action in the classroom. By requiring students to participate rather than observe, the method causes them to communicate with one another and work together. A student finds himself striving for cooperative exploration rather than competitive disagreement. He becomes aware of a responsibility to assist in arriving at a group consensus based on specific facts or information provided in the case. In the process, the student gains experience in group dynamics. He encounters techniques by which a group is moved toward solutions to problems, and he develops a respect for conflicting opinions. The case study method exposes students to various approaches for solving various problems.

Mistakes that are likely to occur on the job are made in the classroom. The experience of making a mistake in the training situation is frequently sufficient to prevent a student from repeating the same mistake at a later time in a real-life situation.

The problem-solving nature of the case study method develops in the student an ability to select facts that relate to specific problems and to perceive factual interrelationships between cause and effect. Students acquire a habit of thinking critically and, in the process, learn also to criticize their own thinking processes and become more amenable to change. As students analyze particular cases, they not only obtain new information but also learn how to use information in practical, problem-solving ways.

The case study method expands a student's potential to discuss and understand opposing points of view and to accommodate them, finally reaching an agreement. The method forces the student to think analytically, to communicate persuasively, to act constructively, and to agree creatively. The case study method is particularly useful in helping students gain experience in making decisions and working with other people.

The case study method stimulates students to discuss the case in advance of classroom discussion and then again after they have participated in reaching a group solution of identified problems. It helps to generate within each student and among the students a type of motivation that facilitates the learning process. Students find that they learn faster and more intently when they discover for themselves possible answers to realistic cases representative of job situations they are likely to confront after completion of training. Instead of listening to theoretical discourses on problems and their possible solutions, the student examines the problems for himself and formulates answers that are shaped by the give and take of many viewpoints.

Perhaps more than any other teaching method, the case study approach requires conscientious student preparation. If the student arrives in the classroom unprepared to participate and contribute to the group discussion, he has deprived himself, as well as his fellow students, of opportunities to learn. For the case study method to succeed, the student must meet his personal obligations in complying with advance study and reading assignments.

●Methods

There are a variety of different ways the case study can be applied. Whatever approach is used, it will at least involve a case that describes a problem to be analyzed, solved, and discussed.

A common approach is to assign a case for students to read and study in advance of a scheduled classroom discussion period. The advance assignment might also include the preparation of a written report and the delineation of proposed solutions to the problems.

A variation of the case study method is the presentation of an incident or a problem in which the student will attempt to discover and analyze circumstances or events leading up to the occurrence of the problem or incident. The instructor does some limited role playing by assuming the identity of one or more persons associated with the hypothesized problem. Students are permitted to ask questions of the instructor who gives additional information that is narrowly responsive to student inquiries. If the right questions are not posed, the students fail to obtain pertinent details. This case study approach parallels real world situations because most on-the-job problem-solving decisions are based on fragmentary information.

●Selecting the Case

Cases in many topic areas are readily available in libraries and book stores. Without too much searching, an instructor should be able to locate prepared cases that are suitable for student study purposes. The instructor might decide, however, that he can achieve better results by writing his own case study.

A case can be short and simple with a single problem, or it can be long, complex, and involve a myriad of problems. The case can be dramatized or placed into writing. It can be augmented with photographs, charts, diagrams, and other supplementary materials. The case can be based on a genuine problem, a hypothetical problem, or a combination of both.

The case should be fairly realistic and should describe an actual problem or situation. When the case is relevant and realistic, the student is better able to identify with the people and circumstances involved. The student must have some expectation that he will face the problem or some similar problem in the not too distant future. It also helps if the case contains a controversial issue. Controversy invariably produces differences of opinion.

●Role of the Instructor

If the students hold center stage in the case study method, what is the role of the instructor? Obviously, a group decision cannot emerge from classroom activities if the instructor dominates the discussion. Too much control and too much structure in classroom activities will inhibit a free exchange of ideas and curb the complete exploration of all possible solutions to case problems. A high level of leadership skill is required to make the case study method work correctly. The instructor knows that he must guide students within certain parameters established by the curriculum, and within those parameters he must involve the students in activities that produce new insights and skills. Overcontrol inhibits learning, while insufficient control results in disorder and frustration. A suitable role for the instructor is that of resource person to the student group.

An important function of the instructor during classroom discussion is to keep students on track. Because too much instructor control is damaging to the case study method, the instructor should use questions to stimulate and direct student actions. Questions that shape and lead student discussions might include the following: "Have you considered what would happen if you did that?" "Is it possible or sensible to address that particular problem before considering the earlier incident of . . .?" or "Does this particular problem have any similarity to problems or issues we have discussed in previous units of instruction?"

As a resource person, the instructor serves as a repository of information about the case and the concepts and skills related to it. Knowing more about the case than his students, he can provide accurate data when necessary.[4] The instructor acts as a subject matter expert and as a facilitator of learning. He ensures that every student is afforded opportunities to speak and to interact with other members of the group. The instructor does not offer a "canned solution" but, through skillful guidance, moves his students toward achievement of established learning objective. Without surrendering his authority as the teacher, he transfers to his students some degree of responsibility for their own learning.

Questions that students ask the instructor can be turned into teaching techniques. A simple technique is to relay a question from one student to another. This helps to get students working together in the sharing of ideas. Equally simple is the use of the question "Why?" The use of that simple word challenges students to reexamine their assumptions and assertions. It makes a student stop to think about the process of analysis he used in arriving at a particular judgment.

Throughout the discussion the instructor should be concerned with making the activity relevant as well as interesting. Not only should a student feel stimulated regarding his activity, but he should feel that an examination of the case contributes to his understanding of the job he is being trained to perform.

THE CRITIQUE

Included within the personal inventory of an instructor are the skills to analyze and judge the achievements of his students. Outside the classroom, the instructor provides appraisal, encouragement, and even criticisms through the process of guidance and counseling. Within the classroom, however, the instructor can use a formalized and structured classroom activity called the critique. The critique provides a way of assessing strengths, weaknesses, and problem areas and informing the student of academic progress.

The objective of a critique is to provide constructive suggestions and directions to students so that student performance levels can be raised. The critique can be used by the instructor to review training objectives or other course standards and to evaluate student performance in relation to them.

The critique can be effective as a follow-up process. Performance activities that lend themselves to follow-up critiques include report writing, briefings, fact-finding, problem solving, repairs, equipment adjustment, and decisionmaking. A critique works especially well immediately following a "hands-on" performance activity. Relevance is added if details of a performance are still fresh in the minds of students.

A critique need not necessarily be limited to follow-up appraisal of student activities. It can be used as a teaching technique in the midst of a student performance. For example, if an instructor notices a student incorrectly performing a particular operation, he should interrupt the student and point out the mistake. The critique then becomes a method of clarifying, emphasizing, or reinforcing important teaching points. When an instructor discovers a need to make on-the-spot corrections repeatedly, he might consider giving greater attention to explaining or demonstrating the skill prior to the exercise. He might also decide to give special attention to the skill in a later critique of the exercise.

A critique need not be extremely long nor need it treat every detail of every student's performance. The instructor must decide what points need to be covered and to what degree of emphasis.

●Types of Critiques

Although the critique is generally used for the benefit of a group, the method can be applied in private for a single student or a small number of students. A *private critique* is sometimes all that is needed to help a problem student back on track. Even with a large group, a critique becomes personal when it focuses upon individual student performances. By using students as examples of how a job function is performed, the instructor personalizes the critique. Not only do individual students benefit from such individual criticisms, but all students observing the critique gain additional insight.

A common critiquing technique uses the *instructor as the central point* of attention. The instructor provides direct leadership and guidance of classroom activities. In much the same way that he would present information in a lecture/discussion session, the instructor directs student attention to specific teaching points. This technique can be expanded upon to permit greater student involvement when the instructor invites members of the class to criticize performances in the previous exercise. This technique allows students to express their ideas and to pool their knowledge.

The instructor must be careful to lead student discussion toward specific purposes. By asking carefully selected questions, he can guide the classroom discussion in the intended direction. When the instructor is satisfied that a particular point has been covered, he summarizes what was said by the class before proceeding to a new point with another question.

The *small group* technique for critiquing breaks up the class into small groups with each group assigned a specific point to criticize. Using guidelines furnished by the instructor, each group analyzes the point in question and then presents its findings to the class.

A further variation of critiquing is the *student-led critique*. A student is assigned to serve as discussion leader. The instructor exercises some control by specifying the format and rules, or he can delegate this responsibility to a student leader. This technique is risky because it depends upon the availability of a student leader who is both a practiced speaker and a respected member of the class. Inexperience on the part of the discussion leader as well as class participants will limit the success of the technique. The instructor, however, can help move the proceedings along productive discussion lines by directing questions to the leader and the class. The student-led critique, when conducted properly, is capable of generating a high degree of interest and learning.

Another technique is to require the individual student to criticize his own performance. One kind of *self-critique* approach uses television. A playback of a video-recorded student performance can be one of the most effective methods of critiquing. Very often a student will not admit to having made a mistake pointed out to him by an instructor or a fellow student. When the student is able to see his mistake through the impartial medium of television he has little alternative but to accept the criticism and, as a consequence, is more likely to work toward correction of the mistake in later performances.

A *written critique*, although infrequently used, has certain advantages. More time and thought can be devoted to its preparation. Points that an instructor intends to cover during an oral critique are sometimes lost in the rush of discussion. Not only does the written critique reduce the risk of omitting important points, it can be used as a record of the performance exercise.[5] If the instructor lacks the time to prepare a written critique for each student, he can instruct all students in the class to prepare their own criticisms of the separate performances of every other student. For example, if the exercise involved each student making a briefing on an assigned topic, each student briefer would be criticized by his fellow students on a performance criteria checklist. The checklist could include such factors as eye contact, bearing, physical appearance, gestures, and voice quality. Each student briefer would then be given a written record of the opinions of his classmates.

●Organization

A logical pattern of organization needs to be followed in the conduct of a critique. Almost any approach is acceptable if it is understandable to the student and the instructor. Without some sense of organization, a critique tends to become disordered, and important comments lose their impact. It is helpful at the beginning for the instructor to tell the class what structure and rules will prevail. A common pattern is to have the order of the critique correspond to the sequence of performance that occurred during the exercise. The various steps followed by students during the exercise become the points of reference for the critique discussions.

The organization of a critique might also relate the exercise to a previous exercise or to a future one. In this way, an exercise can be critiqued in terms of its interrelatedness with skills acquired earlier and skills to be learned at a later time. This gives students the opportunity to conceptualize the exercise, not just in terms of a single skill development activity but as part of a broad, long-range building of skills.

Whatever the structure or pattern of organization selected for the critique, the instructor should be prepared and willing to improvise if necessary. It sometimes happens that a particular step in an exercise is performed poorly by most students. The students are concerned and want to focus upon the problem. Rather than hold to a rigid format, the instructor may find it more rewarding to allow the critique to concentrate on a thorough analysis of the poor performance. Being sensitive to student responses allows the instructor to adjust his presentation so that ideas of concern to students are sufficiently covered. When students show a keen interest in a given area of the critique, the instructor should be prepared to provide a detailed analysis of that area. When students fail to respond to a given point in the critique, the instructor should move on to other points of interest.

A variable that can't be allowed for in preparing a critique is the student reaction to a particular point or defect in the exercise. The instructor may find himself confronted with a problem of what to say, what to omit, what to stress, and what not to stress. He must consider the class situation, student attitudes, training objectives, the amount of time available for the critique, and other factors. The instructor must have the capacity to spontaneously modify and adapt, particularly in response to unexpected challenges that arise from the class.

●Role of the Instructor

The central topic of any critique is the student. Unfortunately, many instructors find it difficult to let students share center stage. Reluctance to break away from traditional teacher-centered instructional methods sometimes prevents them from remembering that effective learning depends more on what students do than on what instructors do. The instructor conducting a critique has to keep in mind that the critique is intended to assess student performance, not instructor performance. The way in which the instructor personally performs a skill is less important than the way in which students perform the skill.

At the outset, the instructor must assure students that the purpose of a critique is to improve their learning. When students fail to appreciate the critique as a learning experience, there is a risk that constructive criticisms will produce negative attitudes towards the instructor or the course.

To be effective in the critique process, the instructor must establish his credibility. Most persons find it difficult to willingly accept criticism, and students are no exception. Before criticism can be taken, much less acted upon, a student must have confidence in the instructor's qualification, sincerity, and authority. Because a critique most usually follows a teaching/learning activity of some type, there is an opportunity for the instructor and student to get to know each other. If the amount of time preceding the critique is insufficient to allow the instructor to establish his personal and professional credentials in the eyes of the students, he will have to rely upon his demeanor, attitude, and the quality of his teaching to attain some degree of respect from the class. Students will usually accept criticism when it is obvious to them that the instructor has taught with conviction and sincerity. The same qualities, from the point of view of the students, are expected to carry over into the critique. An instructor who tries to impress students with his rank or position will find it difficult to conduct a successful critique. Student acceptance of an instructor depends more on demonstrable rather than purported qualities.

The instructor has to be conscious of the students' needs for self-esteem, recognition, and the approval of others. He should never minimize the importance of individual student dignity. To poke fun at a student during a critique can greatly reduce the effectiveness of the critique as a medium for learning. Although an instructor should always be honest in his dealings with students, he should likewise respect their individual feelings. Should an instructor believe that criticism will produce an unwanted emotional reaction, he will look for another time or opportunity to make corrections.

The critique is not a means of determining what a student has learned, but of enhancing learning.[6] It should never be totally negative in content. The good should be discussed along with the bad. Criticisms are more readily accepted and acted upon if they are accompanied by congratulations on successful aspects.

The instructor should be specific with his comments and recommendations. General statements, such as "Your performance at the end was not quite as good as the beginning," have little value. The student needs to know why his performance was not good and what he can do to improve. The instructor should make specific remarks and always have a clear and supportable teaching point in mind. He should express himself firmly and authoritatively, using language that permits little misunderstanding. Specific examples followed by practical suggestions are more helpful than vague generalities. It is helpful also to emphasize a point by demonstrating it. Students cannot be expected to act upon a recommendation made in a critique unless they know precisely what the recommendation is and how it can be implemented. At the end of the critique, every student should have little doubt concerning what he did poorly, what he did well, and what things he can do to improve his performance.

Instructors sometimes allow personal impressions to influence their judgment of students. A critique must be honest and it must be objective. Preconceived judgments, friendship with a student, and conflicts in personality cannot be permitted to prejudice a critique. The matter of bias in a critique can be avoided if critique discussions are based on actual student performance. The instructor should critique not what he expected would happen but what, in fact, did happen. He should concentrate on positive or negative factors that affected student performance and offer constructive suggestions.

The personality traits of a student, favorable or unfavorable, should carry no weight in an evaluation of his ability to perform. For example, if a student successfully completes a complicated problem-solving exercise, it would be very improper for the instructor to criticize the student's personality. On the other hand, if an exercise requires a student to demonstrate skills that promote good interpersonal relationships, it would be appropriate for the instructor to comment upon favorable or unfavorable traits. The important thing to keep in mind in such an instance is that any instructor remarks, congratulatory or critical, should be centered upon the student's ability or inability to perform consistently with established job standards.

Whatever technique is used in a critique, the instructor must be conscious of the need to resolve controversial issues and to correct erroneous impressions. When students are encouraged to participate in critique discussions, allowances must be made for student in-experience and the chance that the critique will fail to cover all the necessary points. When a critiquing technique is student-centered, the instructor should reserve time for himself at the end of the critique to go over those areas that were not adequately addressed.

LECTURE AS A TEACHING METHOD

Although much has been said in this book about the necessity to maintain frequent and intense student participation in learning activities, there are times when the lecture method has usefulness. As a matter of fact, an instructor would find it almost impossible to avoid the lecture method as an instructional approach.[7] This is because many other instructional methods rely to some degree upon the lecture method.

The lecture method is preferred when many ideas need to be presented in a relatively short period of time. It permits rapid presentation of facts and ideas organized in a logical sequence. Lecture is also economical in terms of the material required in support of it. Furthermore, more students can be accommodated in a lecture situation. Economy and convenience seem to be the two most important reasons why the lecture method is frequently selected over other methods of instruction.

●Preparation

More so than any other teaching method, lecture depends almost exclusively upon an instructor's ability to communicate. This fact underscores the connection that exists between student comprehension and the quality of topic delivery. The quality of delivery is a function of how much preparation is invested in the lecture before the instructor enters the classroom. Generally speaking, there are four options available to an instructor regarding the type of delivery he can select for presentation of ideas. First, he can lecture spontaneously and without preparation. This type of delivery requires only a little vanity and a complete disregard for the learning needs of students. Closely related to this type of lecture delivery is the practice of reading from written material. Slightly more preparation is required, however, because the instructor has to remember to bring his written material with him to the classroom. A third kind of lecture is recitation by memory. While this technique requires considerable preparation, the instructor is assured of having little more success than if he taught "off the cuff" or read from a manuscript. All of us at one time or another have been victims of these types of lecture delivery.

The fourth method, the use of a well-prepared outline as an aid to extemporaneously delivered information, will avoid the pitfalls mentioned previously. In this type of delivery the instructor does not read his lecture or recite it from memory. He is prepared because he has developed a written outline of key ideas or teaching points to be covered during his presentation.

In short, preparation is the key to effective lecture. The content of a lecture, its direction, depth, and intensity are dependent upon preparation made well in advance of a scheduled class.

When an instructor is well prepared, he need not commit himself to the use of exact words to express ideas. His lecture is more personal and conversational than if he spoke purely from memory or read directly from prepared material. This conversational manner enables the instructor to observe and interpret facial expressions and other signals of incomprehension or disagreement.

Planning and preparation increase the instructor's personal confidence in making an effective presentation. With confidence comes a willingness to respond flexibly in the classroom. The instructor who is sure of his ability to successfully communicate the essential teaching points will have a greater willingness to occasionally change direction or elaborate upon ideas that have apparent student interest. Also, when an instructor is confident, he is more likely to be enthusiastic about his topic and convey that enthusiasm to his students.

Selecting supporting material. An important factor in preparation is the instructor's selection of supporting material. Because students are able to understand ideas only in terms of their own personal experiences, the instructor chooses examples and comparisons with which his students can personally identify. Information that is asserted without supporting facts or meaningful examples is either rejected or quickly forgotten.

If an idea is important enough to be included in a lecture, it is certainly important enough to be supported with believable examples, comparisons, statistics, quotations, or other testimony that facilitates understanding and acceptance of the idea. Almost every idea needs some form of clarification or proof if the student is to accept it.

One of the best ways to support an idea is to use an *example or illustration*. A teaching point can be supported through the use of a series of short, punchy examples, or a rather lengthy and detailed single example. For example, to make the point that many people serving in the United States Congress are former lawyers, an instructor could name many prominent Senators and Representatives who began their careers in the legal profession. Or to support the same point, an instructor might relate one of the legendary stories of Abraham Lincoln's pre-Congressional career as a backwoods lawyer.

Quotations also constitute supporting material for a lecture. Assertions made on the authority of the instructor take on greater credibility when supported by statements of well-known persons. For a quotation to achieve its purpose, the person being quoted should be an authority in his field. A noted person out of his field of expertise is not truly an authority. To quote W.C. Fields on an issue involving nuclear disarmament would be inappropriate. A quotation is useful only if it helps support the idea being explained. Because quotations are plentiful and diverse, they can add considerable variety to a lecture. Like statistics, however, quotations should be used sparingly or their desired effect will be diminished.

The use of *comparison* is another way to support points made during a lecture. The comparison is like a chain that links a known idea with an unknown idea. The unknown idea can be clarified or explained by pointing out its resemblance to an idea familiar to the student. Comparisons can be used to point out differences as well as similarities. A comparison can be factual or imaginary. An example of a factual comparison would be to explain the similarity between the methods of propulsion used by sea clams and jet aircraft. An imaginary comparison might use an analogy to suggest a parallel between a story and the point under consideration. An analogy might be made, for example, by observing that squirrels store nuts for the winter much like humans save money for a rainy day.

A common procedure for helping students accept information is to cite *statistics*. When used properly, statistics can dramatize a point, particularly if the data are presented in a visual format that is eye-catching and understandable. When overused, however, an audience will tire of statistics. Also, students are accustomed to hearing statistics that are supposed to produce a shock effect. The enormity of a number, for example, is frequently intended to startle students and create concern, but because statistics are so frequently employed for this purpose they usually fail to create the desired effect. The fact that cargo theft losses in the United States last year amounted to twenty billion dollars has limited shock effect. When, however, that same statistic is described as equivalent to the value of a new automobile for every adult male who lives east of the Mississippi River, the statistic has impact because it is couched in personally meaningful terms. When properly collected and judiciously applied, statistics can help an instructor to prove his major points.

Selecting the words. For much the same reason an instructor uses supporting material to clarify, he uses restatement and repetition to explain information in more than one way. Main ideas tend to stand out when they are repeated. In some cases, information can be repeated without any change in actual words used. In other cases, the information needs to be presented in different words and different contexts. The nature of the subject matter and the personality of the instructor determine the character of restatement and repetition. The important thing to remember is that students frequently need to receive information more than once and in different formats.

A lecture is easier to follow when the instructor uses simple rather than complex words. If a topic includes technical terms, the instructor should define each term to leave no doubt regarding its meaning. While it is not necessary or even desirable for an instructor to use perfectly correct English, he should consciously avoid errors in syntax and pronunciation. Profanity and vulgarism similarly detract from a lecture presentation.

Colloquialisms and picturesque words can enliven a lecture. Slang is a colorful part of the American culture and can hardly be excluded from our manner of speaking. Provided they are not abused, colloquialisms add vividness and interest to a lecture.

●Disadvantages

The lecture method has a number of distinct disadvantages. The lecture frequently makes no provision for physical participation by students, and consequently students are not moved towards maximum achievement in certain types of learning. Skills in writing, speaking, analyzing, and psychomotor activity cannot be learned through lecture. Students are able to develop such skills only through application and practice. Neither does the lecture permit the instructor to measure student progress throughout the instruction. The instructor has no reliable assurance that all students have understood the information that was presented. Only after a formal examination has been graded does the instructor discover apparent gaps in student comprehension.

Many instructors will honestly admit to an inability to retain the attention of students throughout an entire class period in which lecture is the primary teaching method.[8] Even the most skillful of speakers will find certain students slipping away from close attention to important material. There is a point at which students are simply unable to absorb any further information presented by the lecture method. The instructor should always weigh the advantages of lecture against its disadvantages. Clearly, economy and convenience do not provide ample justification for the lecture method when learning goals involve action skills. The lecture method has definite application, but only in a limited number of learning activities.

Team teaching can be considered in two major ways—as a method that employs at least two instructors teaching a single subject or as a method using many instructors teaching a series of subjects.

In the first instance, team teaching commonly operates with instructors rotating as speakers, or with a panel of instructors who participate with students in discussions of a topic or problem. A similar type of team teaching occurs when one instructor describes a skill while another instructor simultaneously demonstrates. During applicatory exercises, when students are practicing physical skills, several instructors might be present as evaluators and coaches.[9] Team teaching is also used in small group sessions when each group has its own instructor as a resource person.

The second major way to arrange team teaching is to organize the separate teaching activities of several instructors across a broad range of subjects, over a longer than usual period of time. A teaching team agrees to divide the responsibilities for teaching several units of instruction, using a variety of teaching techniques. A single lesson within the larger block of lesson units can be taught by more than one instructor applying more than one teaching approach. This can be contrasted with the conventional strategy of having one instructor teach one unit by whatever method appeals to the instructor individually.

This second type of team teaching frequently utilizes multiple-track scheduling that places groups of students in different activities at one time. At one place students might be watching a film or listening to a lecture in a large group setting. At another place they might be working in a small group configuration. At other locations students might be engaged in tutorials or individual research projects. Multiple-track scheduling moves people in a planned pattern that provides each student with the same learning activity as all other students. A given learning objective can be reached through the employment of separate, but integrated, teaching methods. For example, a student might be exposed to a subject by reading a text assignment, listening to a lecture, participating in a conference, watching a film or television presentation, researching the subject at a library, working with fellow students on a small group project, conferring with an instructor, role playing a procedure, attending a seminar, practicing a skill, consulting with an advisor or tutor, being critiqued, watching a videotape playback of his own performance of a skill, completing a programmed instruction assignment, or working through a multimedia package at a learning center.

These examples point out a need to assign specific responsibilities to members of the teaching team. For each learning objective, one person should be designated as team leader. The leader is held responsible for ensuring that subject matter information is current, that training aids, student handouts, and other support materials are developed and on hand when needed, and that the other members of the teaching team understand their individual responsibilities for achieving the established learning objectives.

Student learning and interest can be greatly enhanced by team teaching because of the variety and stimulation that result from different teaching personalities applying several instructional approaches. Active participation is an essential ingredient for effective learning, and team teaching techniques make it possible for students to participate and become involved in many different ways.

PEER TEACHING

Has there been a time when you needed an assistant instructor but none was available? If so, you probably selected a student you considered to be a superior learner. Your purpose was to use one student to coach or tutor slower students. Peer teaching uses students to teach other students but is not quite the same as tutoring or coaching. The method utilizes a self-paced movement of a student along a carefully designed sequence of self-contained learning modules. Each module has its own geographical station where a single skill or small set of interrelated skills is taught, practiced, and then performed in a pass/fail test.

Peer teaching follows an approach that requires every student, not just superior students, to teach another person the skills he has just learned himself. Before the peer instructor is allowed to teach another person, he must first demonstrate that he has in fact mastered the particular skill at an acceptable level of excellence. Mastery of the skill is shown through successful passing of a criterion-referenced performance test. The skill being tested is usually divided into a set or series of performance elements. The conditions of performance are identified and standards of competence are specified for each performance element. The performance elements are described in a checklist used by an evaluator who is present during the test.

When the student has passed the performance test, he then becomes the peer instructor for another student who is moving through the same logical and organized schedule, just a step behind him. Simple guidelines help the peer instructor teach his student the required skill. In fact, a written description of the performance test is available to the student and peer instructor for reference. (When performance of a skill is the sole criterion for passing a test, it is only logical that the student know what is expected of him during the test. Revealing the requirements of a performance test has positive rather than negative connotations.) After the peer instructor has explained and demonstrated the particular skill, the student may practice it and decide on his own when he is ready to undergo the test.

Some peer-teaching programs make teaching resources available in addition to the peer instructor. For example, the student who is being coached by the peer instructor might also have a learning center available where he can watch slides, filmstrips, films, or videotapes that depict proper performance of the skill he is attempting to learn.

When the student decides to take the test, his peer instructor is on hand as an observer. He is not allowed to help the student perform the test, but he notes the demonstrated weaknesses which will require remedial training if the student fails the test.

If the student passes the performance test, the peer instructor proceeds to the next teaching/test station where he becomes an incoming student for another peer instructor who is ahead of him in the training sequence. His former student remains at the teaching/test station to teach the next incoming student.

Should any student fail his test, both he and his peer instructor are "frozen" in place until the student has learned the required skill. The evaluator's checklist and the observations of the peer instructor provide guidance on performance weaknesses that need shoring up.

A basic premise of peer teaching is that all students can and will learn.[10] Organizations that have used the peer-teaching method report that slower learners seem to gain more, probably from the experience of being the teacher. The extra practice that results from teaching and demonstrating helps students retain the acquired abilities over a longer period of time.

THE FIELD TRIP

A field trip is a planned learning experience, away from the classroom site, in which students observe procedures or on-the-job operations that involve information presented in class. It is one of the more traditional ways to produce learning. The advantages are apparent. The field trip answers student needs for variety and for seeing concepts in action under genuine job conditions. It places the student on-site at a genuine work location where direct observation can be made of skills that at best are simulated in the training environment.

As our society continues to rapidly increase its capacity to move many people across relatively large distances in shorter periods of time, the instructor finds greater opportunities to use field trips.

The value of a field trip is increased when students are told in advance the important points to look for, when attention is called to those points during the field trip, and when a critique is made after the trip.

Unfortunately, there is no reliable procedure for evaluating the effectiveness of a field trip, because student observations during one field trip are certain to differ from observations made on another trip. The instructor, therefore, is at a disadvantage in constructing a uniform and reliable device to determine the extent of student learning produced by the method. The best that an instructor can hope to determine are very general student impressions. Critiques, group projects, reports, or individual written reports may be useful to the instructor in evaluating a field trip.

ROLE PLAYING

Role playing can be carried out with students as observers of a simulated event, or with students acting as participants or role players. In the former case, the strength of learning for any one student is relative to that student's capacity to identify with a particular role player and to appreciate the significance of what he observes in terms of his own personal involvement in a similar situation.

Role playing that involves each student as a participant provides a high potential for learning. A student who is placed in a fairly realistic situation that requires him to apply principles or skills previously taught will get a taste of what it is like to perform on the job. Role playing can administer heavy doses of meaningful experience. For that reason, it is an excellent medium for stimulating student interest and achieving maximum physical and mental involvement. Role playing is especially effective in teaching tasks that are associated with interpersonal relationships.[11] When a certain type of mental attitude is a critical job requirement, the role-playing technique is helpful in detecting and then correcting attitudinal deficiencies.

An imaginative instructor can take advantage of the natural desire of a person to be someone other than who he is in everyday life. The role-playing technique permits a student to momentarily be someone else. More important, it places the student in a noncritical, nondangerous simulated situation that makes demands upon him to perform in some specified way. The student discovers, through experience, what it is like to perform a particular skill under a particular set of given conditions. Hopefully, the learning he derives through the experience will be transferred later to the job.

For the instructor, the quality of performance demonstrated by the student in the simulated event is visible and therefore measurable. It can be compared with established performance standards of particular job skills. When a student shows a level of acceptable proficiency, he has passed. When he fails to meet the proficiency standard, further instruction and practice are indicated.

PANELS

A chief advantage of the panel is that it can be used with a large audience when extensive student participation is not required. A panel typically consists of from three to nine persons whose individual qualifications give promise of worthwhile contributions to an understanding of the planned topic. A panel might include an outside subject-matter expert, a staff instructor, and a student.

The panel moderator makes sure that panelists concentrate on the issue or problem under discussion. He intervenes as necessary to terminate irrelevant comments and to pose questions or make remarks intended to promote exploration of pertinent ideas.

The student audience observes the panel in action and derives knowledge from the exchange of information.

Other panel method techniques utilize audience reaction teams and listening teams. The audience reaction team is made up of three to five members of the student audience who react to the panelists. The reaction team is permitted, by ground rules, set in advance, to interrupt a panel member to request clarification or amplification of discussion points. The listening team is also composed of audience members. It records main issues covered and summarizes them at the conclusion of panel activities.

The symposium is a panel method that requires special preparation on the part of panelists. Each panelist speaks in turn without interruption, briefly outlining his position and recommendations. The audience is then invited to question the speakers, either to clarify information or to challenge specific assertions. Panel members explain their statements and defend their views. The audience is expected to study the panel topic in advance of the symposium and be prepared to question panel views that do not coincide with their own individual conclusions. This technique can motivate independent student research.

BRAINSTORMING

The primary goal of brainstorming is not simply to produce numerous and unusual ideas, but to engage in a creative problem-solving process that culminates with practical recommendations.[12]

The technique works best when a class is broken up into groups of about five students. The instructor presents a brief overview of brainstorming as a creative problem-solving mechanism. He then announces the brainstorming rules:[13] (1) absolutely no criticism can be made while brainstorming is in process, (2) as many ideas as possible are permitted, (3) the wilder the ideas the better they are, and (4) participants are urged to "hitchhike" on the ideas of other persons.

Each group is given a specific problem which may or may not be identical with that of other groups. The physical setting should be large enough to accommodate all groups and allow them to work separately without disrupting one another.

In each group a secretary or reporter is designated to quickly jot down ideas as they are generated during the brainstorming part of the exercise. On signal from the instructor, the session begins. A set period of time, usually from 10 to 20 minutes, is established. If, at the end of the allotted time, the instructor sees that ideas are still being generated, he may decide to extend the time.

When the brainstorming is complete and all ideas are recorded on paper, the instructor tells the group to examine the ideas and to rank them from the best to the worst. Then, the instructor requires the group to describe its selection process, present its ideas, and propose a solution to the stated problem. The solution put forward is based on an idea or ideas that were generated during the brainstorming session.

The brainstorming technique is very good for generating ideas to solve a problem. It provides opportunity for students to discriminate between ideas tossed out freely and ideas that have been hardened into workable solutions.

NOTES

1. Joseph A. Olmstead, *Small Group Instruction: Theory and Practice* (Alexandria, Va.: Human Resources Research Organization, 1974), p. 94.

2. Thomas F. Staton, *How to Instruct Successfully* (New York: McGraw-Hill Book Co., 1960), p. 88.

3. *Techniques of Military Instruction* (Washington, D.C.: Department of the Army, 1967), p. 33.

4. *Principles and Techniques of Instruction* (Washington, D.C.: Department of the Air Force, 1974), p. 19-3.

5. Ibid., p. 4-4.

6. Ibid., p. 4-1.

7. A 1965 survey of police training academies completed by the National Council on Crime and Delinquency revealed that the lecture method was the predominant mode of instruction. See *The National Manpower Survey of the Criminal Justice System,* Vol. 5 (Washington, D.C.: U.S. Department of Justice, 1978), p. v-294.

8. Allen Z. Gammage, *Police Training in the United States* (Springfield, Ill.: Charles C. Thomas, 1963), p. 209.

9. *Instructor Training, Phase I* (Atlanta, Ga.: Georgia State Merit System), pp. 7-12.

10. J. Richard Suchman et al., *The Development of an Open-Access Performance Oriented Curriculum for Training the Military Policeman* (Alexandria, Va.: Human Resources Research Organization, 1975), p. 13.

11. Thomas F. Staton, *How to Instruct Successfully* (New York: McGraw-Hill Book Co., 1960), p. 125.

12. Dugan Laird, *Approaches to Training and Development* (Reading, Mass.: Addison-Wesley Publishing Co., 1978), p. 143.

13. Michael E. O'Neill and Kai R. Martensen, *Criminal Justice Group Training* (LaJolla, Calif.: University Associates, Inc., 1975), p. 36.

4

PROGRAMMED INSTRUCTION

Types of Programs • Writing a Programmed Instruction Module • Media for Presenting Programmed Materials • When Is Programmed Instruction Feasible?

Imagine a teaching situation in which there is at least one expert instructor per student, with the instructor free to concentrate entirely on teaching. The instructor guides his pupil step by step through the lesson, asking questions each step of the way and confirming answers immediately. When the student has trouble, instruction slows down and difficult ideas are retaught. When the student learns quickly, the pace of instruction picks up. Most important, the teaching does not end until the student correctly learns all the skills and knowledge contained in the lesson.

This ideal teaching situation is possible with programmed instruction. Programmed instruction permits a student to learn without other students present, at his own rate of speed, and with little or no human supervision. The program gives an amount of information; the student responds to the information; and the program supplies an immediate answer.

As a student progresses through the program, he makes one type of response to each planned increment of instruction. A response might be to write a single word or a complete sentence, or to write upon a diagram, sketch, map, or some other graphic representation of information. The student may have to set switches on a device, measure a value, or assemble a piece of equipment.

The program in turn offers the student immediate feedback. If the response is correct, the program moves on to the next teaching point. If the response is wrong, the program may direct the student to restudy the point and try again, or it may supply the same teaching point in a modified form with a new stimulus. Successful completion of each increment moves the student one small step at a time toward completion of the program.

Unlike conventional methods of instruction, the student sets his own pace. He is neither held back nor forced to keep up with faster students. The student is told what he is expected to learn and is guided in the learning process. The programmed approach systematically moves the student, step by step, in the direction of established objectives.

TYPES OF PROGRAMS

Programs are generally classified under two main types, depending on the technique used to elicit student responses. The two types are the linear technique and the branching technique.[1]

●The Linear Technique

Material in linear programming is presented in small steps. Each step is carefully designed to offer as much review as needed to enhance the degree of retention appropriate to the subject matter, the learning situation, and the needs of the students.

A step can consist of a frame or a short series of frames in which information is provided. A frame consists of a single unit of information, such as a fact, which is segregated from other facts by isolating it in some fashion—for example, by placing the information inside a frame. Immediately after completing a response to a frame and before continuing to the next frame, the student checks his response by comparing it to the program answer. The intent of linear programming is to permit each student to progress smoothly, with a sense of satisfaction. If the program designer has thoughtfully constructed his subject matter, the student should learn the information without too much difficulty.

Supporters of linear programming attribute its success to the reinforcement it provides. If a student is reinforced each time he answers correctly, he learns. The more often he is rewarded, the more lasting is the learning. The technique capitalizes on the human tendency to do things that produce satisfying results and to avoid actions that have unpleasant results. The programmer's task is to reinforce (i.e., reward) certain desired responses. The student is consequently conditioned to assign positive personal values to correct responses and negative or low values to incorrect responses.

Another feature of the linear programmed technique is the repetition it uses in presenting a key teaching point. Presumably, if a student encounters the same fact, idea, or concept in a variety of ways, he is more likely to retain the information.[2] In each block of new subject matter presented in a linear program, the initial frames contain obvious hints or cues to correct responses. The average student will find it nearly impossible to make errors. As the program progresses, the cues are gradually eliminated. In the final stages the student is required to supply complete answers without being cued. The following sequence of frames illustrates the linear programmed technique. These sample frames are typical of beginning frames. They offer obvious cues and demand only simple responses, but note that the student is required to write in his answer, not just pick from a small number of offered answers.

	Answer:
1. Measurements are *numbers*. For example, an infant can be described as having a birth weight of 6½ pounds and a length of 20 inches. Two measurements are used in this description. • Suppose during a rainstorm a meteorologist records winds at 56 miles per hour, barometric pressure at 28 inches of mercury, and air temperature at 45 degrees Fahrenheit. How many measurements are recorded?	*three*
2. Measurements describe *characteristics* of persons or things. For example, the 6½ pounds birth weight describes a characteristic of the infant. • A person tells you he is thirty years old. What is the characteristic measured?	*age*
3. A form of measurement is the *counted* measurement. Examples of counted measurements are the number of trials handled by a prosecuting attorney or the number of prisoners released in a month. This type of measurement involves counts of persons or things. • Suppose a highway patrolman investigates 8 traffic accidents. (a) What is the characteristic measured? (b) What kind of measurement is it?	(a) *traffic cases* (b) *counted*

To a person unfamiliar with programmed instruction, this sequence of frames may seem excessively simple. To the beginner who has no knowledge of the subject matter, however, linear programming becomes a kind of game which is impossible to lose. As the student's confidence increases, the game becomes more difficult but never so difficult that satisfactory progress cannot be made in moving through the carefully planned and sequenced material.

• The Branching Technique

Another major approach to programmed learning is called branching or intrinsic branching. Unlike the linear approach, the branching technique presents large segments of material at one time. A frame may consist of a full paragraph or more of important information. This approach recognizes the greater likelihood of student mistakes and, in fact, anticipates that errors will occur, using the errors as part of the learning strategy.

A frame starts with an explanation of the subject matter to be learned. The explanation is followed immediately by a question or problem relating to the explanation. The student is given a choice of two or more possible answers, only one of which is correct. Each possible answer refers the student to a different new frame.

If the student has selected the correct answer, he is referred to a frame that repeats his answer and informs him that his solution was correct. The sense of achievement and self-satisfaction from this feedback is intended to motivate the student to continue learning. The answer frame gives the reason for the correct answer and perhaps some further elaboration. The answer frame also presents a new segment of material to be learned and another problem, with possible choices provided.

When the student's original answer choice is incorrect, he is referred to a frame that explains why the choice is wrong. The frame further tells him how to find the right answer. Some branching programs will direct the student to return to the frame at which he made his original choice and reconsider the problem before making another selection.[3] (See Figure 1.)

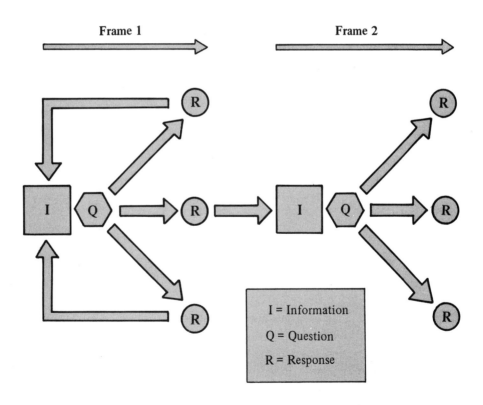

FIGURE 1. A Simple Branching Technique

Let's take a look at a kind of branched program:

1-1 Anthropologists working in an unexplored region of the Amazon discover three unknown primitive tribes. The tribes are the Macos, the Hurus, and the Chingas. The Macos are all less than 5 feet tall and weigh no more than 140 pounds. The Hurus are all shorter than the Macos but weigh more. The Chingas are taller than the Hurus and weigh more than the Macos.

- Which of the following statements is true?

(a) The Chingas are taller than the Macos. (12-5)

(b) The Hurus weigh less than the Chingas. (27-8)

(c) The Hurus are the shortest but not the lightest. (51-12)

The student makes his selection from the three answers given. If he chooses answer (a), the student turns to page 12, paragraph 5. Following is an example of feedback the student might receive.

12-5 You are wrong. Both the Macos and the Chingas are taller than the Hurus, but from the information provided it is not possible to determine which of the two is taller. Go back to 1-1 and try again.

The student would return to the question as directed. Let's suppose he now selects response (b). He turns to page 27, paragraph 8 and finds the following.

27-8 Too bad. Your answer is incorrect. The Chingas and the Hurus both weigh more than the Macos, but from the information given it is not possible to tell which of these two weighs less. Return to 1-1 and select another answer.

The student would again follow the instructions and return to the question. The student would now select the only response left.
Whether response (c) was selected first, second, or last, this is what the student would find.

51-12 Very good. You have found that the Chingas and Macos are both taller than the Hurus, thereby making the Hurus the shortest of the three. You have also concluded that the Hurus are heavier than the Macos, and therefore could not be the lightest.

The anthropologists also discovered that the Macos are the most friendly of the tribes. The Hurus are able to write and the Chingas live in tree houses.

Based on this new information, which of the following statements is definitely false?

(a) The Macos cannot write. (19-3)

(b) The Chingas are friendlier than the Macos. (8-12)

(c) The Hurus live in tree houses. (47-7)

The feedback in 51-12 does a number of things. It provides some rewarding language; it informs the student regarding the correctness of his response; it explains why the response was correct; it gives some new information; and it poses a new question. The student would study the new information and select one of the three responses. In most cases the student would select the correct response on the first try.

Another form of branching is structured in a more complicated manner. The student who makes an incorrect response is carried along a series of relatively small steps that parallel the correct mainstream of ideas. Material presented in the mainstream is designed so that only the superior students will consistently choose the correct response and avoid branching.[4] (See Figure 2.)

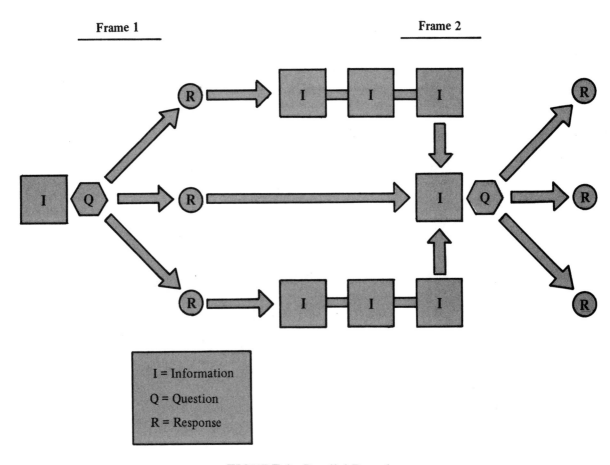

FIGURE 2. Parallel Branches

This method of branching anticipates that students will make errors. An error causes a student to branch along a parallel path that provides extra teaching and feedback sufficient to remedy incorrect thinking. By carefully developing incorrect answer choices, the programmer can provide the assistance that weaker students will often require in order to maintain parity with superior students.

WRITING A PROGRAMMED INSTRUCTION MODULE

Programmed instruction should be used when there is convincing evidence that other teaching methods are likely to be less effective. Student population, the availability of qualified instructors, training objectives, subject matter content, time, and costs are examples of factors that need to be evaluated before deciding to employ a programmed teaching approach. If it is decided to use programmed instruction, the problem is narrowed to that of writing the program and putting it into operation. (See Figure 3.)

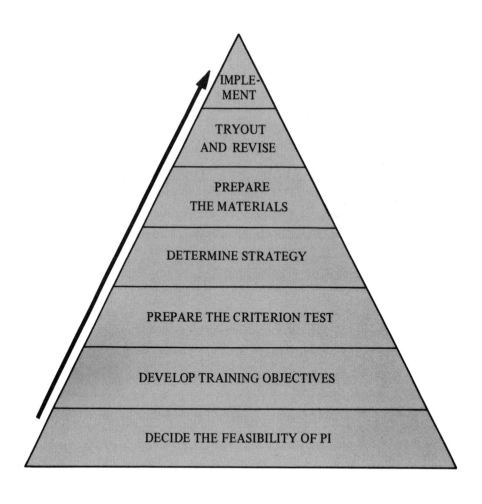

FIGURE 3. Steps in Developing Programmed Instruction (PI)

●Task Analysis

Creating a programmed module for a training program involves a process similar to that used in the development of any instructional program. A first step in the process is task analysis. Not even a single frame should be written until the various tasks involved in the job are identified.

Ideally, job tasks should be observed as they are performed in real life. A solid background of on-the-job experience in the tasks to be taught will greatly assist the programmer in defining the functions or activities that are performed by the student after he leaves training and goes on the job.[5] Field surveys, questionnaires, and similar approaches can help to more accurately define the job, the conditions under which the job is typically performed, and the standards of excellence that constitute satisfactory job performance. Experts, subject matter specialists, and experienced practitioners can provide added insight.

A fundamental intention of any instructional approach should be to develop in the student a form of functional behavior that is necessary for the performance of duties in a particular job. The programmed method of teaching will have succeeded in this fundamental intention when the student has demonstrated an ability to satisfactorily carry out tasks that the programmer defined during task analysis.

Subtasks. It is not sufficient, however, for the programmer to merely describe the job in general terms. Analysis should entail a search for all job aspects, including the implied abilities and operations required in doing a particular job function. For example, if the function requires an employee to prepare a report of an incident, the employee should know when a report must be prepared, what the report must contain, and so forth. These implications are called subtasks. If the programmer records the subtasks in some logical order during the task analysis stage, he is likely to save himself a great deal of trouble during execution of the module.

The programmer's aim is to comprehensively break down all the tasks and subtasks that comprise the job. The breakdown allows the programmer to identify what must be taught in order for the student to perform the job. The emphasis is upon the "what" of teaching. The "how" of teaching is addressed at a later time in the writing of the module. An outline format can be used in making the breakdown. An outline for a single task might appear, in part, as shown in Figure 4.

●Training Objectives

The next step is the development of training objectives. Each task or subtask that was defined during the previous step needs to be converted to one or more training objectives. A training objective is nothing more than a task or subtask with two extra elements added.

```
┌─────────────────────────────────────────────────────────────┐
│ TASK:          PREPARE AN INCIDENT REPORT                     │
│ Subtasks:                                                     │
│     Identify incidents that require reporting.                │
│     Obtain a blank incident report form.                      │
│     Enter the time and date of the incident.                  │
│     Enter the place of the incident.                          │
│     Enter the names and addresses of all parties to the       │
│     incident, including witnesses.                            │
│     Describe how the incident occurred.                       │
│     Describe why the incident occurred.                       │
│     Specify the offense(s) committed, if any.                 │
│     Enter the date of the report.                             │
│     Enter the name and department of the reporting person.    │
│     Enter the names and departments of any assisting persons. │
│     Describe any property stolen, lost, damaged, or recovered.│
│     Attach to the incident report any estimates of property   │
│     stolen, lost, damaged, or recovered.                      │
│     Describe any injuries or deaths.                          │
│     Attach to the incident report any medical reports of      │
│     injuries or deaths.                                       │
│     Sign the report.                                          │
│     Submit the report to the supervisor.                      │
└─────────────────────────────────────────────────────────────┘
```

FIGURE 4. Breakdown of a Task

The first element reflects the conditions under which the task is normally performed. These must take into account the environment in which the task is carried out, as well as the tools used. Any instruments, books, equipment, or other materials normally used on the job in the performance of the task should be identified. The programmer should then determine if the student must have any of the identified materials to be properly trained. When materials (or mockups) are available and appropriate for use in the training, the programmer will need to integrate these items with the module.

The second element reflects the standards of acceptable performance. Standards relate to competency required in the task and the time that is normally consumed in completing the task.

A typical training objective is for a student to learn how to prepare an incident report. Necessary *conditions* would include having an incident, an incident report form, and a writing implement. *Standards* for the task might mention such criteria as legibility, grammar, content, accuracy of facts, and the number of minutes reasonably required to prepare a report of a typical incident. A training objective for one of the subtasks shown previously might read as follows:

(Given) a (hypothetical) incident, an incident report form, and a pen, (the student will) enter the time and date of the incident, with no errors of fact, within 1 minute.

The parenthesized words in the above objective acknowledge that the training environment for teaching this task relies upon simulated conditions.

●The Criterion Examination

After training objectives have been formulated, the programmer needs to establish a means by which achievement of the objectives can be measured. The criterion examination should test those essential job skills that a student must perform to do the job he has been trained for. Training objectives, which are reflections of job tasks, are inextricable elements of a criterion examination. Test items should test each training objective to ensure that skills or knowledge specified in job tasks have in fact been acquired by the student.[6]

During this step in the development of a programmed module, the programmer or module designer may decide it is critical to the success of the training for a student to possess certain skills and knowledge before he undergoes training. The education, past training, and experience of the prospective student have a definite influence on the configuration and content of the module. Style, vocabulary, degree of repetition, and an overall instructional approach are factors affected by the academic and experiential backgrounds of the students.

A sample group of students—fairly representative of all students who will take the training—can be pretested. The criterion examination is administered along with similar tests that measure understanding of subject matter terminology, basic underlying concepts, and other knowledge considered to be necessary for satisfactory progress in the course. Results of the various tests should reveal the entrance abilities of students.

Armed with this information, the programmer is able to do two things:

1. Formulate course prerequisites, primarily with respect to the attainment of minimum scores on pretests. Those who pass the pretest can be expected to complete the course without difficulty. Those who fail the pretests can be steered toward preparatory study or instruction that will correct identified deficiencies.

2. Identify specialized skills or knowledge already possessed by the typical student before the training begins. Information already known by the student can be filtered out of the course, thereby saving valuable training time and resources.

The criterion examination given at the conclusion of, or phases within, the module should be based only on the requirements described in the established training objectives. To show that he has achieved an objective, the student must perform the stated action (task), under certain specified conditions, in accordance with a minimum standard of acceptable performance. A minimum standard does not mean a weak or marginal performance. A minimum acceptable level could be perfection. How extensively and intensively a training objective will be tested on a criterion examination will depend upon how critical the task is to the job.

● **Instructional Strategies**

The next step requires selection and development of appropriate instructional strategies. Based on the results of preceding steps, the designer or programmer must make decisions regarding the methodology of teaching, visual aids and devices, sequencing of content to achieve established training objectives, and similar matters.

Constructing the frames. The information that is written into the programmed materials can be thought of as information which would normally be transmitted to students in a conventional classroom situation. The designer constructs it into sequenced frames that teach and guide students to perform the job tasks, expressed as objectives. Each training objective will have its own single series of frames.

A frame series is called a criterion unit or an achievement unit. The series is described by either of these terms because the frames relate to an objective that is taught and criterion tested, and as such represents achievement of an objective. An average achievement unit in a linear program usually consists of about five to ten frames. A branching program generally has fewer frames in an achievement unit, but the information contained in a single frame is usually larger and more complex.

The final frame in an achievement unit is used to test the student's ability to perform the task or achieve the objective. It is called a criterion frame or a prover frame.[7] The frames that precede the prover frame are called teaching or lead-up frames. The teaching frames provide the student with the information and practice necessary to meet the requirements of the prover frame.

When writing an achievement unit the programmer writes the prover frame first. Each test item that appears on the criterion examination will become a prover frame in the next step. In many cases the language used in a test item on the criterion examination will transfer directly to its corresponding prover frame.

After the prover frame has been written, the programmer needs to write the teaching frames. The teaching frames are intended to lead the student along a learning path that will culminate in proof during the final frame that the student has attained the established objective for the achievement unit.

Choosing the starting point. One problem is knowing where to begin the unit. It is here that pretesting has another payoff. Since the essential idea is to proceed from the known to the unknown, an evaluation of the entrance skills and abilities of the typical student should reveal approximately where to begin the teaching frames. Determining where to start in a programmed approach is the same as determining where to start when teaching in a conventional classroom situation. In a sense, the programmer backs up from the prover frame to a point where he is confident the student has enough foundational knowledge to begin learning new information.

Developing the pattern. The first achievement units in a programmed module should involve the students in learning terms, definitions, and basic concepts that support the tasks to be taught. Similarly, the first frames within an achievement unit should follow the same pattern. These initial learning activities accumulate and build upon one another, and the student is caught up in a process of applying terms and concepts, discriminating among them, solving problems, and drawing conclusions. As the student progresses further into the module, the teaching frames become more complex and demanding.

Teaching frames within an achievement unit must follow a logical line that is evident to the student. Ideally, upon reaching the prover frame, the student should be able to retrace the route he traveled in the unit. The same principle applies to the sequence of achievement units within the complete module.

Selecting techniques. The linear or the branching technique, or a combination of both, might be selected within the overall scheme of instructional strategies. Audiovisual technology, availability of instructors, and subject-matter content are some of the variables that influence strategy choices. As achievement units are written and integrated, minor changes in methodology, sequencing, or content may be necessary.

●Validation

It is advisable to begin validation of programmed materials while writing the module. If the module uses a linear technique, the programmer can begin validation after completing about 100 frames. If branching is used, validation can begin after 25 frames have been constructed. Validation is usually conducted by having selected individuals take the training. The selected persons should be similar in background to students who will later receive the programmed instruction.

Evaluation can focus upon one achievement unit at a time or upon the entire module. A primary purpose of the evaluation is to identify "bugs" that need to be worked out. Persons who take the training on a tryout basis should know this and be encouraged to point out any problems or difficulties that are encountered.

After each tryout, the programmer revises the module to correct errors and otherwise improve upon the product. Materials may be combined, rewritten, or edited. Following each revision of the module, there should be one more tryout. Often a module is tested three times before it is placed into operation. The final tryout preceding implementation should involve as many trainees as possible.

A way of measuring a module's effectiveness is to compute the average score of the test group. When the average score is 90 percent or higher, the programmer can be confident that the module is valid. An average of 90 percent means that 90 percent of the students achieved 90 percent of all training objectives. If more than 10 percent of all persons taking the module fail to achieve a particular training objective, the area of the module pertaining to that objective will need to be rewritten and retested. Only after a final tryout meets the 90 percent standard should the module be placed into operation.

MEDIA FOR PRESENTING PROGRAMMED MATERIALS

A medium for presenting programmed materials is chosen while the module is still in a rough draft. The choice is influenced by the capabilities available for producing various display media. Generally, there are two main media choices. The first medium is paper-and-pencil; the second uses mechanical or electronic display devices.

●Textbooks

Paper-and-pencil modules are most often packaged in textbook form. A programmed text typically uses multiple choice questions to test a student's understanding of information presented in the teaching frames. Linear and branching techniques, or a combination of both, can be used in a programmed text. Questions can be designed not only to check comprehension but also to diagnose any misconceptions that are indicated when a student fails to answer correctly. A multiple choice answer usually provides a page number to which a student must turn to discover if the answer choice was right or wrong. Depending on the answer given, the student is directed to another teaching frame or set of frames with more information to be learned.

The student who answers correctly is given new information that builds upon the previous information. The student who answers incorrectly is given a gentle scolding or brief pep talk. He is then directed to restudy the question and the information upon which it is based, or he might be directed to remedial information which helps him to understand why he was wrong and to learn the intended teaching point.

Programmed texts come in a wide variety of types. An interesting and popular type is the "scrambled book," which uses pages numbered in the usual way but not read consecutively. Each response directs the student to a page in another part of the book. This may lead the student either backward or forward in the book, since the information to be learned is so thoroughly scrambled that no response ever appears adjacent to the question that is answered. The intent is that the student will be challenged to "beat the book."

Some programmed textbooks used hand-held devices that mask out answers until the student has responded. Folded pages, flaps, and other simple items are used to facilitate the presentation of content.

●Mechanical or Electronic Display

A module that presents information through the use of tape-slides, television, film, or computers has the advantage of delivering teaching points to the student in a stimulating or novel fashion. Instead of relying solely on a written form, there is the added impact of images and sound. Also, a student's response to the module can involve something more than putting a pencil to paper. The student can be required to press buttons, turn switches, solve a problem, make a diagram, type on a keyboard, and so forth. The extent of stimulation attainable through the use of such devices is limited only by the sophistication of the equipment itself and the programmer's imagination.

Teaching machines. A special type of electronic or mechanical instrument for presenting programmed materials is the teaching machine. While teaching machines vary in complexity and features, they all use a common instructional method. The student is given problems, exercises, questions, and answers. The machine provides immediate feedback to the student, informing him without delay whether each response is correct or incorrect and permitting him to learn from his errors. Faster students can advance through an instructional sequence very rapidly. Slower students move at their own pace and are tutored with unlimited patience.

The teaching machine not only permits a student to proceed at his own rate, but also controls his action. To complete an instructional module, the student must conform to the rules of the machine. The rules, of course, keep the student moving along preplanned pathways that coincide with specified training objectives.

Cheating is eliminated by the teaching machine. Short of taking the machine apart, the student has no opportunity to progress through the program except by providing acceptable responses. Most teaching machines will provide a hard-copy record of an individual's performance. Responses made by the student throughout the module are recorded in some fashion or other and are thus available for the instructor to use in diagnosing a student's strengths and weaknesses. Proponents of the teaching machine feel that this type of medium provides constant motivation to the student because of the challenge to win against the machine. For training in some jobs a simulator or mock-up can be used as the "teaching machine." For example, a "Link" trainer simulates the cockpit of an aircraft. In this sense, the machine takes on an added dimension because instruction occurs in a situation which more accurately corresponds to actual job conditions.

Because programmed instruction is relatively expensive to produce and validate, there needs to be some assurance that the results of a programmed approach will justify its cost. To have that assurance, the training manager or other person charged with making the decision will need answers to some questions.

First, the decisionmaker will want to know if production costs are likely to be offset by a gain in training effectiveness. If a programmed approach is being considered to replace conventional instruction, the training manager will want to investigate the adequacy and cost of the existing program. It may turn out that what is already in operation is adequate or can be improved with a larger investment in time, materials, or efforts.

Another consideration is standardization of training. An important feature of programmed instruction is the control that it brings to the teaching of a topic. If it is essential that every student receive identical instruction (because, presumably, the job tasks require adherence to identical procedures), then programmed teaching is a good choice. Likewise, if a job task is critical with respect to the saving of lives, and if a programmed approach will permit more effective learning of the task, then the cost of the approach is justified.

Programmed instruction is a desirable alternative when existing instruction proves to be less than satisfactory because of a reluctance by instructors to teach a particular subject. Every training course seems to have at least one subject area that no one wants to handle.[8]

The training manager will also need to inquire as to quantitative improvements likely to be realized through programmed instruction. Can more information be taught in the same or a shorter period of time? Can more trainees be accommodated? Can production costs be spread out over a long period of time in which many people are trained?

A factor that is often overlooked relates to the nature of the subject matter to be taught. Some subjects undergo frequent changes. Report writing, for example, is susceptible to changes in requirements for format, content, writing style, distribution, coding, filing, etc. When a subject matter has predictable instability of teaching points, it is not suitable for programmed instruction.[9]

Nor is it logical to adopt programmed teaching for subjects that are apt to be eliminated from a training course. Sometimes a subject is included in a course on a trial basis or because, unfortunately, the subject conveniently fills up some unused time on a training schedule. Subjects that are likely to be cut should not be programmed, if only from the standpoint of economy.

The decision to adopt or not adopt programmed instruction then rests upon a combination of many factors. Before making such a decision, here are some pertinent questions to ask:[10]

- Will PI increase instructional effectiveness?
- Will it reduce total training time?
- Will it reduce student washouts?
- Will it make efficient use of instructors?
- Will it standardize training over time and between locations?
- Will it free needed classrooms?
- Will it save money, people, or equipment?
- Is it adaptable to the subject matter?
- Does it fit into long-term plans such as new programs, new construction, or new equipment?

To adopt programmed instruction when it is inappropriate, or to shun the method when it is clearly needed, is wasteful. A careful examination of all factors is necessary in arriving at a sensible decision.

NOTES

1. *Techniques of Military Instruction* (Washington, D.C.: Department of the Army, 1967), pp. 73-74.
2. *Principles and Techniques of Instruction* (Washington, D.C.: Department of the Air Force, 1974), p. 11-6.
3. Ibid., p. 11-8.
4. Ibid.
5. Susan Meyer Markle, *Good Frames and Bad: A Grammar of Frame Writing* (New York: John Wiley and Sons, Inc., 1969), p. vi.
6. *Programmed Learning* (Washington, D.C.: Department of the Air Force, 1967), p. 13.
7. *Techniques of Military Instruction* (Washington, D.C.: Department of the Army, 1967), p. 76.
8. An interesting programmed approach to a relatively "dry" subject can be found in *An Approach to Computer-Assisted Instruction,* Military Police Law Enforcement Journal I (Spring Quarter 1974) by John Fay.
9. James E. Espich and Bill Williams, *Developing Programmed Instructional Materials* (Belmont, Calif.: Lear Seigler, Inc./ Fearon Publishers, 1967), p. 11.
10. *Programmed Texts* (Fort Monroe, Va.: U.S. Continental Army Command, 1971), p. 23.

5

USING INSTRUCTIONAL HARDWARE

The Learning Center • Computer-Assisted Instruction • Training Aids
• Summary

The rate at which man is storing up knowledge about himself and his world is spiraling upward at ever-increasing speed. A major force behind the acceleration of knowledge acquisition is technological innovation. Within recent memory, information processing has profoundly altered the procedures of government, the production methods of industry, and the strategies of national defense.[1] To no smaller extent, technology has impacted upon the techniques of teaching. The teacher's everyday working language is peppered with terms like programming, feedback, simulation, loop, and systems.

In contrast with the past, teachers and learners are making more complex and sophisticated demands. Students need to obtain a vast amount of information, and instructors are obligated to deliver it. When the twin facts of increasing student enrollment and rising costs of operating educational institutions are added to the information explosion, the need for new techniques becomes crucial. This chapter explores some of the ways in which technology is helping criminal justice and other educators apply more efficient, cost-effective methods and media in the teaching-learning process.

THE LEARNING CENTER

A learning center, in simple terms, is a self-contained delivery system for programmed or semiprogrammed instruction. Instruction is presented through instructional media controlled by the student. The teaching methods used are frequently simple variations of conventional methods, except that the delivery media are mechanical or electrical devices. The considerable assortment of devices available today makes it possible to set up interesting media combinations for teaching any given set of information.

The predominant characteristic of a learning center is individualized learning. Instruction is usually self-paced and programmed, so that the student has the option of starting, stopping, restarting, and reviewing. The control that a student has over the instruction, and the fact that he sees the instruction as being directed at him personally, helps generate a positive learning attitude.

Two words common to a learning center have been borrowed from the jargon of computer technologists. "Hardware" is used to describe physical equipment contained in the center. Slide, film, overhead, and opaque projectors, audio and video record and playback units, television monitors, head sets, study carrels, and computer terminals are hardware items. "Software" refers to slides, films, filmstrips, tapes, workbooks, study guides, printouts, computer programs, and similar materials.

Although a learning center is nothing more than a special type of classroom, its physical configuration is distinctly different from the traditional classroom arrangement. Instead of an instructor presenting information to many students, a learning center features an array of equipment presenting information to students individually. For a learning center to accommodate more than one student at a time, it is usually broken up into a number of individual areas or cubicles, often called study carrels. They provide physical isolation and are equipped with the teaching devices necessary for students to obtain individual lessons.

●Study Carrels

A study carrel is simply a desk or table with partitions. A good carrel will provide student isolation, reduce outside visual distractions, and reduce outside noises. A study carrel has a writing surface and allows the student to either stand or sit. Some instructional programs might include manipulative actions in addition to mental actions. For example, a student who is being taught how to make a field test of a narcotic substance might be required to mix and apply certain chemicals according to a given procedure. The study carrel in this case would be large enough to permit the student to work with the chemicals and related paraphernalia. Or a table or other work area could be placed in some location convenient to several carrels. On the table would be the materials, tools, or instruments needed in the exercise. The required physical actions could be conducted at the central location, at the carrel, or at a combination of both places.

Some study carrels provide specific electronic equipment or are wired so equipment can be used when an instructional program calls for it. A study carrel that is electrically wired is sometimes called a "wet" carrel. A "dry" carrel has no electronic provisions and in most cases is simply nothing more than a study booth where students can read textbooks or engage in rather simple study operations.

A "wet" carrel can be sparsely or abundantly equipped. It can have earphones only or be a highly sophisticated system with rear screen projection and the capability to record, analyze, and display responses. The display may be in the form of feedback to the learner or it may be feedback to an instructor or computer that monitors student progress.

Whatever the shape and design of a carrel, it should meet a student's need for privacy and minimize external distractions.

●Media Devices

For a learning center to achieve its potential, it should be equipped with media devices that specifically support established learning objectives. This means that a learning center must be designed and created in accordance with a curriculum.[2] A serious flaw would be to develop a curriculum around the capabilities of the learning center. The selection of media devices and the application of them are determined not by their availability but by their appropriateness in producing intended learning outcomes. Also, for much the same reasons that a curriculum depends upon proper and efficient hardware, the hardware in turn needs good software materials. The most technologically advanced equipment can only be as effective as the programmed materials presented by it. Not only should the equipment correspond with the curriculum, but program content should directly address curriculum objectives by requiring the equipment and the student to interact in a planned sequence of learning activities that results in achievement of the specified objectives.

●Multiple Track Scheduling

A great advantage of a learning center is the use of multiple track scheduling. Since software material can be developed in storable and reusable packages, it is possible to create more than one software package for a single general subject area. For example, software packages can be developed at different levels of difficulty. A slower learner can be assigned a software package that moves him through an instructional program at a methodical pace, presenting information in extremely small and easily learned segments. Faster learners can be assigned more demanding software packages that not only meet established objectives but also provide enrichment knowledge. A student who has difficulty completing the requirements of a lesson at a high difficulty level can be placed on another scheduling track at a lower difficulty level.

Another example of multiple track scheduling is the use of different software packages to address specific student job needs. If a single class of students is made up of police officers, correctional specialists, and court officers, it would be advantageous to divorce common interest information from job specific information. A software package for police officers would cover all teaching points that are of equal importance to police, corrections, and court personnel, but the package would also take the police student into job specific skills and knowledge that have little interest or are of no concern to the nonpolice students. The correctional specialists and court officers would each have software packages that address their common and specific training needs. In this sense, learning center teaching has an advantage over classroom teaching.

●**The Instructor's Role**

Teaching methods used at a learning center suffer from the same defect as computer-assisted instructional methods. When taken away from the conventional classroom setting, many students miss personal contact with the teacher. The chance to ask questions or to discuss an idea is not present at a learning center. The depersonalized nature of learning center methods can be counteracted, however, by individual counseling and critiques.

Conventional teaching methods place the instructor in the role of the information giver whose main chores are to develop lessons and deliver them to a class, aiming the lesson content at the majority of students. What little time is left over is taken up with addressing the individual needs of students, particularly slower learners.

The instructor's role is changed drastically by the learning center. Technology assumes a large portion of teaching tasks that have traditionally tied the instructor to the classroom.

Unfortunately, an instructor sometimes perceives the change in role as a threat to his job or self-esteem. The sensible and more accurate way of looking at the change in job functions is to view the instructor as moving to a higher level of competence. More often than not, the instructor develops the software for the learning center. The instructional content of his lesson, already carefully arranged in a lesson plan, must be reorganized in a special format that is compatible with learning center hardware.

Furthermore, although his classroom workload is reduced, the instructor must attain new knowledge and more technical and demanding skills. He must learn audiovisual technologies and their underlying educational philosophies; he must discover how learning center hardware is arranged and controlled; he must be able to develop software packages; and most important, the instructor must have the capacity to psychologically adjust to role changes that accompany learning center teaching methods.

COMPUTER-ASSISTED INSTRUCTION

The term *computer-assisted instruction* (CAI) is frequently imprecisely used to describe any use of a computer for educational ends. For our present purposes the meaning of CAI is restricted to those instructional programs in which the computer is used to interact tutorially with a student. Before looking at CAI as a method, it is first useful to look at the general physical characteristics of a CAI system.

●Physical Characteristics

CAI programs usually operate on a time-sharing arrangement. Time-sharing is an arrangement in which a computer system services more than one user simultaneously. Individual terminals at the user's location are tied into a single, central computer.[3] The user terminals are of several types. The standard teletype unit provides communication between the student and the computer through the medium of typewritten messages. The student types his messages on the keyboard of the teletype unit, and the computer responds by printing messages on a standard roll of teletype paper. Another kind of terminal uses a television viewing screen to display messages from the computer. Still other terminals are linked to slide projectors, closed circuit television, or audio recordings. In other words, communication from the computer to the student is not limited to words or simple concepts. Student responses can also be fairly complex. An electronic pencil, for example, can be used for touching places on graphs or maps that are displayed on the viewing screen or some other electronically sensitized display panel. Although most terminals feature the conventional teletype/television configuration, the possibilities for variety in the communication modes between computer and student seem almost unending.

●Uses and Advantages of CAI

By far, programmed instruction is the predominant theme for CAI application. The endless patience and capacity of the computer provides CAI with an enormous potential for individualizing instruction. Students using CAI particularly like the patience of the computer. There is no embarrassment, no feeling that the instructor or other students are inconvenienced, and no awareness of being slow in learning.

Another great advantage of CAI relates to the reduction of time required for learning. Students who are taught by CAI generally do at least as well as students who are taught by the more conventional methods, but the amount of time required to achieve the specified learning is significantly less with CAI. Even when very small amounts of CAI are added to a regular teaching program, learning occurs at a faster rate.

CAI is clearly at its best when teaching foreign languages. Drill and repetition, the currency of language acquisition, are possible in massive doses for each individual student.

A CAI program typically employs a branching technique. The branching techniques used are very similar to the "pen and pencil" variety described in Chapter 4, "Programmed Instruction." The inherent capability of a computer, however, permits a program to contain branching systems and combinations of branching systems that are far beyond the capabilities of any textbook. For example, conventional textbook branching techniques usually require the student to select from a number of choices that are provided in the book, but the computer is not limited in this way. The CAI programmer is able to allow for many variables. Programs can be produced that more closely correspond with the needs of a broader range of students. Thus, the efficiency of the computer adds tremendous power to the advantages of individualized instruction.

The computer is also very effective in teaching problem-solving skills. After a program presents information about a particular situation or problem, the student can attempt to analyze the situation while getting more and more definitive information from the computer. The nature and quantity of information delivered back to the student is a function of the quality of student responses to stimuli presented by the computer in describing the problem. The situation, of course, is always undergoing change. The character of the change is determined by the student's input. This technique is applicable to the simulation of potentially destructive or expensive activities such as war games. The Air Force uses a form of CAI to put senior officers through their paces.[4] In a simulated command and control room, officers face a huge luminous screen on which the computer displays a mock war in progress. The students command the computer to provide relevant information and make calculations. The students input their decisions as to attack and defense strategies. As the simulated battle rages, the students observe the consequences of their mistakes, alternately brooding and celebrating over skirmishes lost and won.

Despite the real advantages of harnessing computer technology to instructional needs, CAI is not a panacea for all learning problems. CAI works best when it is combined with other learning activities, not when it is used to replace them. The computer's greatest strength is individualization, and it is sensible from a standpoint of efficiency to utilize the computer as a tool of instruction in that area, where it will do the most good.

●Limits and Problems of CAI

While the use of CAI for individualized instruction seems thoroughly desirable, many learning tasks do not lend themselves to the programmed nature of computer-assisted teaching methods. Although improvements continue to be made, many difficult problems still deter widespread use of the method.

Problems that stand in the way of CAI can usually be placed into one of three categories: educational problems, administrative problems, and "people" problems. Educational problems have already been alluded to. CAI is ideal in teaching for content or teaching skills that are facilitated by drill and practice. It is not ideal for teaching interpersonal abilities or skills that require application of content in dynamic, human-to-human situations.

Problems of an administrative nature usually relate to the relatively high cost of CAI. Time sharing, sharing of instructional programs that are written for CAI, and sharing of software materials can reduce the administrative cost of CAI.

The "people" problem usually involves instructors and students. Many instructors resist CAI because they do not understand computerized technology well enough to prepare CAI material. They find it difficult to learn computer language and resent being forced into organizing their subject matter content in ways that correspond with the logic of computer programming. For the student, problems frequently arise because the machine cannot interact with the student and vice versa. Although students will generally experience a motivational lift when initially placed into direct communication with a computer, the effect has little permanence because it results from the novelty of the situation. Students cannot be fooled by the use of their names or the typically saccharine praise that accompanies correct responses. In a nutshell, machines of any type are poor substitutes for teachers in personalizing education.

Like other applications of instructional technology, the computer is only as good as the people who use it. A well-designed computer program of valid content, when appropriately applied in teaching certain kinds of tasks, can be a highly efficient instructional tool.

TRAINING AIDS

Successful instruction depends upon the effective use of workable training aids. The instructor is like a master craftsman. His training aids are his tools. He selects them skillfully because he understands their potential and their limitations. He uses them proficiently because he has spent time in preparation. But while the skilled craftsman uses his tools to turn out a tangible product, the instructor uses his tools to enhance learning.

●Advantages

Training aids help the instructor emphasize important teaching points. To get and retain student attention there must be some appeal to the human senses. Learning begins with stimulation of sensory organs. The more senses that are activated, the greater the opportunity for learning. Words, whether in writing or in speech, are often inadequate to convey subtle meanings and understandings. Training aids can enable an instructor to communicate with students through more than one sensory channel.

People tend to see alike more than to hear or read alike. To illustrate, consider a training situation in which members of a class are required to read a description of how a caliber .38 revolver operates. A written description of the revolver's functions may be extremely accurate, but few members of the class will receive and retain the same mental picture. The same group, however, when given an opportunity to see the functioning of the revolver, will obtain mental images quite similar to the actual facts the instructor is attempting to convey. Visual instruction is much more effective than spoken or written words alone.

Training aids add variety, clarification, interest, and vitality to instruction. Student attention can be directed toward specific points being presented in the lesson. The use of an actual object, a model, or a film not only adds variety to a subject matter presentation, but also provides some element of realism.

A fundamental reason for using training aids is to make learning easier for students. Good aids help to maintain student motivation and enhance a student's state of readiness for learning. Difficult teaching points can be simplified or emphasized through training aids. Student impressions become more intense, resulting in clearer and longer-lasting comprehension. This is true with slow learners as well as with rapid learners. Uniformity and continuity are also important advantages derived from training aids. This is especially true in training situations that require students to recall a certain procedure or steps within a procedure.

●Selection of Aids

Selection of aids should be preceded by a careful examination of the learning outcomes that are expected to occur as the result of training. Instruction should never be modified to correspond to training aids. Quite the opposite, training aids should be modified to conform to the instruction. An analysis of the expected outcome of training will help determine at what point in the training process aids might create confusion.

In planning for the use of a training aid, the instructor should consider the topic, the size of the class, and the place where the aids will be used. He should know when during the instruction the aid should be introduced, and he should also ensure that the class will have no difficulty in seeing and understanding its message.

Training aids should be easy to comprehend and geared to the intelligence level of the audience. When facts and figures appear, they should be accurate, correct, and founded upon established doctrine.

A training aid must support a relevant teaching point. Since teaching points are directly related to established learning objectives, the aid should logically contribute to the successful achievement of those objectives. Training aids should never be used merely for their eye-catching effect, to kill time, or to amuse and entertain students.

In selecting or constructing an aid for use as a memory guide, the instructor should limit the number of points to be covered. An excess of ideas presented at one time or in great detail confuses students.

A variety of aids in the training process increases student learning and interest. An excess of aids or poor timing in the use of an aid, however, interrupts the flow of ideas being developed in a presentation. Too many aids will undermine rather than support a teaching point. The instructor should continually examine his teaching subject to improve and develop only those training aids that support the subject and the methods he elects to use.

For an aid to attract the attention of the student, it should be visually appealing. Neat, readable labels and correct spelling lend eye appeal and cause important words to stand out. Too many words or poorly spaced words detract from the main idea and lead to confusion. When used carefully, contrasting colors can help to emphasize main points. As with words, the use of too much color can be confusing.

One must also be careful to use color selectively. For example, researchers have found that job performance suffers when color is used in training but not in the job to which the training is to transfer.[5]

Aids should be portable enough to carry easily to and from the teaching area. They should also be constructed with durable materials that withstand rough handling. An aid should be simple to operate or manipulate. Intricate or complicated devices have their advantages, but the most effective training aid is usually simple, neat, and practical. An aid that is cumbersome or difficult to handle is distracting.

The benefit of using an aid must justify the expense and effort of its construction. It is not unusual for an instructor to go to great lengths to design and construct an elaborate mock-up when the actual piece of equipment or item will do just as well. The real thing, when available, is sometimes more valuable to learning than a replica. Elaborate models, although attractive to the eye, may in some cases actually detract from training because of their sophistication.

●Presentation

Rehearsal, using aids in concert with the lesson plan, should be repeated as many times as necessary to thoroughly prepare for the actual presentation. An unrehearsed presentation is very rarely successful. Through practice the instructor increases his ability to fully exploit the advantages of training aids.

In a teaching situation that requires more than one instructor to display aids, practice is critical to a coordinated presentation. All instructors should be sufficiently well-rehearsed so that they know exactly what each is to do and when. If one instructor is to assist another by displaying projected aids, a set of prearranged signals should be used so that the projector can be turned on, changed, or shut off at the appropriate intervals.

When using charts, diagrams, throw-overs, or overlays it may be useful to tab the pages with clips or similar devices that assist in identifying the right pages to be used at the right time. Some material can be identified simply by writing lightly on it.

An aid should be displayed so that all students can see it. Obviously, if students cannot see an aid it has no value to learning, no matter how stimulating it may be. A seating arrangement that does not permit everyone to see should be changed. When an aid contains written information, the instructor should, in advance, test the aid in the actual classroom to make sure the printed message can be read from all parts of the class seating area. Some guidelines on readability are shown in Figure 5.

Viewing Distance	Height of Lettering
8 ft.	1/4 in.
16 ft.	1/2 in.
32 ft.	1 in.
64 ft.	2 in.
128 ft.	4 in.

FIGURE 5. Readability of Aids

The instructor should not become so involved with an aid that his remarks are directed at it instead of at the students. Even while assembling or disassembling a piece of equipment the instructor should maintain eye contact with his students. Standing behind or to the side of an aid helps the instructor avoid talking to the aid rather than to the class.

The need to maintain eye contact is just as important when using complex training aids. Elaborate aids are sometimes necessary to illustrate highly complicated and technical material, but they should not be allowed to supersede the subject matter. When an elaborate aid is shown for the first time, it deserves an explanation. Teaching points supported by the aid, however, should not be obscured by an explanation of the aid itself.

A pointer helps to direct student attention toward a particular part of an aid. The pointer should be held steadily on that portion of the aid the instructor wishes the class to observe. If the pointer is held in the hand closest to the aid, the instructor can maintain eye contact. Holding the pointer across the body tends to place the instructor in a position of talking to the aid. When a pointer is no longer needed it should be put away, as it can be very distracting.

Training aids should be covered when not in use. This practice removes a potential distraction. Covering an aid can be done simply by stapling sheets of paper above or over it. If an aid contains printed lines, strips of paper can be placed over individual lines and later removed one at a time. Replicas or actual items that are used as aids can be covered with a cloth or similar material when not actually in use.

●Types of Aids

There are many kinds of training aids. Each has its own special characteristics, advantages, and limitations. Following are brief discussions of various aids commonly used in criminal justice teaching programs.

Actual items. When teaching involves explanation of items such as tools, equipment, or other job essential items, it may be desirable to use the actual items as aids to learning.

Although the "real thing" brings an element of a job environment into the classroom, the instructor may find that too much realism can detract from learning. Equipment that is large or bulky tends to dominate the classroom; items that feature electronic gadgetry may pull student attention away from important discussions; items that are very small may provide limited opportunity for visual examination; items that need to be understood in terms of inner workings may cloud rather than clarify understanding; and items that are hazardous may cause students to do more worrying than learning. For example, a class on bomb identification may operate more effectively if simulated rather than actual explosives are used. Despite some limitations inherent in the use of actual items as training aids, training devices can provide an element of realism and help to reduce learning time on the job.

Models and mock-ups. Models, which are recognizable representations of a real-life place or thing, are frequently used with or in lieu of actual equipment. There is a natural temptation to buy actual job equipment for training purposes, but often a simpler device will do just as well. When there is a possibility of damage to actual equipment or injury to students, a training device may be the only feasible way to practice. Training devices may also be more reliable for practice than actual equipment. For instance, an operator's console in a computerized criminal justice information system is connected to parts of the system, and when another part is "down," the operator's console is affected. With devices that simulate a console, this type of problem is eliminated.

A type of model is the mock-up, which is an imitation of the real thing, but not necessarily a recognizable three-dimensional representation. While a model should be built to scale, a mock-up need not be nor need it be perfect with respect to the item it represents.

Graphic materials. A common form of training aid is the chart, diagram, sketch, cartoon, map, or other graphic material which explains a method or technique related to the idea being taught.

Color enhances the effectiveness of graphic training aids. Figure 6 provides some guidance in using color combinations.[6] Color is used not simply for eye appeal or contrast but to differentiate between separate components of a larger system. For example, if training involves an explanation of the criminal justice system, color codes assigned to various parts of the criminal justice components will assist the instructor in describing important distinctions and relationships.

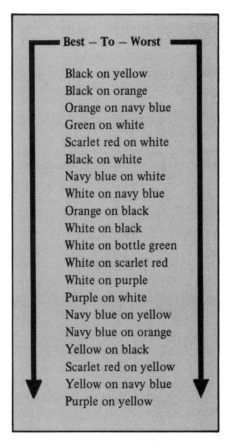

■ Best — To — Worst ■

Black on yellow
Black on orange
Orange on navy blue
Green on white
Scarlet red on white
Black on white
Navy blue on white
White on navy blue
Orange on black
White on black
White on bottle green
White on scarlet red
White on purple
Purple on white
Navy blue on yellow
Navy blue on orange
Yellow on black
Scarlet red on yellow
Yellow on navy blue
Purple on yellow

FIGURE 6. Color Combinations

Displays. A display can also be a training aid. It can be made a permanent part of the training facility environment as well as a periodically used teaching device. A permanent display becomes a functional part of learning by helping to create an atmosphere that will contribute to student desires for learning. To be functional, a display must be thoughtfully designed, carefully exhibited, and supportive of a worthwhile message.

The venetian blind. A venetian blind is a visual aid consisting of several wood slats or posterboard strips arranged in a ladder-like fashion. Words or terms are printed on the strips. This type of visual aid looks like a venetian blind. Venetian blind strips provide mental stimuli for recall of key ideas. They can be very useful in outlining important teaching points and summarizing materials touched upon previously.

Venetian blind strips should be neat, attractive, and orderly. Lettering should be large enough for all students to see and read. Each strip should be exposed one at a time and discussed separately and thoroughly before the next strip is displayed.

The chalkboard. Many instructors fail to remember the most common and most readily available training aid of all—the chalkboard. The chalkboard can be an excellent medium to facilitate student participation. Students are made to feel they are making a positive contribution when their answers, suggestions, or comments are placed on the chalkboard.

A chalkboard can serve the instructor in several ways. Topics, questions, sketches, diagrams, outlines, and other abstractions of teaching points can be written on the chalkboard. Images such as photographs and drawings can be projected on the chalkboard by means of an overhead or opaque projector and amplified with separate writings in chalk or the use of a pointer.

Many chalkboards are designed to be used as magnetic boards, thus providing a way for other types of visual materials to adhere to the chalkboard surface. Posterboard strips and other graphics can be easily attached to a metallic-backed chalkboard with magnetized strips appended to the rear of the visuals. (See "Hints for Using the Chalkboard," p. 89.)

The blanketboard. The blanketboard is similar to the chalkboard. Used to support or hold visuals, it can consist of any kind of soft fabric upon which a velcro or gripping fabric will attach. The velcro can be glued or otherwise attached to the rear of visuals. By using a variety of different fabrics, excellent color contrast can be made with the blanketboard. Black or red velvet can be interspersed with felt of varying colors. By forming a contrasting fabric background, an eye-appealing dimension is added to the visual.

Films and film projectors. An important part of training involves the use of films. Complex combinations of skills, knowledge, and attitudes that are difficult to explain in other ways can be demonstrated through the use of films.[7] The conduct of a criminal trial, for example, involves skills and knowledge that must be applied in combinations. A film that portrays court personnel involved in methods and procedures for conducting a criminal trial can be very effective.

Hints for Using the Chalkboard

- Be sure that everything necessary is obtained before the class meets. It is very easy to overlook the availability of chalk, eraser, template, pointer, and other needed materials.

- Check for chalkboard glare. Be sure that every student will be able to see materials presented. Sometimes it will be necessary to check the lighting and use different combinations of light in order to eliminate glare. The lowering or raising of window shades in a classroom will create or remove glare.

- Before starting a class, the chalkboard should be clean. A dirty chalkboard gives the impression that the instructor is not prepared or is not concerned with the quality of the materials he presents.

- Be sure that materials printed or drawn are legible.

- Maintain uniform letter size. Printing that gradually decreases in size in order to fit on the right margin of the chalkboard is distracting.

- Templates used for writing on a chalkboard need to be accurate or exact. Light pencil markings or tracings drawn on a chalkboard can be written over with chalk during the presentation. The markings or tracings assist the instructor to make a rapid and accurate depiction in chalk of the picture or ideas he wishes to transmit.

- Keep information relatively simple and brief. Concise statements or short terms will often serve to make important points. Oral explanations by the instructor can be used to fully explain ideas represented by a single word or a small group of words. A few well-placed teaching points are more effective than too many points crowded into a small or limited space.

- After points have been discussed, the instructor should erase them so that they will not distract from points to be made later. Using the fingers to erase the chalkboard is extremely irritating to some persons, so use an eraser.

- Use colors for emphasis and variety. Some colors, however, do not show up clearly on certain chalkboards. Testing various colors on a chalkboard in advance is worth the extra effort. Fluorescent chalk used in conjunction with a black light can create special effects.

There is a huge availability of criminal justice education and training films on the market today. Some agencies have organized their own film production units to meet the demand for such films.[8]

More dollars are probably spent for film projectors and films than for any other kind of audiovisual equipment. The film medium has a long history of success. It is a familiar vehicle to both the viewer and the teacher. Many instructors rely on this medium because it combines multiple capabilities designed to produce new knowledge, skills, and attitudes for target audiences. Color, motion, action, plot, and music emphasize information presented in film.

Films can be useful in stirring emotions and changing attitudes. Potentially, they can teach faster, more fully, and can even reach students who have little or no education.

To achieve maximum training value, an instructor should follow certain procedures when using a film as a training aid. The film should be carefully studied and previewed in advance. No training film is perfect in content or direction. By previewing, the instructor is able to identify key points in the film that need to be emphasized. Previewing also allows the instructor to discuss points that were only lightly touched upon in the film or omitted entirely. Careful preview of a film will also identify portions of the film that may be obsolete or require added explanation.

Before a film is shown in the classroom the instructor should make introductory remarks that will direct student attention toward important ideas in the film. The remarks help to ensure that the film will produce the intended effect. It is desirable to include the reasons for showing the film, the key points to be looked for, and the relatedness of the film to earlier and subsequent training. Very often a film will have accompanying written material, such as a short synopsis and suggested discussion or examination questions, to assist in the preparation of introductory remarks. A strong introduction of a film can make the difference between merely showing it for effect and making it work in harmony with instructional goals.

Before the beginning of a class session in which a film is to be used, the instructor should make a final check of the film and the projection equipment. The film should be set up in advance and a short portion viewed to be sure that the equipment is functioning. When the film is ready to be shown, the instructor should make his introductory remarks.

During the showing of a film the instructor may sometimes find it useful to stop and explain an important concept or emphasize a major idea. Motion picture film is essentially a running medium shown from start to finish, but frequently segments of a program are printed on separate loops and referred to as "single concepts." A single concept isolates a key idea which deserves special attention for the learner. A series of single concepts presented in sequence are sometimes used instead of running the film without interruption. The advantage, of course, relates to the emphasis that can be placed upon isolated concepts. Some of the recent criminal justice education and training films employ a technique which allows the instructor to stop at preestablished intervals so that students can respond to situations portrayed in the film. Some projectors have a special feature called "analysis," i.e., the capability to move film through the projector at varying speeds so the viewer can analyze the actions or the details of the image. Speeds range from slow to total stop action. Student responses during the intervals can consist of verbal discussions, writing something down on paper, or engaging in some limited form of physical activity.

At the film's conclusion the instructor should conduct a critique that summarizes important teaching points. In some cases a demonstration by the instructor may help to simplify procedures or techniques shown in the film. Applicatory exercises are a very effective follow-up activity. Such exercises are designed to permit each student to apply skills or knowledge seen in the film. It may even be advisable to follow up such exercises with a second showing of the film, perhaps to critique student performances. Learning and attention are appreciably increased by a second showing of a film, particularly after students have engaged in some form of "hands-on" learning activity.

Filmstrips and filmstrip projectors. A filmstrip consists of a length of standard motion picture film containing still pictures. In days gone by, instructors used filmstrips when motion picture film was too expensive. All too often, early filmstrips were little more than illustrated lectures. But with the advent of improved equipment has come a new generation of programming that offers excellent presentation values, including high-impact photography, graphics, narration, and musical scoring.

It is best to have an assistant instructor operate the filmstrip projector so that the primary instructor is free to explain and to use the pointer to direct student attention to specific ideas within each picture frame. The sequence of picture frames can be stopped at any point for discussion and clarification of ideas not completely understood by students.

Transparencies and the overhead projector. The overhead projector, which projects page-size transparencies onto a screen or flat wall surface, is widely used in criminal justice education and training. Because it can be used in a lighted room, it allows students to take notes.

Another advantage is that the instructor can face the audience while operating the device, thus maintaining eye contact. Furthermore, the transparencies are placed on the projector with the image facing up. The instructor, who must necessarily stand adjacent to the projector, can read messages on the transparencies without having to turn his back to the class. Without moving away from the projector, the instructor can point out features on the screen by placing the tip of a pencil or a short pointer directly on the transparency. The instructor is thereby able to focus and refocus student attention to key ideas without moving to and from the screen.

Making transparencies. Many techniques may be used to construct transparencies for use on the overhead projector. Overlaying transparencies add visually stimulating effects as well as help the instructor establish a smooth pattern of ideas. Cardboard or other opaque materials can be cut into flaps attached to the mounting frame of a transparency so that the instructor can mask out teaching points which are not relevant at a particular moment in his lesson. By lifting or lowering flaps, the instructor can move from one teaching point to the next.

Color transparencies can be made with water-soluble pens, wax pencils, and permanent felt tip pens. Not just any coloring instrument will project in color. Unless specially designed for overhead projection, the pen or pencil marks will tend to dissolve or to project in black only.

An especially stimulating transparency consists of a negative acetate that projects brightly colored images against a solid black background. Another unusual technique is the use of a translucent plastic model placed on the glass face of the projector. The model's components are manipulated to show their relationships.

By use of the acetate roller attachment, which is usually a feature of the standard overhead projector, the instructor can design his own transparencies in response to situations that occur spontaneously in the classroom. All that is required is a grease pencil and some imagination. The instructor is not restricted, however, to using the roller attachment in spontaneous situations only. The instructor can enter the message in grease pencil on the acetate roller well in advance of the class. When he reaches the appropriate moment in his presentation, the instructor can unroll the acetate and make his remarks.

Because transparencies for the overhead projector are relatively easy to make, the instructor is tempted to overuse them or to be indiscriminate in their construction. Since almost any opaque writing or drawing can be quickly converted to a transparency there is a built-in tendency to make too many. The result is to create unreadable, fuzzy, and unneeded visuals. Such output can more properly be called visual hindrances rather than visual aids. A conscientious instructor will carefully determine proper image area, letter size, and message content. The wise instructor keeps his transparencies simple and uncluttered.

Keystoning. Overhead projection is particularly subject to *keystoning*—distortion of a projected image, caused by an indirect angle of the projector in relation to the screen. A keystoned picture is smaller on one of the four sides of the projected image. This problem is relatively easy to correct. For lateral keystoning, the angle of the screen or the projector can be adjusted until the two are aligned properly. For vertical keystoning the overhead projector can be tilted forward or back. Some screens are equipped with a keystone eliminator which can be adjusted to tilt the screen forward until the distortion disappears.

Practical considerations. In deciding to use an overhead projector for a particular teaching situation, the instructor should concern himself with a number of questions:

- How big a picture do I need? If a larger picture is indicated, a good deal of space between the projector and the screen will be required. Such space isn't always easy to find in a conference or classroom. If this is a major problem, the instructor might explore the possibility of obtaining an overhead projector with a wide angle lens.
- Does the projector have a spare lamp? Many overhead projectors have an integral spare lamp that lets the instructor merely flick a lever that removes the defective lamp and places the spare into operating position. If the projector is not equipped with a spare lamp, the instructor should have one with him.
- Does the teaching situation require a portable overhead projector? If the answer to this question is yes, the instructor should be aware that portable models generally have less lamp intensity, resulting in lower image brilliance.

Opaque visuals and the opaque projector. The opaque projector uses the principle of light reflection to create an image of any flat opaque object. Illustrated materials from textbooks, manuals, magazines, newspapers, and other printed material can be projected by the opaque projector. Visual features that are highlighted in color or special print will appear on the screen in the same manner as they appear in the printed form.

The greatest single advantage of an opaque projector is its ability to project from book to screen. The presenter need not convert a page to any other format as is necessary with the overhead projector. The one-step process from page to image makes the device extremely convenient.

The opaque projector can show an item in its approximate size. The projector is moved either forward or rearward until the size of the image is roughly equal to the actual size of the item. This technique can also be used very effectively with maps or diagrams.

Opaque projection also can assist the instructor to fabricate other aids. For example, if drawing the outline of an actual piece of equipment on the chalkboard is desired, the opaque projector can help. A picture of the equipment is placed on the projector, and then the image is projected on the chalkboard. The instructor traces the outline of the equipment as it appears in the lighted image, producing a chalkboard drawing that is fairly accurate in respect to proportions and gross features.

A disadvantage of the opaque projector, however, is that the room must be completely dark. Students are therefore unable to take notes, and the instructor has difficulty observing the class for individual reactions or obtaining student feedback.

One special caution when using the opaque projector: the ever-present temptation to use it for pages of any description should be resisted. Miniscule diagrams and small writing will not project well at all. Opaque materials should be so simple that every element, when projected, will be large enough for every viewer to see clearly. This, of course, is true for every good visual, regardless of the projection technique.

Slides and slide projectors. The slide projector is extremely effective, yet relatively inexpensive. Slides from private collections or commercial sources can be shown with the ordinary slide projector. Some of the best slides are the ones the instructor has created himself. Sound can be added to a slide presentation through recorded scripts that include voices, music, and other sounds appropriate to the subject. Sight and sound together form an example of enhancing learning through more than one sensory channel. A slide projector can also be used in tandem with another slide projector or with the overhead and opaque projectors. The use of more than one projector in a teaching situation adds variety to the topic being covered.

Another effective slide projector technique is to display special "polarized light" slides through a revolving filter placed close to the projector lens. An illusion of motion is created. The effect can be useful in animating images intended to gain student attention.

Optional features of a standard slide projector include remote control, automatic focus, and random access selection of slides. Remote control and automatic focus are relatively inexpensive options and are the rule, rather than the exception, within a good audio-visual inventory. The random access feature generally costs more and is needed less. It permits the automatic selection of visuals for projections in any sequence desired, regardless of placement order in the tray.

The value of a slide presentation corresponds, as it does with just about every audiovisual medium, to the ability of the instructor. Messages in the presentation are only as strong as the skill of the instructor in selecting and employing slides that are meaningful to the student audience.

Front and rear screen projection. Besides being familiar with the more common types of projector devices, an instructor should know something about the two categories of projection: front screen and rear screen. Front screen projection utilizes an image projected on the forward surface of a light-reflecting screen. The image is projected from within or behind the audience area. Rear screen projection utilizes an image projected on the back surface of a semi-translucent screen placed between the viewer and the projector.

The projector is aimed at mirrors which reverse the image for normal viewing in front of the screen. Rear screen installations range from large, permanent in-wall settings to tiny portable screens used on table tops or in attache cases.

Whether projection is by the rear or front screen method, the instructor has to consider audience needs. The width of the viewing screen should be at least one-sixth the distance that the farthest viewer is seated from the screen. The nearest viewer should be two widths away from the screen to avoid eye fatigue.[9] The sight line of viewers is also important. Many presenters like to wrap the audience in the image, so they prefer a large screen. Even so, they must place the screen quite high to prevent the heads of some viewers from obstructing the sight lines of others.

A decision between front screen or rear screen projection is usually made on the basis of architectural considerations rather than the advantages of one method over the other. The constraints of space and light are usually the key determinants in the choice.

Television. Television has become increasingly important in recent years as a training aid. For training or educational purposes, television can be divided into two major types. The first type involves the use of taped programs prepared for specific instructional objectives. Taped programs can either be made through the use of equipment available to the instructor or the training center that supports the instructor, or tape programs can be purchased from commercial sources. In most cases, the production of television programs through internal resources is limited by the high cost of producing such programs.

A second way to use television as a training aid is through videotape record and playback. This method permits the instructor to record on videotape the actual performance of a student or students while practicing a skill. A playback of the student performance is an excellent opportunity for students to critique their own skills. Not only are students able to view their strengths, but they are also able to see their weaknesses.

The potential applications of video are numerous. In addition to permitting students to see themselves, videotaping can be used to capture lectures (one of the least creative applications), to monitor work places so that students can go on a field trip without leaving the classroom, and to provide feedback for sensitivity sessions.

The electronic trade and popular press have helped to promote the "video revolution" made possible by the advent of easy-to-use cartridges, cassettes, and discs. The simplicity and convenience of video software has opened up a whole new ball game for in-house videotape production. Educators and trainers seem anxious to produce videotapes. It is vital, however, that competent professional counsel be obtained before purchasing videotape equipment. The investment can be sizable, and the technology is changing rapidly.

Two main risks are associated with the acquisition of videotape equipment: (1) the system selected and installed will not fully meet learning needs; and (2) future budgets will not maintain the system that has been purchased. The initial financial commitment is the smallest part of the total investment. The organizational budget must include expenditures for operating personnel, maintenance, repair, production costs, updating, inventory, scripts, sets, and outside consultants. In fact, the greatest single mistake can be a commitment to equipment before genuine needs and utilization are defined. Very frequently a videotape system is installed and then underutilized. Without a staff that can produce tapes and a budget that will support in-house production, a perfectly good videotape system will simply gather dust.

Records and phonograph systems. Record players for educational use must be of more durable construction than those found in a family room or den. Heavy duty equipment, although more costly, is a better investment. When choosing a professional record player, the experienced audiovisual buyer will ask to hear the equipment in the environment where it will be used. A phonograph which sounds good in the showroom may not be satisfactory in a classroom or auditorium.

Experienced users also stress the importance of having quality speakers. A good amplifier will produce good sound with quality speakers, but even an excellent amplifier cannot compensate for poor speakers.

Another critical element of a record player system is the record itself. Records are the most vulnerable elements of the system because they are easily damaged. Without proper care, records will scratch, dent, warp, and melt. It helps to direct phonograph operators in the proper handling of records. Records should never be stacked flat; the grooves should not be touched; a record should be inserted carefully into its paper sleeve before returning it to the album jacket; and records should be regularly cleaned.

The needle or stylus of the player is also a consideration. Because stereo records have become standard in recent years, a phonograph will require a stereo needle. Even though the phonograph may be monaural, a stereo needle should be used because it is compatible with monaural as well as stereo records. A monaural needle will work with monaural records only.

Audiotapes and tape systems. Audiotape equipment is rapidly replacing the phonograph as the primary sound medium for education and training. There are four general types of audiotape systems now on the market: the reel-to-reel tape deck, the compact cassette, the eight-track cartridge, and the continuous cartridge.

Reel-to-reel is the oldest member of the quartet. It utilizes tape and runs at speeds that vary, depending on the playback machine. User preferences for reel-to-reel tape systems have dropped off remarkably in recent years with the growing acceptance of cassette and cartridge systems.

The internationally-standard compact cassette has the advantages of portability, relatively low cost, program flexibility, and ease in storage, playing, and replaying.

Cassette running time is determined by the length of its tape even though cassette casings are all the same size. As a general rule, the longer the running time the thinner the tape. A C-60 cassette holds 30 recorded minutes on each side of the tape. A C-120 cassette gives 60 minutes on each side of a thinner tape. Instructors with experience using cassette systems report that any tape thinner than C-60 stock sacrifices sound quality and jam-free winding.

The eight-track cartridge utilizes a continuous loop inside a plastic housing. Eight separate tracks can be recorded across the width of the tape. The wider tape moves more rapidly than that in the cassette format. Because the faster speed provides somewhat better sound fidelity, the cartridge format is usually the first choice of the music industry.

The fourth type of audiotape system is the continuous cartridge. It employs a tape loop for repeated playback of a recorded message. The continuous cartridge is useful for displays and exhibits. The tape length varies with the total time of the recorded program and the carrying capacity of the cartridge housing.

Audiotape record/playback systems vary widely in quality and performance. The first concern should be with quality; without it the full message cannot be received. Quality depends on a good amplifier and good speakers. Performance characteristics of a system can be found in specifications and life expectancy statistics of critical parts such as the drivemotor, recording and playback heads, and internal circuitry.

SUMMARY

We have discussed the characteristics of the learning center, the instructional possibilities of computer-assisted instruction, and an approach to the use of training aids. Although we have discussed the major forms of aids with definite application to training, we have by no means covered them all. There are many simple devices an instructor can use to enhance learning.

But of the ingredients that go into the creation of effective training aids, the most important ingredient is the instructor himself. If an instructor lacks the dedication required to create and use training aids, then his teaching cannot achieve its fullest potential.

NOTES

1. Alvin Toffler, *Future Shock* (New York: Bantam Books, 1970), p. 30.
2. *Principles and Techniques of Instruction* (Washington, D.C.: Department of the Air Force, 1974), pp. 11-15.
3. Ibid.

4. Gilbert Burck et al., *The Computer Age* (New York: Harper and Row, Publishers, 1965), pp. 30-31.

5. Ronald W. Spangenberg et al., *The State of Knowledge Pertaining to Selection of Cost-Effective Training Methods and Media* (Springfield, Va.: Human Resources Research Organization, 1973), p. 21.

6. Dugan Laird, *Approaches to Training and Development* (Reading, Mass.: Addison-Wesley Publishing Co., 1978), p. 210.

7. Robert T. Flint, *Instructional Techniques for Using Behavioral Training Films* (Schiller Park, Ill.: Motorola Teleprograms, Inc., 1975), p. 4.

8. A modest approach to in-house filmmaking is appropriate for the majority of criminal justice agencies. Eastman Kodak's *Movies with a Purpose* provides many good tips on producing low-budget, single-concept films.

9. Dugan Laird, *A User's Look at the Audio-Visual World* (Fairfax, Va.: National Audio-Visual Association, Inc., 1974), p. 30.

6

WRITING A LESSON PLAN

Elements of a Lesson Plan • Writing the Lesson Plan • Summary

The term "lesson plan" means just what it says—a plan of a lesson. It is more than just notes or an outline of ideas. A lesson plan accounts for everything that the instructor and students will do from the moment the lesson starts until the moment it ends. Indeed, a lesson plan may even cover preclass and postclass activities by specifying additional, out-of-classroom assignments.

The price of lesson plan quality is careful preparation. A prosecuting attorney spends hours preparing a case before he presents it in the courtroom; a correctional specialist prepares schedules of activities for inmates; and a police officer participates in the development of a narcotics raid plan. A process as complicated as learning certainly deserves no less attention than is given to other important criminal justice activities. There is no question about it —an instructor spends much time and effort in preparation.

A course of instruction consists typically of a number of instructional units. A unit is sometimes called a lesson, a topic, a block, or some similar name that denotes it as an element of the course curriculum. Groupings of units are sometimes called phases, levels, or sections. Each instructional unit or lesson has, or should have, one or more learning objectives. A learning objective is stated as an action to be performed by the student. The learning objectives for a single lesson represent what each student must minimally achieve. A curriculum usually states in explicit terms the learning objectives for each unit of instruction. In some cases, instructors are permitted to formulate specific learning objectives based on broadly stated objectives in the curriculum. (The option of permitting instructors to establish learning objectives is becoming less frequent. As pressure mounts on teaching managers to produce students capable of performing actual jobs, curriculums are written with greater specificity and attention to job standards and conditions. More and more, learning objectives are being formulated by persons close to the job situation, who may or may not be instructors.)

Everything that is contained in a lesson plan is geared to one essential outcome: the achievement of established learning objectives. Before anything else can be done, the instructor must clearly know the objectives of the lesson so that he can select and arrange teaching activities that permit his students to achieve the goals set for them.

The use of learning objectives conditions the instructor to develop a plan that focuses on what the student is to learn rather than what the instructor is to teach. The phraseology of a lesson objective, because it is a reflection of what the student will be expected to do on the job, forces the instructor to consider his lesson plan in terms of student activity rather than instructor activity.

In preparing his plan the instructor should take into account what his students already know. If the course itself was well planned, the entering skills and knowledge of the average student will be known. If the starting level is too low, students are likely to be bored; if it is too high, the students may get lost at the very beginning. The complexity of the material and the general level of the students will determine the instructor's overall teaching approach.

Another important prerequisite to the development of a lesson plan is research. Not only should research material be relevant to learning objectives, it should also have some value in helping students achieve the objectives. If an instructor selects research material because it is fascinating and interesting, he will end up with a lesson plan filled with intriguing ideas that may or may not have learning value for the student. At the other extreme, dry and uninteresting facts or statistics may add nothing to a student's capacity for accomplishing the lesson objectives. "Nice to know" or enrichment information should be kept at a minimum. A simple test for the lesson planner to use in deciding what research material is supportive of lesson objectives is to ask this question: "Will the information help the student achieve the learning objective?"

ELEMENTS OF A LESSON PLAN

Lesson plans come in all sizes and shapes. Rather than attempt to cover a variety of lesson plans, a single, widely used, time-tested format will be discussed. It contains elements common to most lesson plan approaches in use today.[1]

This format has three major components:

1. INTRODUCTION
2. BODY
3. REVIEW

●The Introduction

The introduction component has four subcomponents:

- Gain Attention
- Training Objective(s)
- Lesson Tie-in
- Motivation

Gain attention. The gain attention subcomponent is intended to capture student attention at the outset of the class and to transfer that attention to the next subcomponent. Ways to gain attention are limited only by the imagination of the instructor. Telling a story or joke, asking a rhetorical question, or conducting a skit are common attention gainers. Gimmicks, tricks, and startling demonstrations make marvelous attention gainers, but they also tend to rivet student consciousness on the attention gainer instead of on the lesson content. The instructor who uses a card trick or sleight-of-hand runs the risk of not being able to refocus student attention from the tricks to the topic. The author recalls an instructor who opened his class on bomb identification by exploding a dynamite cap without advance notice to the students. For the remainder of the class, the students kept waiting for the next explosion, more concerned with safety than the subject being taught. The students are likely to remember the instructor but not likely to recall much about bomb identification.

An attention gainer has to be constructed with three things in mind: (1) the personality of the instructor, (2) the student audience, and (3) the nature of the topic.

Creating an attention gainer that blends with the personality of the instructor is one of the keys to good lesson preparation. Some instructors are good at jokes or stories while others are masters of the low key comment. An instructor who can't tell jokes should avoid them. An instructor should work from his strengths and shy away from his weaknesses.

The student audience has to be considered when devising an attention gainer.[2] A class full of trial judges might be more easily attracted to the topic and the instructor if class attention is gained by citing cases that helped shape the American criminal justice system rather than by presenting a skit in which a judge is shown to be interested in the vital measurements of a buxom blonde defendant. The attention gainer should be consistent with the intellectual level of the class and should never offend student sensibilities. Profanity and off-color remarks about religion, politics, and race are strictly taboo.

The nature of the topic is also important when constructing an attention gainer. Using an opening gambit that has no relevance to the training subject is like mixing apples and oranges. The "eye for an eye, tooth for a tooth" concept quoted from the Bible might be a good lead-in to a class on correctional philosophy, but it would be less effective if the subject deals with inmate recreational programs.

Training objectives. The second subcomponent of the introduction section of a lesson plan is intended to inform students of what they are expected to do during the lesson. Students usually have general expectations regarding a particular teaching subject. The title, descriptions in course announcements, and conversations with former students provide general clues, but students need to know in specific terms what each of them will do during the lesson. Their need for this information is based on the principle of personal accountability, i.e., making a student responsible for his own learning. When a person knows what is required of him, he is better able to meet the requirements. When requirements of training are not stipulated in advance or in sufficiently explicit language, students become confused, with frustration and discouragement sure to follow.

It is important, then, for a student to know at the very outset of a class what is expected of him. The language of a training objective should express an action to be performed by the student. This places a deserved emphasis on the student's role in the training process. The instructor's role or function is to create learning activities that permit students to achieve the established objectives.

A training objective can be one of two types: cognitive or psychomotor. The cognitive type of objective requires the student to demonstrate a knowledge. The psychomotor type of objective requires the student to demonstrate a physical action. For example, a cognitive training objective might be "The student will specify the five elements of proof required to sustain a charge of conspiracy"; while a psychomotor objective might be "The student will prepare an inmate transfer report." In either case, whether the objective is cognitive or psychomotor,[3] the student is required to do something that can be evaluated by the instructor. The student might specify the five proof elements of conspiracy by verbally naming them, writing them down, marking multiple choices, or even by pressing buttons on a display panel. The student who is required to prepare an inmate transfer report demonstrates his performance by preparing the report. Both objectives require student performance, but the character of performance varies according to the nature of the action specified in the objective.

Although it is true that a training objective is expressed in student-centered language, the language also has a strong influence on the instructor's choice of learning activity. When an objective says that a student will prepare an inmate transfer report, the learning activity must include an opportunity for every individual student to prepare an inmate transfer report. Thus a training objective has implications for student and instructor. It gives specific directions as to what the instructor can or cannot do. A mutual accountability between student and instructor is built into the training objectives concept. In a very real sense, the learner and the teacher are locked together in the training enterprise. Each has a stake in the outcome. The learner's stake is to achieve the objectives, and the teacher's stake is to prove that his teaching was successful—as evidenced by what the student is able to do.

Most carefully designed courses of instruction will specify training objectives. Writing the training objectives subcomponent of a lesson plan is usually a matter of copying the training objectives from the course curriculum, program of instruction, or whatever document is used to describe the lesson units contained in the course.

When training objectives for a lesson do not exist, the instructor is at a disadvantage.[4] He is expected to arrive at some learning outcome, but is not told how to get there. Nor does he have any way of knowing if and when he has arrived. It helps, of course, when an instructor is both an academician and a practitioner. His on-the-job experiences will reveal to him the critical job tasks that must be learned by the student. For example, the instructor who is assigned to teach police recruits how to make an arrest might conclude that the lesson should address at least two tasks: a search incidental to the arrest and the application of handcuffs. Each of these tasks is a training objective.

Whether training objectives have been formulated for or by the instructor, it is extremely important that they be included in the lesson plan. Because the objectives are central to the training process and because they interconnect with other subcomponents of the lesson plan—as we shall see in this chapter—it is essential that they be emphasized in the introduction stage of the lesson presentation.

Lesson tie-in. A training course typically consists of a series of instructional units, with each unit representing a single subject or topic. For each unit there is at least one lesson plan. When a subject is taught in multiple sessions or taught by several instructors, more than one lesson plan for that unit is needed. A single lesson plan does not stand alone: every lesson plan is related to at least one other lesson plan. The first unit in a course has an impact on one or more units that follow it. The last unit is influenced by one or more preceding units, and middle units are influenced by surrounding units. If a course is designed properly, it will account for the relationships that exist among instructional units in a course. The topic of criminal interrogation, for example, would be preceded by a unit dealing with the law as it relates to a suspect's rights and might be followed with a unit that teaches an investigator how to testify in court with respect to an obtained confession. Learning is facilitated when new skills and knowledge are built on a foundation of previously acquired skills and knowledge. This means that training must be delivered in a sequential pattern. The interrelatedness of instructional units has critical implications for the success of training. The student who has failed to acquire an understanding of laws pertaining to interrogation will find it difficult, if not impossible, to satisfactorily perform in the unit that teaches him how to interrogate. Connections exist between separate lessons, and the instructor and students need to be reminded of them.

The instructor needs to know of lesson tie-ins in order to (1) ensure that his teaching builds a foundation for following units and (2) check student understanding of knowledge that forms a foundation for the unit he teaches. The student needs to know lesson connections because of the effect they have on his ability to pass the course.[5] But more than this, students frequently have trouble seeing the "big picture." Their images and impressions of the job come largely from the training environment. Since training is conducted in units, the students tend to conceptualize in units, i.e., their perceptions are fragmentary. A student who is uninformed of tie-ins among and between separate job tasks will be ill prepared to carry out the overlapping and interconnecting functions that comprise the total job.

Motivation. At this point in a lesson presentation, the instructor has obtained the attention of his class, told them the objectives of the instruction, and placed the topic within the context of all topics and the job they are being prepared to fill. Now the students need to be awakened to the importance of the topic. The purpose of the motivation subcomponent is to motivate students to apply themselves. Unless a student perceives some personal worth in a subject, he has little incentive to concentrate. The amount of energy put forth by him is proportional to the value he places on the end results of his efforts. If a student has no interest in a particular subject or thinks it pointless to pursue training objectives related to the subject, the instructor will be fighting an uphill battle. There are many reasons why a student will place zero value on a training subject. He might be asking himself "Why should I pay attention? This subject is too simple, and anyway I've studied stuff like this before." Or "What good is this subject? Chances are I'll never have to do this on the job." The instructor's task is to answer questions like this before they get in the way of learning.

One way to arouse motivation is to relate the subject to job functions the student will perform after he graduates. A student has a strong inclination to identify with his chosen profession. An instructor comment that begins "This subject is important because someday when you are on the job. . . ." is likely to evoke in the student a mental picture of himself doing challenging work. Natural interest is harnessed and put to constructive use.

An appeal to pride is another motivator. It capitalizes on every student's hope to eventually become competent in his field. Professionalism underlies the pride that a student frequently takes in his studies, even without encouragement from instructors. All people have pride. An instructor lets pride boost learning by reminding students that professional excellence is founded upon education and training.

Fear is sometimes used as a motivator. Fear is employed when an instructor encourages his students to learn on the grounds that a failure to do so might result in unfortunate consequences. For example, an instructor might point out that a failure to develop proficiency with a handgun can result in injury or death. Fear as a motivator has its advantages, but it also has occasional disadvantages. The student who imagines himself involved in some future shootout situation is as likely to be distracted from learning as he is to be motivated.

Fear as a motivator of learning is not as evil as it sounds. The concept of reward and punishment has fear as a major premise. Fear of academic failure, fear of lost prestige, and fear of admonition or reprimand are just a few of the reasons that make students want to excel. There is no question that fear is an influence on human behavior. A good instructor knows this. He takes fear into account, but does not abuse it.

●The Body

The body component is the largest and most important part of the lesson plan. The introduction and review components are subordinate to the body in the sense that one is a lead-in and the other is a recap. While the introduction and review may take up a combined total of about 15 minutes, the body consumes most of the available time for teaching. The body has two subcomponents:

- Supporting Knowledge
- The Practical Exercise

Supporting knowledge. The term "supporting knowledge" is derived from the concept that knowledge supports abilities. The abilities to be supported in a lesson plan are the tasks expressed in the training objectives subcomponent. This subcomponent contains that body of knowledge or information the student must know in order to perform the tasks specified in the training objectives subcomponent. If an objective requires a student to "name two primary facts that must be determined upon receipt of a crime in progress call," then the supporting knowledge must reflect teaching points that cover the two primary facts.

An outline format is usually followed when writing supporting knowledge.[6] The teaching points are grouped according to their importance in this fashion:

Main Teaching Point No. 1
    Sub-point
        Sub-sub-point
        Sub-sub-point
    Sub-point

Main Teaching Point No. 2
    Sub-point
    Sub-point
    Sub-point
      Sub-sub-point
    etc.

Many instructors work only from an outline. Sometimes an instructor will speak of an outline as a lesson plan—which it is not. An outline becomes a lesson plan when it is coupled with an introduction and a review, when it includes opportunities for student participation and practice, and when it integrates teaching points with approved objectives. An outline is a part of a plan, but is not the plan itself.

Writing the supporting knowledge subcomponent is the most tedious part of lesson plan preparation. It involves research, organization of material, revision, and at least some attention to the rules of grammar.

To be sure, an instructor who finds writing difficult will struggle with supporting knowledge. Struggle in this case does not mean failure, nor does it justify not writing a lesson plan. It simply means that writing of supporting knowledge involves putting forth some effort.

To help him decide how much to include in the supporting knowledge subcomponent, the writer uses the lesson's objectives as a guide. Information that contributes to the objectives belongs in the supporting knowledge subcomponents; information that does not contribute is a fair target for editorial slashing. Deciding what to cut can be as important as knowing what to include. By limiting information to facts that support established objectives, the writer is safeguarding against two risks. First, he reduces the amount of nonessential information that tends to creep into lessons. Second, he restrains his presentation from straying off into subject matter areas covered by other objectives contained in other instructional units.

The practical exercise. If one lesson plan subcomponent deserves to be singled out as the most important of all subcomponents, the practical exercise (PE) would be it. Everything done by students and the instructor in preceding steps of the lesson has led to this important training activity. The PE is a powerful teaching tool because it is an experiential activity. It requires students to "exercise" their newly attained knowledge or skills in "practical" ways. They experience the *doing* of something. Because the strength of learning is proportional to the quality of the experience that produces it, an instructor has a duty to use the practical exercise teaching method to its fullest advantage.

The PE subcomponent marks a turning point in an instructor's presentation. Until now the lesson plan has called for things that the instructor should say or do, but the PE is concerned with what students do. Instead of telling and showing students how something is done, the instructor sets up a situation in which students practice what was told and shown.[7]

●Writing and Preparing

Writing the PE subcomponent is best done in a "by the numbers" fashion. The planned exercise should be broken down into short, logical, and sequential steps. The steps should be numbered and described in sufficient detail to leave no doubt as to the mechanics of the exercise.

To illustrate, let's set up a hypothetical PE for an instructor who wishes to teach his students how to lift weights. Specifically, the objective requires the student to bench press at least 110 pounds. In the classroom the students have been taught the principles of bench pressing, they have seen a short film on the topic, and they have seen and handled bench pressing equipment. The supporting knowledge subcomponent of the lesson plan has concluded, and it is now time for the practical exercise. The PE might read like this:

1. Proceed with the class to the gymnasium.
2. Upon arrival at the gymnasium,

    a. direct the students to the locker rooms and allow 15 minutes for them to put on gym clothing, and

    b. the primary instructor and assistant instructor will check to ensure that the following equipment is on hand:

    (1) five weightlifting benches with bar supports,

    (2) five weightlifting bars with weights, each balanced to weigh 110 pounds.
3. Place the five benches in a line, keeping enough distance between benches so that the weightlifting bars will not pose a safety hazard to adjacent benches.
4. Place the five weightlifting bars in the bar supports above and at the end of each bench.
5. Assemble the students around the benches.
6. Demonstrate the exercise. The assistant instructor will demonstrate while the primary instructor describes.
7. Line up the students in rows behind the benches.
8. Have the first student in line at each bench assume the supine position on the bench, with his or her head facing upward below the bar supports.
9. The five students on the benches will simulate what their actions will be when the order is given to proceed with the exercise.

10. The assistant instructor will be prepared to assist any student who needs help.
11. The primary instructor will give the order to proceed.
12. The student will raise the bar from within the supports, and with arms extended, balance the bar.
13. The student will take a deep breath, hold it, lower the bar until it touches the chest, and continue to hold the breath.
14. The student will then push the bar directly above the chest and place the bar in the bar supports. As the student pushes the bar upward, the air held in the lungs is exhaled.
15. The primary instructor will give the order to perform four more repetitions (steps 12 through 14) without stopping.
16. At the end of the fifth repetition, the primary instructor will give the order to stop.
17. Allow the students to rest for 1 minute.
18. Conduct one more set of five repetitions.
19. Repeat steps 8 through 18 for each of all students remaining in line.
20. After all students have completed the practical exercise, assemble them around the benches and conduct a critique.

When a PE is written as illustrated above, the PE writer is forced to consider all the ingredients needed to make the exercise work properly and to ascertain what is available. He is reminded of the need to have five benches, five bars, five sets of weights, and an assistant instructor. His needs include having the gymnasium reserved and providing transportation. He is also reminded of the need to have a watch and perhaps a whistle. The written PE accentuates the importance of knowing what resources are available and arranging to integrate them in an activity that produces intended learning.

Including all lesson objectives. The instructor should try to include all lesson objectives, psychomotor and cognitive, in a single practical exercise session. Even if cognitive objectives are to be tested later by written examination, the students will at least have had the benefit during a PE to practice the knowledge. When all lesson objectives cannot be attained in a single exercise, the instructor will have to construct more than one PE. This can be time consuming and cumbersome. Rarely should this be necessary. Usually it occurs because dissimilar objectives have been incorrectly grouped within a lesson unit, or because the instructor can't think of a way to combine the tasks in one exercise. While the former reason represents a flaw in curriculum design and is usually beyond the instructor's control, the latter reason is something that can be worked out. An instructor's ability to create a practical exercise involving several tasks largely depends upon his understanding of how the tasks are performed on the job and how imaginative he is in setting up a scenario for their execution.

There are, however, some instances when it is not desirable to include all lesson objectives in a single PE session. If a curriculum called for 40 hours to teach firearms, the instructor would set up several similar practical exercises. If the curriculum included repair and maintenance of firearms, the instructor might set up a separate PE because of subject matter complexity. Or the curriculum might require night firing in addition to daytime firing. In any of these cases, the use of more than one PE is justified, but at the same time there is justification for the use of separate lesson plans.

The nature of a practical exercise for a unit is usually decided before an instructor is even assigned to teach the unit. Although instructors are often encouraged to create practical exercises, the fact is that the character of the exercise is determined during the curriculum design stage in the development of a course. When a curriculum designer writes an objective that says "the student will achieve a qualifying score with the .38 caliber revolver using the double action pistol course," the nature of the exercise has been pretty much settled. The content of a PE is directed at attainment of what the objectives specify. Objectives that contain action verbs like "prepare," "draw," "write," "make," or "name" mean what they say. The instructor's obligation is not to lend his own interpretation to objectives, but to see that they are met.

Using PE as a test. The practical exercise can be used for practice, for testing, or for both. Ideally, a training objective specified in an instructional unit is met through student performance under conditions that simulate the real-life environment. The job-related task expressed in the objective is performed by the student and evaluated by the instructor. If the purpose of the PE is to provide practice, the evaluation is informal in nature, i.e., the instructor guides and advises. If the purpose of the PE is to make a pass/fail determination, the evaluation is formal. And when the purpose is to practice and then evaluate for achievement, the PE does double duty.

Many training administrators find it difficult to formally evaluate achievement without the written examination. For this reason, the practical exercise method is not always used to its fullest potential. Generally, we find psychomotor training objectives being formally evaluated by the PE and cognitive objectives being tested by written examination. The fault with this procedure is that valuable opportunities for practice of cognitive skills are lost when the PE is used exclusively for practice of psychomotor skills.

There is nothing terribly wrong about written examinations, except when they are used as substitutes for practical exercise. Few people would argue that a written examination can determine a student's accuracy with a pistol. The proof of that ability can only be shown at the firing range. Even so, there are some who would demand an expert pistol shooter to answer written questions that relate to trigger squeeze, breath control, sight pattern, and so forth. Some instructors are just not satisfied with demonstrated performance. They need to reassure themselves by requiring students to explain knowledge or skills that can be or have been proficiently applied in practical exercise.

At least one good reason for including formal testing within a practical exercise is the time that is freed by not holding written examinations. For the same reason, where it is possible to test all lesson objectives in a single practical exercise, the instructor should do so. This is usually not difficult because the training objectives within a lesson or instructional unit will have many things in common. For example, a unit on firearms might have three objectives requiring students to achieve qualifying scores with the pistol, shotgun, and rifle. The conditions for each objective are similar enough to allow all three objectives to be achieved within one practical exercise session. Suppose also that an objective for firearms required each student to name the circumstances that justify the use of deadly force. This is a cognitive objective that tests a student's understanding of when to use a gun, as opposed to the psychomotor skill of shooting it. There is no reason why the cognitive objective cannot be tested within the same PE. *Further discussion of the practical exercise appears in Chapter 7, along with specific suggestions for constructing the PE.*

●**The Review**

The review consists of three subcomponents:

- Retain Attention
- Summary
- Closing Statement

Retain attention. This lesson plan element is similar in purpose to the attention gainer used at the outset of a presentation. It is intended to capture student attention and focus it on a summary of major teaching points. Keep in mind that the immediately preceding subcomponent, the practical exercise, consists of experiential activities. The instructor must now regain the collective focus of the class. The transition from doing to listening and discussing can be handled in many ways. A simple "Let me have your attention, please" can be just as effective as a joke, a story, or an admonition. Whatever the tactic, it is briefly described in writing and called the retain attention subcomponent.

Summary. The main part of the lesson review is the summary. Important knowledge and skills discussed, demonstrated, or practiced during the body section of the lesson are now summarized. The summary is also a time when students are encouraged to ask questions to clarify points not clearly understood.

Although an important part of a lesson plan, the summary is unfortunately downplayed by some instructors. Skimming over or just naming the lesson's key points does not fulfill the purpose of the summary. If an instructor remembers that the summary is his last chance to get the message across, he will take care to make a solid summarization.

The summary should not introduce new ideas or teaching points. Information relevant to the topic is taught prior to the lesson's review and only briefly touched upon in the summary. If a new or unfamiliar concept is unveiled during the closing moments of a lesson, students become concerned that they have missed something that might be tested later.

An outline format is suitable when writing the summary subcomponent. The outline should not be as long or as detailed as information set out in the body component, but it should reflect the major points that directly address the lesson's training objectives. If student performance (i.e., the ability to perform job tasks) rests upon the student possessing certain information, then the instructor has an obligation to summarize that information. The summary, however, need not and should not be long and drawn out.

A discussion of the summary subcomponent must necessarily include a related matter called the *summary sheet*, which is a record of the major points taught during the lesson. A summary sheet is not technically part of a lesson plan, but is an appendix to it. Whereas a lesson plan is written for and used by instructors, the summary sheet is written for and used by students. It is handed out to students, usually at the conclusion of a class.

Closing statement. A smooth ending to a lesson presentation is just as important as a smooth beginning. Sometimes an otherwise flawless teaching performance will be marred at the very end by a poor closing. If at the conclusion of a lesson an instructor does something ludicrous or embarrassing, the students are apt to remember the incident rather than what was taught. A crude joke, a profane story, or a flippant remark can devastate an excellent presentation.

If the instructor is mindful that training is effective only to the extent that it produces human improvement on the job, he will use the closing statement as a final chance to drive home the importance of the knowledge and skills covered during the lesson. Information and skills acquired through training but not applied in the work situation represent an enormous waste. A strong closing statement stresses the value of the lesson and motivates the student to apply his newly developed abilities. The instructor exits on an upbeat, positive note.

●**Handouts**

Part of writing a lesson plan is the planning and preparation of handouts. Student handouts are generally of three types: (1) the advance sheet; (2) the classroom issue; and (3) the summary sheet.

The advance sheet is given to students before a particular class. It may tell the students to read a particular chapter, view a film, perform an experiment, bring or wear something to class, meet at a particular place, etc.

The classroom issue is given to students during the class. It can be used as a prestructured outline in which students record definitions of key ideas as the instructor articulates them; it can be used to describe steps in a procedure that is taught, demonstrated, or practiced during the class; or it can be used as part of a PE to describe a situation for student analysis and response.

The summary sheet is given to students at the conclusion of class. Its main purpose is to provide information that will help students prepare for an examination. By including the central points of a lesson, the summary sheet indicates what information will be tested. It may also be useful as a job performance aid. For example, a summary sheet that details the procedures for making plaster casts of tire prints can be helpful in readying students for an examination, and it can be helpful on the job when circumstances would require the making of such plaster casts. The summary sheet is a logical extension of the summary subcomponent. The same major teaching points, in perhaps the same language appearing in the lesson plan summary, are appropriate for inclusion in the summary sheet.

WRITING THE LESSON PLAN

An instructor need not be an Ernest Hemingway to write a lesson plan. It is not necessary to write down every single word the instructor will utter as he teaches from his plan. Neither is it desirable to make a plan so sparse as to create uncertainty regarding the meaning of a word or term listed in a supporting knowledge outline. The lesson plan writer needs to aim at some middle point between too little and too much description.

To illustrate how a lesson plan is actually written, we will be assisted by a fictitious lesson plan writer named Larry Cranston. For the sake of simplicity, Mr. Cranston will write a plan that is short and uncomplicated. The unit is titled "The Criminal Justice System"; it is two hours long; it covers "The major functions and interrelationships of police, courts, and corrections, with emphasis on conflicts and problems that impede efficient operation of the system." The unit has one training objective which requires each student to "Describe at least one major problem within each component of the criminal justice system which impedes efficient operation of the system."

●**The Introduction**

You will recall that we said an attention gainer should

- be appropriate to the topic, and
- conform to the personality of the instructor.

Our fictitious lesson plan writer, being a reasonably serious person, at least as far as his topic is concerned, prepares an attention gainer as follows:

I. INTRODUCTION

A. Gain Attention.

Some people will argue that the American criminal justice system is not a system at all. They point out that the definition of a system requires its component parts to operate with coordination, purpose, and a sense of direction. The detractors of the system we call criminal justice will cite case after case in which the system fails to act in accordance with the meaning of the term. It is my belief, and I hope at the conclusion of this lesson you will share it with me, that the criminal justice system does work and can be made to work better if the people who comprise it will come to understand and fulfill their roles and responsibilities. To be sure, the system has its imperfections, but with clear thinking and fortitude we can improve it and in the process enhance the quality of American life.

Writing of the training objectives subcomponent is strictly a matter of copying the objective(s) directly from curriculum specifications.[8] This lesson unit has one objective:

B. Training Objective.

As a result of this instruction, you will be able to:

Describe at least one major problem within each component of the criminal justice system which impedes efficient operation of the system.

Even though this is a very simple objective, it is nonetheless quite specific. It calls for a student action that is not easily misinterpreted, that can be made visible, and is measurable. The objective is cognitive, and Mr. Cranston plans to test it by written examination on Monday following the week in which it is taught.[9]

Curriculum specifications also assist in writing the lesson tie-in. The curriculum tells us what subjects are taught before and after each unit. One preceding unit and several succeeding units have tie-ins with the subject. A lesson tie-in is prepared that looks like this:

C. Lesson Tie-in.

In a previous unit of instruction you have been given an overview of the American form of government. Now you will see how the criminal justice system operates within the framework of federal, state, and local governments. In later units of instruction you will build upon today's lesson. You will learn the major functions performed by police, courts, and corrections, and the system of laws that constrain and limit those functions.

It is not necessary to name specifically the units that are interrelated. It is the interrelationships that are important.

The motivation subcomponent is intended to awaken students to the importance of the subject. Mr. Cranston prepares the following motivating statement:

D. Motivation.

An understanding of the criminal justice system is important to you because it will help you to perceive the part you play within your particular component of the system, and within the total system. Whether you are a member of the police, courts, or corrections, you will derive from this unit a better understanding of how your job impacts on other members of the system and on the offenders who are being processed by that system.

The introductory portion of the lesson plan is now complete. It is short and sweet. Even very complicated and very long lessons have brief introductions. The time needed for the introduction portion will rarely exceed 15 minutes. For most lesson plans it will fluctuate within the vicinity of 5 minutes. Mr. Cranston calculates his introduction to require between 3 and 5 minutes.

●The Body

Supporting knowledge. The next step is to write the supporting knowledge subcomponent of the body. A safe and simple method is to structure the supporting knowledge so that it corresponds rather directly with the unit's training objectives. In other words, start the outline of teaching points by selecting and grouping those points that support the ability reflected in the first training objective. When that has been done, do the same for the second objective, and so forth. If a teaching point has relevance to more than one objective, as it frequently does, the instructor will need to include it in the outline in several places. In his presentation, however, he will find himself placing less and less emphasis upon the points, returning them to his class's attention when necessary with a brief mention of their relationship to subsequent discussions.

This method of writing the supporting knowledge is safe because it helps to ensure that information supportive of objectives is included. It is simple because it tends to exclude extraneous ideas. The method reflects a concern with student success rather than instructor preferences. It seems to express in its style and format an awareness that some concepts have greater importance than others; and that the important concepts come first, are taught well, and are repeated as often as necessary to strengthen them in the student's mind. And, at least from the point of view of a beginning instructor, this method of writing a teaching point outline is helpful because it tells the instructor where to start, what to include, where to put information, and when to stop. A fault with the novice lesson plan writer is a propensity to leave out main ideas by writing too little or to cloud them with many tangential points.

Mr. Cranston decides to use this method of constructing supporting knowledge in relation to objectives. His task is not difficult because his unit has only one objective. This is what he writes:

II. BODY

    A. Supporting Knowledge.

        1. The Police

           a. Functions

               (1) Arrest, search, seizure

               (2) Patrol

               (3) Traffic

               (4) Investigations

               (5) Social services

           b. Interrelationships with courts

           c. Interrelationships with corrections

           d. Major problems confronting the police

               (1) Lack of public support

               (2) Lack of public understanding

               (3) Inadequate financing

               (4) Rising crime rates

        2. The Courts

           a. Constitutional foundations

               (1) Due process

           b. Judicial systems

               (1) U.S. Supreme Court

               (2) Federal court

               (3) State supreme courts

               (4) Court of Appeal

  (5) Superior courts

  (6) Civil and criminal courts

 c. Grand jury functions

 d. Interrelationships with police

 e. Interrelationships with corrections

 f. Major problems confronting the courts

  (1) Lack of public understanding

  (2) Inadequate staffing

  (3) Increase in crime

  (4) Breakdown in law enforcement

  (5) Recidivism

  (6) Clogged calendars/workload

  (7) Lack of inclination to make reforms

3. Corrections

 a. Philosophy

  (1) Past

  (2) Present

  (3) Future?

 b. Goals

 c. Organization

  (1) Institutional

  (2) Community-based

 d. Interrelationships with police

 e. Interrelationships with courts

 f. Major problems confronting corrections

  (1) Lack of public support

  (2) Inadequate funding

  (3) Poor staffing

  (4) Overcrowded conditions

  (5) Failure to rehabilitate

  (6) Lack of desire to reform

4. Purpose of the criminal justice system

 a. Philosophic core

  (1) Impartial and deliberate process

 b. Nature of the process

  (1) Visible and invisible administrative procedures

5. Needs of the system

 a. Financing

 b. Technical resources

 c. Coordination

 d. Public support

 e. Innovation

In writing the supporting knowledge Mr. Cranston relies exclusively on the use of short terms, phrases, and words. Each term represents an idea to be presented to the class. The details of each idea are in Mr. Cranston's head. As his eye moves down the lesson plan, details are triggered. This is a technique that lends itself to a dynamic and flexible oral presentation. The instructor does not read word for word from a lesson plan but speaks conversationally and spontaneously, using a few key words or expressions to actuate discussions of important teaching points.

There is, however, one potential problem in using an outline of key words. What means something to one person may mean something altogether different to another person. The problem usually arises when an alternate instructor fills in for the primary instructor. Therefore when writing supporting knowledge, the instructor should pause at each word and ask himself this question, "Will a replacement instructor know what I mean when I use this word?" When the answer is less than a definite yes, the instructor will need to provide more detail in the outline. For example, the last word in Mr. Cranston's supporting knowledge is innovation. If he felt a replacement instructor might be confused, Mr. Cranston could expand the outline in this way.

Innovation.

The criminal justice system needs to find new ways to attack old problems. Effective remedies a few years ago are no longer appropriate. To meet the challenges of a rapidly changing society in a technological boom, fresh ideas and a willingness to experiment are needed.

The extent of detail in the supporting knowledge section should lie somewhere between the extremes of a highly skeletal outline and a highly detailed manuscript. When key words have wide and uniform understanding, there is less need to expand upon them. When a word is obscure or ambiguous, detail is needed.

One last thing should be said about supporting knowledge. The amount of discussion, emphasis, and detail given to an idea depends not on how much the instructor knows about it but on what the students need to know. Many an instructor has made the mistake of trying to teach his students everything he knows about an idea. The result is that students are given too much information. They spend valuable time acquiring "nice to know" information that has no present or immediate value. Also, undue emphasis is placed on some ideas to the detriment of others. Nothing is wrong with an instructor imparting knowledge derived from valid job experiences which relate directly to his subject. But it is unwise for him to consume most of his teaching time covering certain points and only lightly touching upon others that are just as important.

Practical exercise. What is taught in the supporting knowledge phase of the instructor's presentation is applied during the practical exercise phase. The nature of the application activity will depend on a variety of factors. These factors are covered in depth in Chapter 7, dealing with construction of practical exercises. For now, it is enough to say that a practical exercise is influenced by these factors:

- time
- number of students
- space
- logistics
- assistant instructors

Mr. Cranston concludes that he needs one instructional hour (50 minutes) for his practical exercise. Note that time is allocated first on the basis of what the PE will require and not on the basis of what the supporting knowledge phase will require. Regrettably, this point is not always understood or followed. Many instructors hold a PE only when there is time remaining after the lecture. Lecture thereby becomes the dominant teaching method and, as a consequence, student learning suffers. Instructors who believe that people learn more from doing than from listening and watching will set aside less time for talking and more time for practical application.

A rule of thumb is to allocate to the PE at least 50 percent of the total time specified by the curriculum for teaching of the unit. This means that the introduction, review, and supporting knowledge combined get no more than 50 percent of the available teaching time. This realization leads Mr. Cranston to allot 5 minutes to introduce, 40 minutes to cover the teaching points, 50 minutes to practice, and 5 minutes to summarize.

Mr. Cranston's next considerations in developing a PE are the number of students, a place to hold the PE, materials or equipment needed, and assistants needed. He notes that the class averages thirty students, and there is only one cognitive objective. He is sure he can arrange for all thirty students to simultaneously practice the knowledge described in the objective and that the exercise can be conducted in the classroom using only pencils and paper. Mr. Cranston concludes that one assistant instructor would be helpful during the exercise but not essential.

In looking at his objective, Mr. Cranston observes that it requires students to possess one type of knowledge—knowing the major problems—as it relates to three areas: the police, the courts, and corrections. He decides to create separate written hypothetical situations for the police, courts, and corrections. The students will study the situations in terms of the problems discussed during the supporting knowledge phase of the lesson. In addition to reading and studying each situation, students will be required to provide written responses reflecting their understanding of the problems.

●The Handouts

Mr. Cranston realizes he will have to put the written situations in the format of a student handout. Since Mr. Cranston's purpose is to give students something to analyze and respond to, the suitable handout is of the classroom issue type.

THE CRIMINAL JUSTICE SYSTEM
Classroom Issue I

SITUATION A.

The following article appeared in a local newspaper:

"Last night the Bakersville city council voted to disapprove a budget proposal that would have provided the police department with a new $2,550,000 communications center. The proposal, if approved, would have seen Bakersville contribute 10% in matching funds, with the federal government providing 90% of cost. Chief Farnsworth said 'We have missed a wonderful opportunity to obtain a much-needed communications capability. It is incredible to me that the city council acted so irresponsibly.'

"The budget request ran into early trouble when an unidentified lady citizen in the audience demanded to know why the police department needed so much money 'to build a fancy communications center at a time when it isn't safe for women to walk the streets of Bakersville.' Her remarks drew much applause from those present."

REQUIREMENTS FOR SITUATION A.

1. Allow yourself 10 minutes to read and complete the requirements for this situation. Work alone. This is an individual exercise.

2. Based on your understanding of the situation and of problems that were discussed in class regarding the police component of the criminal justice system, do these things:

a. On the line below, name one problem present in the situation.

_____

b. With regard to the problem named above, what in your opinion helped cause it? Write your answer on the lines below.

_____
_____
_____
_____

c. On the line below, name a second problem present in the situation.

_____

d. With regard to the problem named above, what in your opinion helped cause it? Write your answer on the lines below.

_____
_____
_____
_____

e. On the line below, name a third problem present in the situation.

_____

f. With regard to the problem named above, what in your opinion helped cause it? Write your answer on the lines below.

_____

_____

_____

_____

g. Be prepared to discuss your responses in a critique that follows this exercise.

SITUATION B.

In the same newspaper, another story appeared.

"Accused drug kingpin Rolly Dutton was freed yesterday when Judge Herman Redeker ruled on a defense motion that Dutton's constitutional right to speedy trial had been violated. Dutton was free on bond for the full 28 months it took to bring the case to court.

"Assistant prosecutor Mel Oglesby lamented after the trial that 'Based on Dutton's long history of drug trafficking, it was an injustice that he escaped conviction on a technicality.' Mr. Oglesby also went on to say 'Rising drug violations have reached proportions that are beyond the ability of the police to control, and unless changes are made in the way criminals are coddled in court, we are all headed for God knows what.'

"Judge Redeker, when asked to comment on Oglesby's strong criticisms, called Oglesby 'A young man imbued of high idealism who has not yet gained sufficient appreciation of criminal procedure.'

"Immediately following dismissal of the case, Dutton called a press conference in which he praised the judicial system for exonerating him."

REQUIREMENTS FOR SITUATION B

1. Allow yourself 10 minutes to read and complete the requirements for this situation. Work alone. This is an individual exercise.

2. Based on your understanding of the situation and of problems that were discussed in class regarding the courts component of the criminal justice system, do these things:

a. On the line below, name one problem present in the situation.

_____

b. With regard to the problem named above, what in your opinion helped cause it? Write your answer on the lines below.

_____

_____

_____

_____

c. On the line below, name a second problem present in the situation.

_____

d. With regard to the problem named in c, what in your opinion helped cause it? Write your answer on the lines below.

_____
_____
_____
_____

e. On the line below, name a third problem present in the situation.

_____

f. With regard to the problem named above, what in your opinion helped cause it? Write your answer on the lines below.

_____
_____
_____
_____

g. Were any other problems present in the situation? If so, briefly describe them on the following lines.

_____
_____
_____

3. Be prepared to discuss your responses in a critique that follows this exercise.

SITUATION C

Assume you are a correctional officer at a county correctional facility. The minister for the church you attend has asked you to make a brief talk at a small fellowship meeting next week. The warden thinks it is a good idea. He suggests that your talk include mention of problems that confront the field of corrections in general.

REQUIREMENTS FOR SITUATION C

1. Write an outline of a short speech that includes at least four major problems of corrections. Make the outline brief by using key words or phrases in lieu of lengthy explanations. Write the outline on scratch paper.

2. Allow yourself 15 minutes. Work on your own.

3. Be prepared to discuss your responses in a critique that follows this exercise.

Now, let's take a look at certain features of the classroom issue prepared by Mr. Cranston. First, we notice the Roman numeral I following the heading. Since it is possible to have several classroom issues for a single unit, the number differentiates one issue from another. Mr. Cranston might decide to use a classroom issue to guide students in taking notes during a supporting knowledge portion of his lesson, or he might decide to use a separate classroom issue for each of the three situations he has created. In either case he will want to number the issues to keep track of them.

A noticeable feature of Mr. Cranston's handout is the time he has allocated to the students for completion of the situations comprising the PE. With 10, 10, and 15 minutes consumed working the exercise, Mr. Cranston has built himself a cushion of 15 minutes in which to critique the exercise.

In Situations A and B, the students are presented with information that is described as having come from a newspaper. The information could as well have come from any source or with no attribution at all. The situation can be presented as a factual, real-life case, a fictitious case, a simulated case, or any scenario that presents an issue relevant to the subject. In Situation C the student is asked to assume a role in the conceptual sense. A situation can be structured in almost any form. The important thing is for it to have relevance to one or more of the unit's training objectives.

Another feature of the classroom issue is the specificity of instructions in the requirements that follow the situations. Note that the requirements are in detail, arranged in a step-by-step fashion, and provide space for student responses. This helps to clarify what is expected of the students and to reduce the number of questions they will ask of the instructor while the PE is in progress. Even more important, responses are put in writing, providing the instructor with the opportunity to collect the written responses for evaluation purposes. A classroom issue designed to provoke and capture student responses does double-duty by operating as a learning tool for students and as an assessment tool for the instructor.

A classroom issue is not a part of a lesson plan. The lesson plan is written for the instructor; a classroom issue is written for the student. A classroom issue is referred to in a lesson plan and attached as an exhibit. The relationship of the classroom issue to the lesson plan is demonstrated in the Practical Exercise subcomponent as written by Mr. Cranston:

B. The Practical Exercise

1. Hand out Classroom Issue I. (Note: See copy of Classroom Issue I which is attached to this plan as an exhibit.)

2. Brief the students on how the exercise is to be conducted. Answer student questions as necessary.

3. Begin the exercise. Allow 35 minutes for the students to complete the requirements of all three situations in Classroom Issue I.

4. At the end of 35 minutes stop the exercise.

5. Conduct a 15-minute critique of the exercise.

The PE subcomponent need not be long or complicated. Most of the preparation for a PE is done before the start of class. Equipment or materials, including classroom issues, have been made ready. The lesson plan simply states how and in what order they will be used during the exercise. Documentary items attached to the lesson plan may include a list of tools, equipment, or visual aids; diagrams or sketches that depict the physical layout of a PE area; and advance sheets, classroom issues, and summary sheets.

●**The Review**

The more difficult portion of lesson plan writing is now behind us. All that remains to be written is the review component. You will recall that the review has three elements:

- Retain Attention
- Summary
- Closing Statement

The retain attention subcomponent focuses class attention on a summarizing of important points. It need not be long or elaborate, just effective. Mr. Cranston's attention getter is as follows:

III. REVIEW

   A. Retain Attention.

     Let me have your attention, please. We have examined and discussed a number of concepts, and we have also practiced some of that knowledge in a PE.

The summary subcomponent is the heart of the review. It is the only reason for having a review. The summary can be thought of as a mini-version of the supporting knowledge phase. It need not cover every teaching point presented in the supporting knowledge, but it should include all points that relate to objectives. An outline format, similar to that used in the supporting knowledge, is appropriate for the summary. Keep in mind that the selected points are only briefly recalled. Here is Mr. Cranston's summary outline:

B. Summary

   1. Major functions of the police

   2. Major problems of the police

     a. Lack of public support

     b. Lack of public understanding

     c. Inadequate financing

     d. Rising crime rates

   3. Major functions of the courts

   4. Major problems of the courts

     a. Lack of public understanding

     b. Inadequate staffing

     c. Increase in crime

     d. Breakdown in law enforcement

     e. Recidivism

     f. Workload

     g. Unwillingness to make reforms

   5. Major functions of corrections

6. Major problems of corrections
   a. Lack of public support
   b. Inadequate funding
   c. Poor staffing
   d. Overcrowding
   e. Failure to rehabilitate
   f. Inability to make reforms
7. Needs of the system

All that remains to be done by an instructor who has reached this stage of a lesson is to gracefully exit. The closing statement serves that purpose. It allows the instructor to cap off his summary with a strong and positive statement. Mr. Cranston's closing remarks are as follows:

C. Closing Statement

At the outset of this class I said it was my hope that you would come to share with me a belief that the criminal justice system, despite its many problems, can be made to work effectively and serve the needs of all citizens. As a consequence of today's instruction, I am confident you have made a strong first step toward attaining the level of commitment required by any person who would call himself a criminal justice professional.

The summary sheet should be distributed during or at the close of a lesson. When the instructor comes to the point where he or she plans to hand out a summary sheet, he should have a note to that effect.

There is no reason why every unit of instruction should not have a summary sheet. If information is worth teaching, it is worth retaining, and the summary sheet helps fulfill that purpose. An example of Mr. Cranston's summary sheet appears on page 129.

●Notes

It is nearly impossible to have a lesson plan without notes of some type. Notes remind the instructor to display a training aid, ask a question, write something on the chalkboard, demonstrate a procedure, show a film, and so forth. Some instructors keep their notes separate from a lesson plan because they change their notes frequently or they feel comfortable working with notes that are written on flash cards. When notes are used separately from a lesson plan, they should not substitute for the lesson plan. Nor should they transcend the boundaries of a unit's scope or ignore the key points that support the unit's objectives. Separate notes must conform to the lesson plan. They are part of the plan, not independent of it; they complement the plan, not supplement it; and they are subordinate, not superior to the plan.

A way to integrate notes with a lesson plan is to use a format that places the notes in a margin created for them. This procedure allows an instructor to change his notes without having to disturb his written plan.

Mr. Cranston's department uses a preprinted form that allows for margin notes. As Mr. Cranston transcribes his developed lesson plan onto the form, he also inserts his notes. His complete lesson plan, with notes included, begins on page 130.

● Cover Sheet

One final matter remains before a lesson plan is finished. A cover sheet should be made that provides certain administrative information. School administrators, office personnel, alternate instructors, and outside evaluators frequently need to know things like the filing code for the unit; what written materials were used by the writer of the plan; what are the books needed by students; what are the training aids and student handouts; when was the plan written or revised; who wrote it; who approved it; who are the primary and alternate instructors; and other details. An example of a lesson plan cover sheet is on page 130.

SUMMARY

Before concluding this examination of lesson planning, let's take a final look at the important points covered.

We have seen that a lesson plan reflects what is taught, in what order or sequence it is taught, and what teaching methods are used. A plan ensures that instruction is properly organized. It has definite value to the instructor who prepares it and an even greater value to a replacement instructor.

An instructor does not read directly from his plan; he uses it as a guide in staying on track and moving in the direction of planned learning outcomes. A lesson plan is an instructor's tool. It is to be used by him and not vice versa. Rigid conformity to a lesson plan and not having a lesson plan at all are extremes to be avoided.

A lesson plan consists of an introduction, a body, and a review. The introduction is brief. It sees the instructor gaining student attention, explaining training objectives, tying in the lesson, and instilling motivation.

The body is the heart of the lesson plan because it provides for the presentation of knowledge followed by practice of the tasks supported by that knowledge. The knowledge to be presented is arranged in an outline format. Separate teaching notes are commonly used to supplement the supporting knowledge part of the lesson plan's body. A sensible way to write supporting knowledge is to organize ideas according to the training objectives they support.

The latter (and usually largest) portion of the lesson plan body is used for practice of the tasks named in the lesson's objectives. The practice can be cognitive or psychomotor in nature; it can be for familiarization, development, or mastery; and it can be practice in preparation for a test or it can constitute the test itself.

A review of the lesson is brief. Because a review immediately follows a practical exercise, it helps to regain student attention before summarizing important points covered in the body. A summary sheet is normally handed out to students to use in preparing for an upcoming examination. The instructor makes a positive, motivating statement to close out his lesson.

This sequence of lesson plan use can be seen in Figure 7.

A last word needs to be said about the lesson plan in terms of its use as a management instrument. Training practices must be continuously measured and evaluated.[10] The lesson plan is a measuring device for management because it describes in fairly specific language the design and intent of the teaching enterprise. Training managers (or their quality control representatives) who visit the classroom need only compare what they see against the lesson plan. Managers (or those who supervise on their behalf) need only compare job performances of former students against the learning outcomes expressed in lesson plans. Where there is discrepancy between the plan and its proper execution, management intervention may be indicated.

Many of the skills and much of the knowledge that go into lesson plan preparation are covered elsewhere in this book. The use of questions, critiques, motivation, practical exercises, and training aids are but a few ingredients of lesson planning that are closely examined in other chapters. The instructor using this chapter as a guide in writing a lesson plan should also examine other chapters.

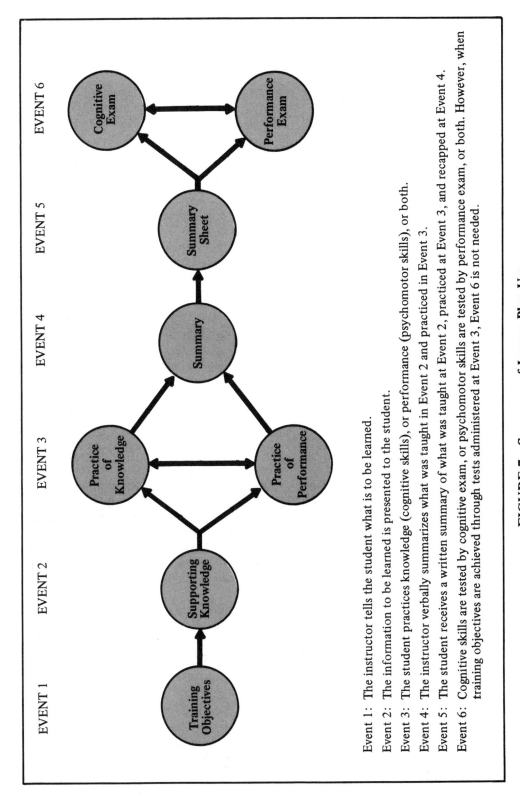

EVENT 1   EVENT 2   EVENT 3   EVENT 4   EVENT 5   EVENT 6

Event 1: The instructor tells the student what is to be learned.

Event 2: The information to be learned is presented to the student.

Event 3: The student practices knowledge (cognitive skills), or performance (psychomotor skills), or both.

Event 4: The instructor verbally summarizes what was taught in Event 2 and practiced in Event 3.

Event 5: The student receives a written summary of what was taught at Event 2, practiced at Event 3, and recapped at Event 4.

Event 6: Cognitive skills are tested by cognitive exam, or psychomotor skills are tested by performance exam, or both. However, when training objectives are achieved through tests administered at Event 3, Event 6 is not needed.

FIGURE 7: Sequence of Lesson Plan Use

NOTES

1. This recommended format is similar to a format generally used at police academies in Georgia. See John Fay, *Police Instructors Guide* (Atlanta, Ga.: Peace Officer Standards and Training Council, 1978).

2. *Executive's Handbook of Humor for Speakers,* Preface (Waterford, Conn.: Bureau of Business Practice, 1971).

3. In Bloom's *Taxonomy of Educational Objectives* (New York: Donald McKay Publishers, 1964), three categories of objectives are cited: cognitive, psychomoter, and affective. The affective objective relates to job tasks that require the learner to develop attitudes or feelings. Examples of such objectives are "Tolerates human resistance to change," "Forms ethical judgments," "Pays attention to complaints," "Develops techniques to control aggression," and "Speaks up in staff meetings."

4. Dugan Laird suggests in *Approaches to Training and Development* (Reading, Mass.: Addison-Wesley Publishing Co., 1978), pp. 110-111, that the writing of objectives is a team chore to be shared by the client (e.g, chief of police, warden, and judge), supervisors of the workers to be trained, typical workers, a training and development person, and a learning-system designer. The client, supervisor, and worker representatives provide information about the job; the T & D member provides the expertise in writing objectives that reflect job tasks; and the learning-system designer develops instructional strategies that are appropriate for carrying out the objectives. Having an instructor "on the team" ought not be arbitrarily ruled out, but the value of the instructor would reside mainly in making contributions that carry out the team functions described by Laird.

5. The importance of objectives is once again apparent. Mager has this to say about it. "An additional advantage of clearly defined objectives is that the student is provided the means to evaluate his own progress at any place along the route of instruction and is able to organize his efforts into relevant activities." From Robert F. Mager, *Preparing Instructional Objectives* (Belmont, Calif.: Fearon Publishers, 1962), p. 4.

6. Ideas can be organized in descending order, i.e., start with the big (most general) idea and under it place supporting ideas in order of their importance. On p. 58 of *Writing for Results* (Reading, Mass.: Addison-Wesley Publishing Co., 1975), Dugan Laird suggests an inverted pyramid method for organizing ideas.

7. Several good ideas for developing structured learning experiences are contained in *Criminal Justice Group Training,* by Michael E. O'Neill and Kai R. Martinsen (La Jolla, Calif.: University Associates, Inc., 1975).

8. It was noted earlier that a well-planned course described its objectives.

9. It would make great sense at this point to write test questions, or ascertain what they are. The questions must necessarily go to the heart of the objective. By determining at the outset what students will have to know, the instructor can construct a lesson plan that helps students acquire the needed information.

10. David A. Hansen and Thomas R. Colley, *The Police Training Officer* (Springfield, Ill.: Charles C. Thomas, 1973), p. 18.

THE CRIMINAL JUSTICE SYSTEM

Summary Sheet

1. An overall purpose of the police service is to preserve domestic peace consistent with rights secured by the Constitution. Within that purpose the police discharge a number of functions which may include patrolling, investigation, crime prevention, traffic enforcement, temporary detention, civil process, disaster assistance and community service referral. The types of functions performed by the police are influenced by local needs.

2. Major problems of the police may at various times and to varying degrees include lack of public support and understanding, inadequate funding, rising crime rates, and police personnel turnover.

3. The courts operate as a focal point for the criminal justice system. Courts regulate the flow of criminal process under governance of the law. Activities of the police and corrections are restrained and shaped by rules and procedures of the courts.

4. Major problems confronting the courts include a general lack of public understanding regarding the criminal process, inadequate staffing, increases in crime, breakdowns in enforcement of law, recidivism, high workload, and clogged court calendars. Adding to these problems is the inability and unwillingness of the courts to make basic changes in their methods of operation.

5. Corrections is the least known component of the criminal justice system. It operates prisons, jails, rehabilitative programs, and probation and parole agencies. The term corrections may be a misnomer in the sense that many offenders are in fact not corrected by the system.

6. Major problems affecting corrections include an unwillingness of taxpayers to support correctional operations, poor staffing, overcrowding, an inability to rehabilitate inmates, insufficient resources, and an inability to make needed reforms.

7. The criminal justice system, if it is to efficiently serve society, needs public backing, a larger commitment of financial support, greater use of technical resources, internal coordination, and innovative problem-solving approaches.

LESSON PLAN COVER SHEET

Unit Title	Unit Code
The Criminal Justice System	BCJ-2

Course	Hours	Date
Basic Criminal Justice Course	2	Prepared/Revised

Prepared By	Approved By
L. Cranston	Kevin Kennedy

Primary Instructor	Alternate Instructor
L. Cranston	Margo Lane

Scope

The major functions and interrelationships of police, courts, and corrections, with emphasis on conflicts and problems that impede efficient operations of the system.

Training Objectives

BCJ-2-1   Describe at least one major problem within each component of the criminal justice system which impedes efficient operation of the system.

Instructor References	Student References
Criminal Justice, Kaplan.	None.

Training Aids	Student Handouts
Overhead transparencies 1-4; court system wall chart; chalkboard.	Classroom Issue I; Summary Sheet.

LESSON PLAN

Unit Title The Criminal Justice System	**Unit Code**
Course Basic Criminal Justice Course	**INSTRUCTOR NOTES**

I. INTRODUCTION

  A. Gain Attention.

   Some people will argue that the American Criminal Justice System is not a system at all. They point out that the definition of a system requires its component parts to operate with coordination, purpose, and a sense of direction. The detractors of the system we call criminal justice will cite case after case in which the system fails to act in accordance with the meaning of the term. It is my belief, and I hope at the conclusion of this lesson you will share it with me, that the criminal justice system does work and can be made to work better if the people who comprise it will come to understand and fulfill their roles and responsibilities. To be sure, the system has its imperfections, but with clear thinking and fortitude we can improve it, and in the process enhance the quality of American life.

  B. Training Objective(s).

   As a result of this instruction, you will be able to:
   Describe at least one major problem within each component of the criminal justice system which impedes efficient operation of the system.

  C. Lesson Tie-in.

   In a previous unit of instruction you have been given an overview of the American form of government. Now you will see how the criminal justice system operates within the framework of federal, state, and local governments. In later units of instruction you will build upon today's lesson. You will learn the major functions performed by police, courts, and corrections, and the system of laws that constrain and limit those functions.

  D. Motivation.

   An understanding of the criminal justice system is important to you because it will help you to perceive the part you play within your particular component of the system, and within the total system. Whether you are a member of the police, courts, or corrections, you will derive from this unit a better understanding of how your job impacts on other members of the system and on the offenders who are being processed by that system.

Unit Title	Unit Code
The Criminal Justice System	

Course	INSTRUCTOR NOTES
Basic Criminal Justice Course	

II. BODY

  A. Supporting Knowledge

    1. The Police

      a. Functions

        (1) Arrest, search, seizure

        (2) Patrol

        (3) Traffic   *Display overhead transparency no. 1 (Functions of Police).*

        (4) Investigations

        (5) Social Services

      b. Interrelationships with courts

      c. Interrelationships with corrections

      d. Major problems confronting the police   *Display overhead transparency no. 4 (Problems of Corrections).*

        (1) Lack of public support

        (2) Lack of public understanding   *Q: Lack of public support is an outgrowth of lack of public understanding. Explain what this means.*

        (3) Inadequate financing

        (4) Rising crime rates   *A: People do not support what they do not understand.*

    2. The Courts

      a. Constitutional foundations

        (1) Due process

      b. Judicial

        (1) U.S. Supreme Court

        (2) Federal court   *Show wall chart depicting the system of courts. Use chart to explain the judicial system.*

        (3) State supreme courts

        (4) Courts of appeal

        (5) Superior courts

        (6) Civil and criminal courts

      c. Grand jury functions

      d. Interrelationshps with police

      e. Interrelationships with courts

Page 2

LESSON PLAN

Unit Title	Unit Code
The Criminal Justice System	

Course	INSTRUCTOR NOTES
Basic Criminal Justice Course	

f. Major problems confronting the courts
 	
    (1) Lack of public understanding
    (2) Inadequate staffing
    (3) Increase in crime
    (4) Breakdown in law enforcement
    (5) Recidivism
    (6) Clogged calendar/workload
    (7) Lack of inclination to make reforms
3. Corrections
  a. Philosophy
    (1) Past
    (2) Present
    (3) Future?
 	
  b. Goals
  c. Organization
    (1) Institutional
    (2) Community-based
  d. Interrelationships with police
  e. Interrelationships with courts
  f. Major problems confronting corrections
    (1) Lack of public support
    (2) Inadequate funding
    (3) Poor staffing
    (4) Overcrowded conditions
    (5) Failure to rehabilitate
    (6) Lack of desire to reform
	Display overhead transparency no. 3 (Problems of Courts).
	
	Q: In what ways are the problems of the courts similar to those of the police?
	
	A: The ways in which the public views them.
	
	Use the following as a discussion point: A philosophy of corrections is sometimes expressed as "The offender is a patient and treatment is a part of correction." Explain this philosophy.
	
	Display overhead transparency no. 4 (Problems of Corrections)
	
	Use as a discussion point: "Positive efforts toward prison reform are usually accompanied by a belief that treatment should fit the needs of the individual inmate."
	
	Page 3

Unit Title	Unit Code
The Criminal Justice System	

Course	
Basic Criminal Justice Course	**INSTRUCTOR NOTES**

4. Purpose of the Criminal Justice System
    a. Philosophic core
        (1) Impartial and deliberate
    b. Nature of the process
        (1) Visible and invisible administrative
            procedures

Instructor Note: Use as a discussion point: "Plea bargaining is an example of an invisible administrative procedure." Explain.

5. Needs of the system
    a. Financing
    b. Technical resources
    c. Coordination
    d. Public support
    e. Innovation

Instructor Note: Go to chalkboard. Get the students to state the system's needs. Write student comments on board. Discuss.

B. The Practical Exercise
    1. Hand out Classroom Issue I.

Instructor Note: Note: See copy of Classroom Issue I attached to this plan.

    2. Brief the students on how the exercise is to be conducted. Answer student questions as necessary.
    3. Begin the exercise. Allow 35 minutes for the students to complete the requirements of all three situations in Classroom Issue I.
    4. At the end of 35 minutes stop the exercise.
    5. Conduct a 15-minute critique of the exercise.

Page 4

Unit Title	Unit Code
The Criminal Justice System	

Course	
Basic Criminal Justice Course	**INSTRUCTOR NOTES**

III. REVIEW

   A. Retain Attention.

     Let me have your attention, please. We have examined and discussed a number of concepts and we have also practiced some of that knowledge in a PE.

   B. Summary

     1. Major functions of the police

     2. Major problems of the police

       a. Lack of public support

       b. Lack of public understanding

       c. Inadequate financing

       d. Rising crime rates

     3. Major functions of the courts

     4. Major problems of the courts

       a. Lack of public understanding

       b. Inadequate staffing

       c. Increase in crime

       d. Breakdown in law enforcement

       e. Recidivism

       f. Workload

       g. Unwillingness to make reforms

     5. Major functions of corrections

     6. Major problems of corrections

       a. Lack of public support

       b. Inadequate funding

       c. Poor staffing

       d. Overcrowding

       e. Failure to rehabilitate

       f. Inability to make reforms

     7. Needs of the system

Instructor Notes:

Hand out Summary Sheet. (See copy attached to this lesson plan.)

Page 5

Unit Title	Unit Code
The Criminal Justice System	

Course	INSTRUCTOR NOTES
Basic Criminal Justice Course	

C. Closing Statement

At the outset of this class I said it was my hope that you would come to share with me a belief that the criminal justice system, despite its many problems, can be made to work effectively and serve the needs of all citizens. As a consequence of today's instruction, I am confident you have made a strong first step toward attaining the level of commitment required of any person who would call himself a criminal justice professional.

Summary Sheet
(See page 129.)

Page 6

THE PRACTICAL EXERCISE

Knowledge—Cognitive Objectives • Performance—Psychomotor-Based Objectives • Feedback • The SPO Concept • Practical Exercise Handbook for Interviews

This is a good place to make some observations concerning our use of the word "objective." Up to now, we have applied the word in a general way. For example, in the chapter on lesson plan writing we see the term "training objective" used in much the same way that the term defines itself, i.e., as an objective of training. The modifier, "training," is interchangeable with similar adjectives, such as "instructional" or "teaching." The author happens to prefer the feel and sound of "training objective," although other terms might be just as appropriate.

In some uses of the word "objective," however, we are obligated for the sake of accuracy to attach particular modifiers. A case in point occurs in this chapter: here we use the terms cognitive *and* psychomotor *to describe two kinds of objectives that have important implications within the context of learning through practice. Other modifiers are used in other contexts, and they too have certain essential implications.*

The many different terms that contain the word "objective" can be confusing, especially when some training authorities create their own pet names for objectives. The decision to use a particular term involving the word "objective" sometimes seems to depend as much upon the personal preferences of the speaker as upon the precision of language.

The following chart shows some *of the adjectives currently in use. In a simplified way, the chart also provides conceptual relationships. To obtain more precise definitions, please turn to the glossary or use the subject index.*

When learning is at these levels...	SUB-TASKS AND TASKS	TASKS	DUTIES
these adjectives are often placed in front of the word "objective"	Enabling Enroute Subordinate	Behavioral Performance Training Cognitive Psychomotor	Terminal Learning outcome
and these commands help to define the relationships.	Simple to learn Very many Very detailed Nuts and bolts	Challenging Many Specific Important parts	Complex to apply Few General Major components

This chapter presents a discussion of practical exercises in general and concludes with step-by-step guidance on how to construct a specific practical exercise. The initial discussion will first define the term *practical exercise* (PE).

A PE is a learning activity in which students practice a task or tasks. There are two key elements in this definition. The first is practice. The nature of practice is almost unlimited in variety and scope. Practice can involve performance of tasks—

- in an actual job environment or a simulated job environment;
- with real equipment, mockups, or no training aids at all;
- with instructors or without them;
- with media or no media; or
- in an unsupervised activity using programmed methods.

Whatever method of practice is used, it will follow a cue/action/feedback sequence. The cue is a signal to the student to take some form of action. The action is the response to the cue. Feedback is the indicator of correct or incorrect response by the student. More will be said about the cue/action/feedback sequence, but for now it should be stated that any practical exercise should provide something for the student to respond to; the response should be job related; and the student should be informed of the quality of his response.

The second key element is the *task* or tasks, i.e., the object of practice. Synonymous with task is the term *training objective*. During curriculum development, detailed descriptions of job-related tasks are prepared. Tasks that are selected for teaching are expressed as objectives of training. The task itself constitutes the basis for the design of a learning activity in which the student practices the task.[1] If an on-the-job task, for example, requires an employee to prepare an incident report, the training objective would require the student to prepare one. When, after sufficient practice, the student has mastered the task and can correctly prepare an incident report, it can be said that the objective was achieved.

Objectives are of two types, and the types are reflections of tasks. The *cognitive objective* relates to a task that is carried out by thinking. The *psychomotor objective* relates to a doing or physical action task.

Distinguishing between cognitive and psychomotor tasks is often confusing for several reasons. First, any psychomotor objective must necessarily involve thinking. The police officer who directs traffic is involved in a psychomotor task, but in order to do it correctly he needs to know the gestures, which hand to use and when, where to point, and so forth. Second, cognitive objectives frequently are not directly related to tasks at all. A cognitive objective might require a student to identify seven of ten major problems confronting the criminal justice system, but the student will probably never be asked as a criminal justice practitioner to identify any of the major problems. Then why have such objectives? The answer is that learning should begin with an orientation of the student to the job as a whole. A whole-to-part learning sequence helps the student see himself and the functions he will perform in relation to the overall job. Identifying seven of ten problems may not literally represent a job task, but being able to achieve the task is an indication of the student's understanding of his job within the functional context.

KNOWLEDGE–COGNITIVE OBJECTIVES

●The Practice of Knowledge

The practice of knowledge means that a student gives symbolic responses to cues, and as a consequence receives feedback as to their correctness. Knowledge is symbolized by words, numbers, formulas, codes, pictures, etc. The symbols of knowledge represent such information as the functions of equipment, location of controls and parts, safety precautions, step-by-step procedures, or principles that underlie a job task.

Usually, the greater part of training is consumed in presenting knowledge rather than practicing it. The advantages of presentation over practice are usually stated as (1) a great deal of information can be delivered in a short time; (2) a single presentation can reach many students at the same time; and (3) presentation costs less than practice.[2] These apparent advantages are somewhat illusory because presentations are often made at such an abstract level, or with such rapidity, that students fail to grasp the essential points. Or, just as frequently, the level of a presentation is so elementary that students are unchallenged. Even at an excellent presentation, some students fail to pay attention. Since presentation is a one-way street, the method provides no surefire way to assess student learning. Only when students practice the tasks is there an opportunity to determine if learning has occurred. Presentation without practice in the training environment is risky because it provides no proof that the graduates are capable of performing adequately in the work environment.

Unquestionably, students learn more and retain more when presentation is followed with heavy doses of practice. Ideas that may only vaguely interest a student take on new dimensions and more powerful meanings when they are placed into practice, even if only in a simulated fashion. This does not diminish the importance of the presentation. In fact, the organization and appropriateness of information and to what extent it corresponds to the class level will influence the practice situation.

●Transfer of Knowledge

Practice of knowledge will transfer to the execution of a task provided the knowledge is thoroughly learned. The degree of transfer of knowledge depends upon the degree of mastery of the knowledge. To attain mastery and thereby produce transfer generally requires practice and lots of it.

An agreeable feature of practicing knowledge is its relative economy. Often, little more than pencil and paper are needed to conduct a knowledge-centered PE. On the other hand, a performance-centered PE generally requires tools, equipment, space, assistants, and time.

When knowledge is to be acquired as a foundation for performing a psychomotor task, the transfer of the knowledge to the task will reduce the time needed to learn and practice the task. A student driver who learns road signs and markings before he gets behind the wheel of a motor vehicle does not have to spend valuable practice time driving to places to observe particular road signs and markings. This means that transfer of knowledge can reduce requirements for training equipment, supplies, or even fuel.

●Techniques for Practicing Knowledge

The usual pattern for the practice of knowledge is to present the student with a requirement to do something (cue), have him do it (action), and then tell the student how he performed (feedback).

In programmed instruction, cues can be provided by frames in a scrambled text, slides, audio or video formats, and computer devices. Student responses are registered by writing, typing, verbalizing, pressing buttons, or punching holes in a card. Feedback in programmed techniques usually follows a format corresponding to that used in presenting the cues. Programmed instruction is very effective in presenting and practicing cognitive skills. (See Chapter 4.)

Practice of knowledge can be provided by simple feedback devices. A common technique is to provide every student with four or five cards, each of a different color or with a different number. The instructor poses a series of questions or problems (cues) verbally or with media. Out of several suggested reponses, there is one correct response. Each student holds up the card that corresponds to the response he has selected. The instructor looks at all the cards and provides feedback. A more sophisticated application of this method has the student manipulating a switch or some other control at his desk. A master panel at the podium shows the instructor all student responses. An advantage to a master panel is that each student's response is concealed from the other students. This helps minimize unwanted competition, embarrassment, and the social pressure placed upon persons whose thinking is at variance with the group majority. The instructor can provide feedback individually to those who need it or direct it to the class as a whole.

A very popular form of exercise for practicing knowledge is to cue students with a written document that describes a hypothetical situation. The situation offers details for analysis and requires that students respond. The response may be covert or overt. When making a covert response the student thinks out the answer but does not register it visibly. Although visible responses are often preferable, the covert option works if the instructor gives a strong critique so that students can compare their thinking with optimally correct responses. When the overt option is taken, the situation document is used to capture the student's written response. In addition to holding a classroom critique, the instructor can collect the situation sheets and later examine or grade them.

Peer instruction is a practical exercise technique that seems to be gaining popularity. In this technique one student performs the role of instructor or coach while another student is the learner.[3] The student instructor asks questions and provides feedback, sometimes with a script or guide and sometimes spontaneously. With rotations, all students get to play learner and instructor. The method reportedly works well because the trainees learn during both roles. Interest is added to peer instruction when scores are kept as to the number of correct responses. A trainee can thereby compete against himself in successive trials and against the rest of the group. (See "Peer Teaching," page 55.)

PERFORMANCE–PSYCHOMOTOR-BASED OBJECTIVES

●The Practice of Performance

The practice of performance is the practice of a psychomotor-based task. A task has a clear beginning, a clear ending, and is a recognized unit of job performance. It is an activity or a few closely related activities that have a common purpose.

In planning a practice of performance exercise, the instructor will need to select appropriate equipment. For a discussion on training aids, see Chapter 5, page 82.

Practicing a complex task may involve such skills as dexterity, balance, timing, coordination, speed, and strength. The student will need to practice on genuine equipment or highly replicative devices that permit the practice of all subtasks or closely related tasks. For example, the student driver of an armored personnel carrier will need to practice the skills of braking, accelerating, changing gears, and steering. He can only practice those skills if he has a carrier or a realistic simulator.

Some of the procedural tasks within a complex task can be practiced ahead of time, using only rough approximations of equipment. For instance, the student driver of the armored personnel carrier must learn to turn the engine on and off. He can begin practice for that task by studying photographs, diagrams, and captions mounted on a board. This preliminary practice reduces the practice time he will need on the actual carrier.

●Transfer of Performance

What is learned and practiced during training is meant to be transferred to the job situation. Properly designed and executed practical exercises will provide the desired transfer.

When retention of a skill is particularly critical, it is desirable for the student to overlearn. Overlearning occurs through practice after the performance standards of a training objective have been met. When initial learning cannot be followed by periodic practice throughout a training course, overlearning will help to preserve the skill until it is refreshed through practice on the job. In addition to aiding retention, overlearning will keep a skill from breaking down under difficult conditions. For example, the skill of administering artificial resuscitation, when overlearned, is less likely to deteriorate during a stressful emergency.

FEEDBACK

A student usually has a personal hypothesis about what he should do in a practice situation and how he should do it. The guesses he makes may result in misleading feedback. It is therefore important to correct wrong impressions about a PE as soon as possible. The instructor has to anticipate student confusion and to eliminate guesswork.

One course of action is to provide students with a clear understanding of training objectives (tasks). Another is to provide an accurate description of the practice activity and any equipment or devices employed in it.

Feedback increases the rate of learning and the level of performance. Almost without exception, a student who receives feedback learns faster and attains greater skill development than a student who has not received feedback. Motivation is clearly effected because feedback produces a challenge and adds interest for the student. (When motivation becomes intense, however, a student may be inclined to cheat or take advantage of a weakness in the evaluation method of a PE.)

The more specific the feedback, the faster the improvement and the higher the performance level. When feedback is specific to the quality of a student's response, the student will more likely work to correct his errors. Detailed feedback works very well during the latter stages of practice in the development of a skill when the student has a greater capacity to understand the details and act upon them. In an early stage of skill development, feedback that is too detailed or specific may be confusing. General feedback is seldom helpful at all. To tell a student that his response was erroneous but not tell how he can correct it has little benefit.

The longer the delay in providing feedback, the smaller its effect. This principle is often violated. Delays in releasing test scores, failure to break out test scores so students can see their mistakes, and failure to hold critiques following a PE are examples of withholding feedback. If the nature of a PE makes it impossible to provide feedback immediately following every response, the feedback should be given as soon as possible. Long sequences without feedback should be designed out of a PE whenever possible.

It is important that feedback follow practice of a task by an appropriate but short interval. The optimum interval is often found by experimentation. A short delay in feedback will not seriously reduce performance unless the interval between response and feedback is taken up with an activity that diverts the student's attention. When a slight delay in the delivery of feedback is unavoidable, a quiet, undistracting waiting time should be provided.

●Natural and Artificial Feedback

Feedback can be observed in two ways: as natural feedback or as artificial feedback.[4] Natural feedback is the evidence of the student's own senses as he interacts with the task environment. His ability to perform a task depends upon his recognizing this feedback when it appears. Sometimes the feedback is very apparent, and sometimes it is subtle. Natural feedback that is easily sensed might be the sound of a radio signal as a student adjusts tuning controls, or the emergence of latent prints as the student dusts with fingerprint powder. A subtle kind of natural feedback would be the color change produced when an chemical reagent is added to a suspected narcotics substance. If the student has not been told and shown what to expect, he will miss the less apparent forms of natural feedback.

Artificial feedback does not arise out of the task itself but is provided by additional means. It can consist of spoken words from instructors and fellow students, test scores, written critiques, or special signals such as lights, bells, and buzzers. Artificial feedback should be employed with caution because it can have an unwanted effect at a later time when the student performs the task on the job. Artificial feedback during practice of a task in training will likely raise or maintain the level of performance, but on the job the task is likely to decline in quality due to an absence of the same feedback. A student who has come to expect instructor encouragement and who is motivated by it will experience a loss of enthusiasm when he fails to obtain at work the same rewarding feedback he enjoyed at school. In other words, too many "attaboys" are not good.

When artificial and natural feedback occur together in a task, there is less tendency for performance to drop off when the artificial feedback is withdrawn. Natural feedback compensates for the loss of artificial feedback. If that natural feedback is present on the job and is a powerful reinforcer for learning, it should be designed into practice activities. Actual equipment or devices that simulate job activities can produce natural feedback and should be made a regular part of any practice session.

●Feedback in the Practice of Knowledge

Feedback is usually examined in relation to psychomotor or performance-centered tasks, but it has just as much value and relevance to the acquisition of knowledge. Types of feedback typically present in the practice of knowledge are (1) giving the student a correct definition or description of a chosen alternative, (2) giving a reason why a chosen alternative was best or not best, and (3) pointing out the probable consequences of a chosen alternative. Instead of just telling the student he is right or wrong, or just reporting a correct answer, the feedback should include explanations or reasons.

Feedback is a principal medium for making knowledge meaningful, a critical factor in the acquisition and retention of knowledge. The more personally meaningful information is to the student, the easier it is for him to grasp it and later recall it. Knowledge that is related to student experience has more meaning than that which is not; knowledge that is shown to have strong value to a job task has more meaning to the student than knowledge which cannot be shown as valuable to job performance; and knowledge that blends with significant student goals has more meaning than knowledge that does not coincide with student goals.

An instructor should not be dismayed when he discovers his students do not make use of all the feedback he provides. The student will latch onto feedback that is important to him personally and pay little attention to feedback that he believes he does not need. A student who is confident of his response may not even bother to look for the feedback that informs him of how well he answered. This does not suggest that feedback should be withheld; it simply indicates that students differ in their needs for it. Those who can use it generally look for it and take it. Those who don't need it don't take it, and they are not disadvantaged as a result.

THE SPO CONCEPT

A great distance lies between formulating a training objective and bringing it to fruition. The curriculum designer specifies the objectives of training, and the instructors see that the objectives are achieved. Usually, the instructors have no difficulty in setting up appropriate practical exercises. It sometimes happens, however, that an instructor will find himself murmuring, "How am I ever going to do that?" It is then that the SPO concept comes to the rescue.

SPO stands for student performance objective. An SPO takes an objective and describes it in terms of what the student performs. In fact, an SPO is nothing more than a training objective (task) with two elements added. The two added elements are (1) the conditions that affect the task and (2) the level of proficiency required in performing it.

When compared to an SPO, a training objective is somewhat general. A training objective, although stated in explicit language, does not state the circumstances under which the task is to be performed, the equipment or tools that will be needed, or whether the task environment will be simulated or genuine. Neither does a training objective define what is considered satisfactory performance.

The three parts of an SPO are called—

- action (task),
- conditions, and
- standards.

The action or task element is the heart of the SPO. It has a clear relationship to a job task. It is an act that is done in its own right as part of a job, and when successfully exercised, it has a value in and of itself.

The conditions element reflects essential aspects of the real-life environment in which the task is performed. For example, if the training objective specifies a task requiring the directing of traffic, the instructor would logically conclude that essential features of a traffic-directing environment would be an intersection or other outdoor locale having vehicular and pedestrian traffic and varying light and weather. The conditions would also include such job equipment as a whistle, a traffic baton, a reflectorized vest, and foul weather clothing. These are all genuine job conditions that should be simulated to the maximum extent possible. Practice of the task is best done under actual conditions with supervisory guidance. A lesser version would be practice in a parking lot or some other safe area where conditions are more controllable.

The standards element of the SPO states the degree of precision the student is expected to demonstrate in doing the task. There are two kinds of standards: accuracy and speed. Accuracy is present in all SPOs; speed is usually present. Firing on the pistol range involves both accuracy and speed, but certain continuous tasks, such as directing traffic, do not involve speed as an indicator of proficiency. Some standards can be determined with relative precision and others cannot. Calibrating a meter, writing a traffic citation, setting a camera, and doing a math problem are examples of tasks for which accuracy and speed can be determined with little trouble or disagreement.[5] Counseling an inmate and cross-examining a witness will have less definable standards because they rely on subjective judgments.

Any standard should reflect a consensus of agreement among experienced practitioners of the task in question. The instructor who is in doubt regarding a task's standards would do well to inquire of people who regularly do the work. When perfect agreement cannot be reached regarding a standard, the lowest of those suggested is the safest to select. The benefit of doubt belongs to the student because a standard in training is usually less, and never more, than the same standard on the job. It is simply not reasonable to expect students, who are novices, to perform tasks with greater accuracy and speed than experienced persons.

●Writing an SPO

In writing an SPO it is convenient to use a format like this:

> Given certain conditions, the student will perform a certain task, in accordance with certain standards.

The format follows an order of conditions, task, and standards. Of the three, the task element is immediately known because it is provided by the curriculum. Let's assume an instructor is writing an SPO for the task "Prepare an inmate delinquency report." The instructor makes a first attempt as follows:

> Given certain conditions, the student will prepare an inmate delinquency report, in accordance with certain standards.

Now, what are the conditions present on the job which impinge upon the task? To what extent can those conditions be duplicated in the training environment? The instructor concludes that the man on the job will need a blank inmate delinquency report form and an incident that involves a delinquent inmate. Comparing these conditions with what is available in the training environment, he is satisfied that he can set up a realistic PE. He intends to simulate an incident of inmate delinquency through the use of a written situation. His SPO takes shape as:

> Given a blank inmate delinquency report form and a hypothetical written situation, the student will prepare an inmate delinquency report, in accordance with certain standards.

In considering standards for the task, the instructor knows that the correctional facility not only uses a particular incident report form but also has an established operating procedure for preparing the report. Being a former correctional officer himself, the instructor knows that the average incident report requires about 20 minutes to prepare. He is sure that 30 minutes will be sufficient to practice the task once. In addition, he knows that acceptable task performance involves the who, what, when, where, how, and why elements of basic report preparation. The instructor intends to write ten pertinent facts into the simulated situation and require the student to accurately mention at least seven of them in his report.

The completed SPO now reads:

> Given a blank inmate delinquency report form and a hypothetical written situation, the student will prepare an inmate delinquency report, in accordance with report writing operating procedures, specifying seven of ten pertinent facts, within 30 minutes.

When writing an SPO, it really doesn't matter if the task is psychomotor or cognitive oriented. What matters is whether the cognitive task will in fact be practiced or tested as a part of practice. If any practice of a cognitive task is planned, an SPO similar to the one just written is appropriate. A cognitive task to be practiced might have an SPO that reads like this:

> Given a written situation involving court administration, the student will describe the procedures for establishing a trial court docket, with not more than three errors, within 15 minutes.

If, however, the curriculum does not intend for a cognitive task to be practiced but only tested by written examination, the SPO is written as follows:

> Given a written examination, the student will describe the procedures for establishing a trial court docket, with XX percent accuracy.

The mechanics of executing the written examination type of SPO are a function of the exam itself. The questions, of any number or variety might be weighted. The time standard is included within the total time allowed for testing all cognitive tasks covered by the exam. The accuracy level of a cognitive task tested by written examination should correspond to the importance of the task in real life. If the consequences of not knowing something are relatively minor, the accuracy required could be as low as 70 percent; but if the consequences are serious, the accuracy level should be high. A failure to correctly describe trial docket procedures does not have the same weight of consequences attendant upon a failure to know when or when not to shoot at someone.

Page 148 shows examples of conditions and standards. With a little imagination it would not be difficult to discern tasks associated with them.

EXAMPLES OF CONDITIONS	EXAMPLES OF STANDARDS
Conditions	**Standards**
Given a traffic intersection having light-to-moderate traffic. . . .	. . . .within 20 minutes.
Given a simulated traffic intersection. . . .	. . . .achieving a score of 70 percent or higher.
Given an open paved area measuring 300 by 500 feet. . . .	. . . .with no mistakes of fact.
Given handcuffs with keys. . . .	. . . .in accordance with principles delineated during classroom teaching.
Given a mock crime scene. . . .	. . . .to the satisfaction of two subject matter experts.
Given a written situation. . . .	. . . .with seven out of ten correct responses.
Given a hypothetical case. . . .	. . . .in accordance with procedures described in the Police Reference Notebook.
Given a verbal briefing. . . .	. . . .to the satisfaction of the primary instructor.
Given ten items of mock evidence. . . .	. . . .with not more than four typographical errors.
Given a mock courtroom environment. . . .	. . . .correctly computing all measurements.
Given an accident report form. . . .	. . . .including correct compass directions.
Given a pencil and paper. . . .	. . . .using correct grammar, punctuation, and spelling.
Given grid coordinates and a map. . . .	. . . .in their order of priority.
Given a requirement to respond to. . . .	. . . .containing all elements of the title block.
Given the Motor Vehicle Identification Manual of the National Automobile Theft Bureau. . . .	. . . .with not more than 12 inches deviation.
Given a nomograph, a clipboard, notepaper, pencil. . . .	. . . .in accordance with established departmental rules.
Given an evidence receipt, an evidence bag, tweezers. . . .	. . . .using the prescribed marking tools and devices.
Given a resource person to role play as a witness. . . .	. . . .without error.
Given nighttime conditions, an outdoor firing range. . . .	. . . .achieving four out of five correct matches.
Given a list of twenty possible sources of information. . . .	. . . .in not less than 10 minutes and not more than 15 minutes.
Given a fellow student to role play as a patrol partner. . . .	. . . .with no observable cross-contamination of evidence.
Given a gymnasium or suitably equivalent area. . . .	

The chief value of an SPO is the preparation forced upon the instructor. Writing an SPO channels the instructor's attention toward the logistical space and time factors important to an effective PE. The SPO also makes the instructor establish the criteria of successful task performance, and devise a method for measuring and scoring the criteria.

If the curriculum designer has done a good job, the instructor will find that all or almost all training objectives in an instructional unit will have almost identically worded SPOs. This means that several tasks can be combined for practice in a single PE. Collecting an item of evidence at a crime scene and then tagging it for identification purposes are two separate job tasks. The conditions and standards of performance, however, are so similar that they can and should be practiced together.

To summarize: An SPO reflects the means and methods of achieving the training objectives; an SPO should be written for each training objective; every SPO must be carried out; most SPOs are carried out by PE; cognitive SPOs can be carried out by written examination; and similar SPOs should be practiced together.

Where an SPO describes tasks, conditions, and standards that must be present in the PE, it does not describe how to bring the SPO elements together in a coherent, logically organized fashion. This is where the experience and creativity of the instructor come into play. The instructor who has personally done the tasks and is gifted with imagination and a willingness to innovate will have little trouble in thinking of an appropriate scenario for his PE. An instructor lacking these attributes will be working from a disadvantage, but with perseverance and trial and error he can succeed.

As in preparing a lesson plan, let's follow a fictitious instructor through the mechanics of constructing a PE. The instructor's name is Mr. Kent, and his assigned subject is described in the course curriculum as follows:

Interviews (4 hours)

Scope: The application of basic psychological principles in the obtaining of information from complainants, victims, witnesses, and suspects. Emphasis is upon a proper and legally accepted method for making preinterview rights warning advisements.

Training Objectives

Administer a rights warning to a suspect person. Demonstrate an approved interviewing technique.

Mr. Kent writes an SPO for each of the training objectives:

Given a simulated interview room, a table, two chairs, a rights warning card, a waiver of counsel form, a person to role play as a suspect, and a written situation requiring a custodial interview, the student will administer a rights warning to a suspect person, with no procedural errors, obtaining a signed and witnessed waiver of counsel form, to the satisfaction of the instructor, within 10 minutes.

Given a simulated interview room, a table, two chairs, a person to role-play as a suspect, a complainant, victim or witness, and a written situation requiring an interview, the student will demonstrate an approved interviewing technique, in accordance with principles taught in class and contained in Chapter 5, "Interviewing Techniques," to the satisfaction of the instructor, within 15 minutes.

The two SPOs are so similar that Mr. Kent is certain he will be able to set up a simple PE to practice both tasks. He has allowed 10 minutes for the rights warning task because it usually takes no longer than 5 minutes for the experienced officer to perform. He has allowed 15 minutes for the second task. The training objective does not require a full interview but merely that the student practice an interviewing technique. Mr. Kent figures the student will need no more than 15 minutes to demonstrate his ability at this task. Mr. Kent also notes that interviewing techniques are applicable when making a rights warning. Deciding that the two tasks can and should be carried out simultaneously, he calculates that the amount of time for a single repetition of both tasks is 15 minutes.

Combining the two tasks in this way will be helpful because time is a critical factor. Mr. Kent has only 4 hours to teach his topic. (Four hours represents 200 minutes of instructional time, allowing for class breaks.) He has to determine how much time to allocate to presentation and how much to practice. The easiest method would be to "guesstimate" the amount of time needed for presentation, with whatever is left over going for practice. He is too conscientious, however, to take that approach. He knows that the PE is where the real learning takes place and that presentation is nothing more than a prelude to practice. Mr. Kent figures he'll need at least 50 percent of all available time just for practice.

Mr. Kent knows there will be twenty-five students in the class. If it requires 15 minutes for each student, the time needed for all students to perform the tasks will be 375 minutes. This doesn't even allow for time to get set up. Obviously, this won't work. What will work, however, is to have the tasks performed at several locations simultaneously. The classroom happens to be large enough for simulated interview rooms in its four corners and center. With five stations, five students can practice the tasks. Allowing another 5 minutes for set up and changeovers, all twenty-five students will perform the exercise, and the total time consumed will be 100 minutes—exactly 50 percent of the unit's instructional time.

If only five students are practicing the tasks at any given time, what are the rest of the students doing? In an interview situation there are always at least three persons present: the person being interviewed, the interviewer, and an assistant interviewer who is a corroborating witness. In addition, Mr. Kent will place an observer at each station and will permit five students to be on break during each repetition. This accounts for all twenty-five students at any given time: five will be interviewing; five will be assistant interviewers; five will be interviewees; five will be observers; and five will be on break. Mr. Kent believes this will work well for several reasons. First, the students will learn more by functioning in several roles besides that of the primary interviewer. Second, putting some students on break while the exercise is in progress frees 20 minutes of time that would normally be used for hourly break periods. The extra time is available for more practice or to offset unexpected delays or interruptions.

Time obviously has an impact upon resources. Less time translates into a need for more simultaneous practice stations, which means more space, more equipment, more materials, and more resource persons and assistant instructors. For "interviews," there is not much difficulty. The classroom is big enough, student desks and chairs can be used, rights warning cards and waiver of counsel forms are on hand, and students can be used as resource persons. Mr. Kent can develop written situations, and although an assistant instructor would be helpful, he is confident he can get by without one because all interviewing stations will be in his range of view.

When resources are so limited that a PE cannot be conducted at many locations simultaneously, it may be possible (although not desirable) to shave some minutes from the time standards. A better alternative is to extend the length of the PE. In either case, the effect intended is to reduce the number of locations needed. Great care should be taken when modifying a time standard. Time specified in an SPO is determined by the amount of time judged to be required for a student to perform a particular task. It would not be reasonable to expect a student to demonstrate approved interviewing techniques in only 5 minutes.

This raises an interesting question. What does the instructor do when he finds that he cannot, for whatever reason, implement a practical exercise in accordance with an SPO? The answer is to rewrite the SPO to reflect conditions and standards that are capable of being applied. It is for this reason that the responsibility for SPO writing rests with the instructor. Of all people, he is most familiar with the constraints and limitations peculiar to his school.

All the ingredients for a PE are now present except one. A scenario or cue is needed to elicit from the student a response that will constitute achievement of the unit's objectives. Mr. Kent recalls from his former experience as a patrolman that a single serious crime frequently requires interviews to be made of suspects, witnesses, and victim. He decides to create a hypothetical robbery in which three suspects, one witness, and one victim are to be interviewed. These five roles will be played by students at the five simulated interview rooms set up in the classroom. Each role player will be given a situation sheet (in the form of a classroom issue) to use in assuming an identity and answering questions. Separate but corresponding situation sheets will be used by the primary and assistant interviewers.

The observers will also be put to good use. Mr. Kent intends to use them to collect information regarding the correctness of actions taken by the primary interviewers. Observers will be given checklists for the two tasks. As the tasks are performed, the observer checkmarks the actions performed by the primary interviewer. The checklist forms become the basis for evaluation and feedback by Mr. Kent.

It is easier to understand Mr. Kent's PE when it is put down on paper. Also, the instructor who someday substitutes for him will need specific guidance in setting up and conducting the exercise. For these reasons, Mr. Kent decides to write a short handbook as a guide. He makes an entry in his lesson plan as follows:

LESSON PLAN

Unit Title	Unit Code
Interviews	BCJ-28

Course	
Basic Criminal Justice Course	**INSTRUCTOR NOTES**

| C. The Practical Exercise. 1. Follow procedures set forth in the Practical Exercise Handbook for Interviews. 2. At the conclusion of the PE, conduct a critique of student performance. | A copy of the PE Handbook for Interviews is attached to this lesson plan. |

A replacement instructor would turn to the attachments of the lesson plan to find the handbook prepared by Mr. Kent. See page 155.

A number of things in Mr. Kent's PE handbook are worth noting. For one thing, he has left little to chance or interpretation. Enough specificity and detail are provided so that almost anyone could administer the exercise. Every participant has written instructions; training aids and evaluation devices are shown and explained; task locations with equipment are described; and a clearly articulated schedule moves the students between the task locations. The instructor is told what goes where, who does what, when and for how long, and to what degree of satisfaction. The handbook operates like a sheet of music, with each player doing things in harmony with others.

The PE provides for those students who can perform their tasks faster than others. The "lock-step" feature of the exercise has students moving in a timed sequence; however, when the primary interviewer has finished, he is allowed to switch roles with the assistant interviewer so that maximum use is made of the available practice time. Thus, students who are borderline performers might get more practice, and when the exercise is graded, their chance of passing is increased if they have more attempts to succeed.

The roles in the exercise are simple, yet permit interviewers to employ several techniques. Depending on personal inclinations, the role-playing suspects can adopt attitudes ranging from hostility to docility. The victim is role played as being frightened and confused, and the witness is reluctant. When role playing, the student retains his own identity and is not expected to assume a personality other than his own. There is very little to remember concerning facts of the hypothetical case, and the freedom of role players to improvise in response to interview techniques facilitates spontaneity.

Also apparent in Mr. Kent's PE is the cue/action/feedback sequence. The cue is provided by the hypothetical case and is given to the students through the medium of classroom issues. The action is the performance of the two job-related tasks specified in the unit's training objectives. Performance of them is assisted by training aids (rights warning card and waiver of counsel form) that duplicate the real-life task environment. Feedback is dispensed in several ways. There is the natural feedback that occurs when the suspect agrees to waive his rights to counsel in response to an advisement. It is also present, to a lesser extent, when any of the interviewees provide information in response to proper questioning techniques. Artificial feedback takes the form of guidance given by the instructor as he monitors student performance; it occurs extensively during the critique that immediately follows practice; and it is part and parcel of the checklist forms that evaluate the students.

●The Role of the Instructor

Instructor actions in a PE are not at all similar to things he does during a presentation of knowledge.[6] When presenting knowledge the instructor functions as the primary repository of information, and the students are necessarily dependent upon that repository for the knowledge they need. During practical application, however, the focus is no longer upon the instructor as a central point of reference but upon the students individually.

What counts in a PE is the activity of students. The instructor's value is chiefly as a facilitator of learning. He provides the planning and preparation; he arranges to acquire and set up the PE area; he has equipment and training aids on hand; he briefs and assigns assistant instructors; and he attends to the myriad of details and inevitable snafus. In making the transition from presentation to practice, the instructor instantly changes from teacher to manager.

For some instructors, the transition is easily made, indeed gladly welcomed. The switch from talking to doing provides a respite for instructors as well as students. Some instructors find the facilitator role difficult. It is essential that they try to overcome such difficulties. Whatever the reasons for them, they are less important than the fact that conducting an effective PE requires the instructor to exercise a wide range of skills.

NOTES

1. Harold G. Hunter, *The Formulation of Training Problems* (Washington, D.C.: Human Resources Research Office, The George Washington University, 1966), p. 2.

2. *How to Prepare and Conduct Military Training* (Washington, D.C.: Department of the Army, 1975), p. 99.

3. Thomas F. Staton, *How to Instruct Successfully* (New York: McGraw-Hill Book Co., 1960), p. 94.

4. In *Design of Instructional Systems* (Washington, D.C.: Human Resources Research Office, The George Washington University, 1966), author Robert G. Smith, Jr., makes this distinction between feedback that is either natural or artificial.

5. *Basic Teaching Principles* (Washington, D.C.: Department of the Navy, 1967), p. 98.

6. This point is supported by Odiorne who states, "Traditional methods of education, including the college classroom in most of our educational institutions, engage in a form of behavior on the part of the teacher that isn't producing a result on the part of the student. That is, the lecture form of education is obsolete. This is a bit of an exaggeration to emphasize the increasingly important role of action training techniques" (*Training by Objectives*, George S. Odiorne [Westfield, Mass.: MBO, Inc., 1975] p. 27).

PRACTICAL EXERCISE
HANDBOOK FOR
INTERVIEWS

I. Purpose of the Exercise:

A. This exercise is intended to provide student practice for the following training objectives:

Administer a rights warning to a suspect person.

Demonstrate an approved interviewing technique.

II. Conditions of the Exercise:

A. This exercise is conducted during the latter portion of a 200-minute instructional period.

B. The exercise requires 100 minutes to administer.

C. The exercise should take place in the classroom.

D. The exercise is designed for a class of 25 students or less.

III. Personnel and Equipment Required to Conduct the Exercise:

A. One primary instructor. Assistant instructors would be helpful but not essential.

B. Five stations set up in the four corners and center of the classroom. Each station requires chairs, desks, or tables sufficient to accommodate an interviewee, a primary interviewer, an assistant interviewer, and an observer.

C. Four students at each station as resource persons to role-play as interviewee, primary interviewer, assistant interviewer, and observer.

D. A classroom issue that provides instructions for the interviewers at all stations (see Attachment 1).

E. A classroom issue that provides instructions for the interviewee at Station A (see Attachment 2).

F. A classroom issue that provides instructions for the interviewee at Station B (see Attachment 3).

G. A classroom issue that provides instructions for the interviewee at Station C (see Attachment 4).

H. A classroom issue that provides instructions for the interviewee at Station D (see Attachment 5).

I. A classroom issue that provides instructions for the interviewee at Station E (see Attachment 6).

J. A classroom issue that provides instructions for the observers at Stations A, C, and E (see Attachment 7).

K. A Rights Warning Advisement form for primary interviewers at Stations A, C, and E (see Attachment 8).

L. A Waiver of Counsel form for primary interviewers at Stations A, C, and E (see Attachment 9).

M. A classroom issue that provides instructions for the observers at all stations (see Attachment 10).

N. A chart depicting the rotation of students from station to station during the progress of the exercise (see Attachment 11).

O. A supply of Rights Warning Checklist forms (see Attachment 7).

P. A supply of Interviewing Techniques Checklist forms (see Attachment 10).

IV. Procedures for Conducting the Exercise:

A. Set up chairs, desks, or tables at the four corners and center of the classroom.

B. Identify the locations as Stations A, B, C, D, and E.

C. Place material at each station as shown in the station chart, p. 155.

D. Assign a number to each student, starting with 1 and ending with the last student. Make sure that each student knows his number.

E. Announce to the class which student numbers are assigned to what stations for the first repetition. Post a chart on the classroom wall that describes the rotation of students from station to station during the five repetitions. (A chart showing the five repetitions is located at Attachment 11.)

F. Call attention to the fact that instructions and all needed materials are on hand at each of the five stations.

G. Explain to the students that this exercise will permit them to practice proper interviewing techniques and administer a rights warning advisement.

H. Demonstrate a rights warning advisement using proper interviewing techniques.

I. Assign assistant instructor(s), if available, to monitor student activities at the five stations.

J. Instruct the students to move to their assigned stations.

K. Begin the first repetition.

L. Monitor student performances. Interrupt and guide as necessary.

M. After 16 minutes, stop the first repetition.

N. Allow 4 minutes for the observers to fill out the checklist forms and for changeover of students in accordance with the posted chart. Collect the completed checklist forms from the observers.

O. Begin the second repetition. Repeat the procedure until all five repetitions are completed.

P. If this exercise is to be used for testing purposes, the checklist forms completed by the observers are to be graded in accordance with Paragraph V of this handbook.

V. Directions for Grading:

A. Grading for the training objective "Administer a rights warning to a suspect person."

1. Organize the completed Rights Warning Checklist forms in packets according to student names.

2. Where a "no" block has been checked, the task for that particular performance has not been achieved in accordance with the accuracy standard. If a student does not have at least one checklist form reflecting all "yes" checkmarks, he has failed the test.

B. Grading for the training objective "Demonstrate an approved interviewing technique."

1. Organize the completed Interviewing Techniques Checklist forms in packets according to student names.

2. Notice that in parentheses adjacent to each checkmark block is a number. The number represents the score value for that item.

3. Add up all the score values for items that were checkmarked.

4. Add up the total score values of all checklist forms for an individual student. Divide that figure by the number of forms so that an average score is computed for the student.

5. A passing grade is 14 or higher. (Maximum score value is 20 points. 14 points equal 70 percent.)

Station A

- Instruction sheet for the interviewee who role plays as a suspect (Attachment 2).
- Instruction sheet for the interviewers (Attachment 1).
- Instruction sheet for observers to use in scoring the rights warning (Attachment 7).
- Instruction sheet for observers to use in scoring interview techniques (Attachment 10).
- Rights Warning Advisement form (Attachment 8).
- Waiver of Counsel form (Attachment 9).
- Rights Warning Checklist form (Attachment 7).
- Interviewing Techniques Checklist form (Attachment 10).

Station B

- Instruction sheet for the interviewee who role plays as a victim (Attachment 3).
- Instruction sheet for the interviewers (Attachment 1).
- Instruction sheet for observers to use in scoring interview techniques (Attachment 10).
- Interviewing Techniques Checklist form (Attachment 10).

Station C

- Instruction sheet for the interviewer who role plays as a suspect (Attachment 4).
- Instruction sheet for the interviewers (Attachment 1).
- Instruction sheet for observers to use in scoring the rights warning (Attachment 7).
- Instruction sheet for observers to use in scoring interview techniques (Attachment 10).
- Rights Warning Advisement form (Attachment 8).
- Waiver of Counsel form (Attachment 9).
- Rights Warning Checklist form (Attachment 7).
- Interviewing Techniques Checklist form (Attachment 10).

Station D

- Instruction sheet for the interviewee who role plays as a witness (Attachment 5).
- Instruction sheet for the interviewers (Attachment 1).
- Instruction sheet for observers to use in scoring interview techniques (Attachment 10).
- Interviewing Techniques Checklist form (Attachment 10).

Station E

- Instruction sheet for the interviewee who role plays as a suspect (Attachment 6).
- Instruction sheet for the interviewers (Attachment 1).
- Instruction sheet for observers to use in scoring the rights warning (Attachment 7).
- Instruction sheet for observers to use in scoring interview techniques (Attachment 10).
- Rights Warning Advisement form (Attachment 8).
- Waiver of Counsel form (Attachment 9).
- Rights Warning Checklist form (Attachment 7).
- Interviewing Techniques Checklist form (Attachment 10).

Classroom Issue I

INSTRUCTIONS FOR THE PRIMARY AND ASSISTANT INTERVIEWERS

I. Instructions for Station A Interviewers

A. At about 9:00 a.m. today you and your patrol partner arrested three suspects as they fled from a convenience store robbery.

B. One of the suspects is now waiting to be interviewed by you and your partner.

II. Requirements for Station A Interviewers

A. Using the method discussed and demonstrated in class, the primary interviewer will administer a rights warning to the suspect and obtain a waiver in writing.

B. The assistant interviewer will act as a witness to the obtaining of the waiver.

C. Twenty minutes are allowed at this station. If the warning and waiver are completed in less than 20 minutes, the primary and assistant interviewers will switch places and repeat the exercise in the time remaining.

III. Instructions for Station B Interviewers

A. At about 9:00 a.m. today you and your patrol partner arrested three suspects as they fled from a convenience store robbery.

B. The sales clerk at the convenience store is now waiting to be interviewed by you and your partner.

IV. Requirements for Station B Interviewers

A. Using interview techniques discussed in class, the primary and assistant interviewers will obtain basic information from the sales clerk.

V. Instructions for Station C Interviewers

A. Follow directions contained in Situation A.

VI. Requirements for Station C Interviewers

A. Follow directions contained in Situation A.

VII. Instructions for Station D Interviewers

A. At about 9:00 a.m. today you and your patrol partner arrested three suspects as they fled from a convenience store robbery.

B. A witness to the convenience store robbery is now waiting to be interviewed by you and your partner.

VIII. Requirements for Station D Interviewers

A. Using interview techniques discussed in class, the primary and assistant interviewers will obtain basic information from the witness.

IX. Instructions for Station E Interviewers

A. Follow directions contained in Situation A.

X. Requirements for Station E Interviewers

A. Follow directions contained in Situation A.

INTERVIEWS *(Attachment 2)*

Classroom Issue II

INSTRUCTIONS FOR THE INTERVIEWEE AT STATION A

I. SITUATION

A. At about 9:00 a.m. today you and two accomplices robbed a convenience store. As you and your two accomplices tried to make a getaway, you were all arrested. You are now at the station where an interview is about to begin.

II. REQUIREMENTS

A. The objective is not for the students to conduct a full interview, but to get practice in making a rights warning and obtaining a waiver.

B. Be as cooperative or uncooperative as you like, but be sure to waive the rights and sign the waiver. Use your own identity.

INTERVIEWS *(Attachment 3)*

Classroom Issue III

INSTRUCTIONS FOR THE INTERVIEWEE AT STATION B

I. SITUATION

A. You are a sales clerk at a convenience store that was robbed at about 9:00 a.m. today. The robbers were caught. You are now at the station to provide a statement.

II. REQUIREMENTS

A. Play the part of a person who has been frightened by the experience of being held up. Act confused on details, but be cooperative. Use your own identity and try to integrate your own personality into the role.

B. The objective is for each student to apply basic interviewing techniques that are likely to overcome the problem of obtaining information from a confused person. When a student uses a proper technique, you should respond with more accurate details regarding the incident.

INTERVIEWS

Classroom Issue IV

INSTRUCTIONS FOR THE INTERVIEWEE AT STATION C

I. SITUATION

A. At about 9:00 a.m. today you and two accomplices robbed a convenience store. As you and your two accomplices tried to make a getaway, you were all arrested. You are now at the station where an interrogation is about to begin.

II. REQUIREMENTS

A. The objective is not for the students to conduct a full interview, but to get practice in making a rights warning and obtaining a waiver.

B. Be as cooperative or uncooperative as you like, but be sure to waive the rights and sign the waiver. Use your own identity.

INTERVIEWS

Classroom Issue V

INSTRUCTIONS FOR THE INTERVIEWEE AT STATION D

I. SITUATION

A. At about 9:00 a.m. today you were present in a convenience store that was robbed by three men. You are now at the station to provide a statement.

II. REQUIREMENTS

A. Play the part of a person who dislikes policemen. Be uncooperative and slightly abusive to your interviewers. Use your own identity.

B. The objective is for each student to apply basic interviewing techniques that are likely to overcome the problem of obtaining information from a reluctant witness. When a student uses a proper technique, you should respond with more accurate details regarding the incident.

Classroom Issue VI

INSTRUCTIONS FOR THE INTERVIEWEE AT STATION E

I. SITUATION

A. At about 9:00 a.m. today you and two accomplices robbed a convenience store. As you and your two accomplices tried to make a getaway, you were all arrested. You are now at the station where an interrogation is about to begin.

II. REQUIREMENTS

A. The objective is not for the students to conduct a full interview, but to get practice in making a rights warning and obtaining a waiver.

B. Be as cooperative or uncooperative as you like, but be sure to waive the rights and sign the waiver. Use your own identity.

Classroom Issue VII

INSTRUCTIONS FOR OBSERVERS AT STATIONS A, C, AND E

I. SITUATION

    A. You are a silent observer to an interview of a robbery suspect.

    B. The interviewers will administer a rights warning and obtain a waiver of counsel.

II. REQUIREMENTS

    A. Immediately following this paragraph is a Rights Warning Checklist form. A supply of these forms is available from the instructor. Obtain sufficient copies of the form to rate the interviewers as they administer the rights warning.

RIGHTS WARNING CHECKLIST FORM

Name of Primary Interviewer:

	Yes	No
1. Did the interviewer identify himself as a police officer?	_____	_____
2. Did the interviewer make known the offense which he was investigating?	_____	_____
3. Did the interviewer inform the suspect he was a suspect for that offense?	_____	_____
4. Did the interviewer inform the suspect he has the right to remain silent?	_____	_____
5. Did the interviewer tell the suspect that anything the suspect says can and will be used against him in a court of law?	_____	_____
6. Did the interviewer tell the suspect that he has the right to talk to a lawyer and have him present while being questioned?	_____	_____
7. Did the interviewer inform the suspect that if he cannot afford to hire a lawyer, one will be appointed to represent him before any questioning, if he so desires?	_____	_____
8. Did the interviewer tell the suspect that he can decide at any time to exercise these rights and not answer any questions or make any statements?	_____	_____
9. Did the interviewer ask the suspect if he understood each of the rights explained?	_____	_____
10. After the suspect's reply did the interviewer ask if he was willing to talk?	_____	_____

11. Did the interviewer have the suspect sign a waiver form after he agreed to talk?

12. Did the witness (assistant interviewer) also sign the waiver form upon request from the interviewer?

13. Did the interviewer use the waiver card or form provided?

THE MIRANDA WARNING *(Attachment 8)*

1. You have the right to remain silent.

2. Anything you say can and will be used against you in a court of law.

3. You have the right to talk to a lawyer and have him present with you while you are being questioned.

4. If you cannot afford to hire a lawyer, one will be appointed to represent you before any questioning if you wish.

5. You can decide at any time to exercise these rights and not answer any questions or make any statements.

6. After the warning and in order to secure a waiver, the following questions should be asked and an affirmative reply secured to each question.

7. Do you understand each of these rights I have explained to you?

8. Having these rights in mind, do you wish to talk to us now?

I, _____ , have been informed by the undersigned law enforcement officers, prior to being questioned by them,

1. That I may remain silent and do not have to make any statement at all.

2. That any statement which I might make can and will be used against me in Court.

3. That I have a right to consult with an attorney before making any statement and to have such attorney present with me while I am making a statement.

4. That if I do not have enough money to employ an attorney, I have the right to have one appointed by the Court, free of charge, to represent me; to consult with him before making any statement; and to have him present with me while I am making a statement.

5. That if I request an attorney, no questions will be asked me until an attorney is present to represent me.

6. That I can decide at any time to exercise these rights and not answer any questions or make any statements.

After having my Rights explained to me, I freely and voluntarily waive my right to an attorney. I am willing to make a statement to the officers. I can read and write the English language and fully understand my Rights to an attorney. I have read this Waiver of Counsel and fully understand it. No threats or promises have been made to me to induce me to sign this Waiver of Counsel and to make a statement to the officers.

This _____ day of _____, 19____.

All of the above Rights in the above Waiver of Counsel were read and explained to the above defendant by me and he freely and voluntarily waived his right to an attorney. No threats, promises, tricks, or persuasion were employed by me or anyone in my presence to induce him to waive his rights to an attorney and to make a statement without an attorney. He freely and voluntarily signed the above Waiver of Counsel in my presence after having read it.

_____

_____
(title)

Witnessed by: _____

_____

Classroom Issue VIII

INSTRUCTIONS FOR OBSERVERS AT ALL STATIONS

I. SITUATION

A. You are a silent observer to an interview.

II. REQUIREMENTS

A. Immediately following this paragraph is an Interviewing Techniques Checklist form. A supply of these forms is available from the instructor. Obtain sufficient copies of the form to rate the interviewers.

INTERVIEWING TECHNIQUES CHECKLIST FORM

Name of Primary Interviewer:

Name of Assistant Interviewer:

1. Did the interviewer demonstrate any of the following POSITIVE techniques?

		YES	
a.	Patience	___	(3)
b.	Persistence	___	(3)
c.	Effort	___	(3)
d.	Understanding	___	(2)
e.	Firmness	___	(1)
f.	Confidence	___	(2)
g.	Fairness	___	(1)
h.	Impartiality	___	(1)
i.	Control of temper	___	(3)
j.	Courtesy	___	(1)

Rotation of Students from Station to Station   *(Attachment 11)*
(Each student is assigned a number)

FIRST REPETITION

	A	B	C	D	E
Interviewee	1	2	3	4	5
Primary Interviewer	6	7	8	9	10
Assistant Interviewer	11	12	13	14	15
Observer	16	17	18	19	20
On Break	21	22	23	24	25

SECOND REPETITION

	A	B	C	D	E
On Break	5	1	2	3	4
Interviewee	10	6	7	8	9
Primary Interviewer	15	11	12	13	14
Assistant Interviewer	20	16	17	18	19
Observer	25	21	22	23	24

THIRD REPETITION

	A	B	C	D	E
Observer	4	5	1	2	3
On Break	9	10	6	7	8
Interviewee	14	15	11	12	13
Primary Interviewer	19	20	16	17	18
Assistant Interviewer	24	25	21	22	23

FOURTH REPETITION

	A	B	C	D	E
Assistant Interviewer	3	4	5	1	2
Observer	8	9	10	6	7
On Break	13	14	15	11	12
Interviewee	18	19	20	16	17
Primary Interviewer	23	24	25	21	22

FIFTH REPETITION

	A	B	C	D	E
Primary Interviewer	2	3	4	5	1
Assistant Interviewer	7	8	9	10	6
Observer	12	13	14	15	11
On Break	17	18	19	20	16
Interviewee	22	23	24	25	21

8

CURRICULUM DEVELOPMENT THROUGH

TASK ANALYSIS

A Training Curriculum • Task Analysis • Conclusion

A distinction needs to be made between the "how" of teaching and the "what" of learning. Instructional approaches and all the methods and techniques implied by that term are the "how" elements of teaching; they represent a process—a process which results in students being able to do at the conclusion of training something they were not able to do at the start. The "what" elements are the outcomes intended for the student to learn; they represent a product, a result, an achievement. These intended learning outcomes are expressed in a training document usually called a curriculum and sometimes called a program of instruction. The "how" and "what" are contrasts between instruction (a process) and curriculum (a product).[1]

Much of this book has focused on the teaching process, and we have discussed the product of learning only in the context of training objectives. To really grasp the importance of objectives and why particular objectives are selected, we need to know what a curriculum is and to understand the methods by which it is created. Without that foundation, an instructor is unable to fully appreciate why particular objectives are selected for teaching.

A curriculum does not appear in some miraculous way, like Moses's tablets. There is both rhyme and reason underlying a curriculum, and that is what this chapter is about. We will look first at the curriculum itself. Then we will look at task analysis as a method for determining curriculum content.

A TRAINING CURRICULUM

As much as anything else, a curriculum is a management tool. It allows managers (including those who manage courses and those who supervise course managers) to carry out two important functions: planning and control. The planning function is assisted when the curriculum defines the units of instruction, places them into a logical sequence, prescribes student learning outcomes, and delineates in instructor guides the strategies for reaching the intended outcomes. A well-written curriculum will also identify instructional aids, establish practice sessions, and specify achievement tests and other events that are planned to occur at predetermined intervals during the course. The control function is strengthened because managers are able to compare actual course activity and progress against the curriculum's specifications, and to take corrective action when variances are observed.

The importance of the curriculum is evident in the chart on the following page. Note that a curriculum is the product of many pre-instruction activities.

A curriculum is a management tool in one other sense. It can provide evidence against charges of negligent training. When a curriculum includes instructional units that result in learning outcomes critical to the job, such as instruction in deadly force, a built-in defense of sorts is established. This defense, however, works like a double-edged sword. When a curriculum calls for certain critical instruction which was proved not to have been given or to have been given imperfectly, an accusation of negligence can be supported, and perhaps even directed at the particular training officials who failed in their responsibilities.

Designing a curriculum for adults involves several essential elements. Curriculum design requires understanding the needs and interests of the learners and understanding the workplace in which they will apply the learning. The curriculum designer produces a careful statement of the subject matter to be covered and a clear statement of objectives in a form easy to understand for learner and instructor. Where does the curriculum designer obtain the necessary information? How does this person determine the needs and interests of learners or come to understand details of the workplace? The answers can be found with task analysis.

TASK ANALYSIS

What we commonly refer to as task analysis is in fact a broad range of analytic procedures used to describe work in terms of tasks.[2] These procedures are rooted in the various practices of industrial engineers and have parallels in managerial practices, such as "management by objectives" and "critical path method." Task analysis has many applications in addition to developing training programs.

The common denominator of all task analysis techniques is the use of task statements. The centrality of the task to the technique requires us to know the definition of a task. A task

- is a group of related manual activities directed toward a goal.

FIGURE 1: A Course from Start to Finish

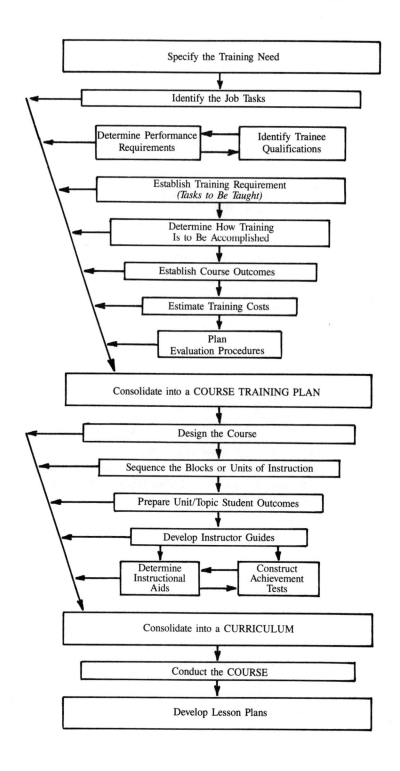

- usually has a definite beginning and end.
- is usually of relatively short duration.
- involves a person's interaction with equipment, other people, and/or media.
- results in a meaningful product. (A product need not be tangible. For example, a "correct decision" is an intangible, but meaningful product.)
- includes a mixture of decisions, perceptions, and/or physical activities.
- may be of any size or degree of complexity, but is always directed toward a specific purpose.
- is performed independently of other tasks, although it may be related to one or more other tasks.
- is visible and therefore measurable.

Unfortunately, a task is sometimes confused with other concepts like goal, assignment, or qualification. It is none of these things; neither is it a job or a duty, although a task is related to these terms. The following chart shows the relationships between job, duty, and task. It also shows that a task can be dissected into further subdivisions.

DIVISIONS OF WORK ACTIVITY

Job	A group of related duties.
Duty	A large segment of closely related tasks.
Task	A part of a duty.
Subtask	A part of a task.
Sub-Subtask	A supporting knowledge or skill.

To illustrate these work activity divisions, look at Figure 2, a hypothetical job structure chart.

To further understand the chart, let's assume that a law enforcement organization has a position called police dispatcher (job). The dispatcher receives messages, sends messages, and maintains records (duties). Within the send messages duty, the dispatcher communicates by telephone, radio, and teletype (tasks). When communicating by radio the dispatcher must set the frequency, use the microphone, and adjust the squelch (subtasks). To use the microphone, the dispatcher must know the call signs and the 10 series and must be able to transmit messages (sub-subtasks).

We could go down one level further in the chart by observing that to transmit messages the dispatcher must know how to hold the microphone and depress the key, but we would then be at the point of triviality. How to hold a microphone and push a button are actions so simple as to require not more than cursory interest.

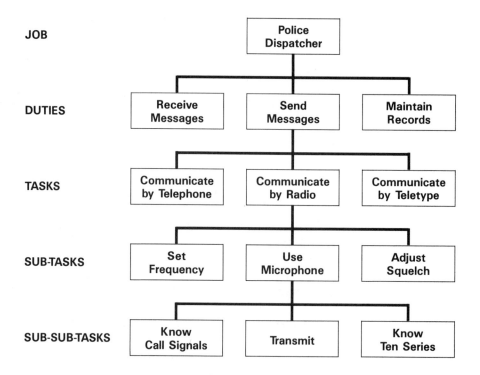

FIGURE 2: Job Structure

The way we are able to differentiate between job, duty, task, and subdivisions of a task is to apply the task definition. To send messages cannot be a task because messages are sent by several pieces of equipment, each of which is operated differently. The function of sending messages is broad, logically encompassing more than one task. The action of using a microphone (a subtask) is narrow. It does not meet the definition of a task because it has no work value unless performed in concert with other actions such as turning on the transmitter, setting the frequency, and adjusting the squelch.

This technique of breaking a job down into its separate parts has the effect of locating tasks as they exist in the order of real-life work activities. The technique also facilitates an identification of the skills and knowledges upon which performance of the task depends. For example, the breakdown in Figure 2 discloses that the police dispatcher must know communication codes, be skillful in speaking and interpreting the codes, and be manually adept at operating the radio's controls. The curriculum designer can use this technique to discover these aspects of the job and to program learning of them into the course curriculum.

Now that we know something about tasks and the part they play in planning and executing instruction, let us look at the process through which tasks are written, analyzed, and eventually selected for inclusion in a training program. Although methodology may vary from one task analysis project to another, the general sequence of steps in a task analysis is as follows:

- Develop an inventory of tasks comprising the job.
- Rate the tasks.
- Analyze the ratings.
- Select the tasks appropriate for training.
- Assign performance criteria to the tasks.

• Developing a Task Inventory

A task inventory is usually prepared from information obtained through interviews with job incumbents and persons close to the job, and by studying job-related written materials such as job descriptions, policies and procedures, prescriptive memorandums, reports and forms prepared as part of the job, and existing training materials.[3] Also revealing are the job's tools, supplies, and equipment.

Each task entered on the list is in the form of a statement. The statement has three elements which appear in the order shown below:

1. An action verb that describes what is done.
2. A brief identification of what is being acted upon, i.e., the object of the verb.
3. Any qualifying phrase which may be needed to remove confusion or ambiguity as to what the task is. In many cases, a qualifying phrase will not be necessary.

A task is written as a simple declarative statement. It is in the present tense, with the subject understood to be "I". The statement is brief and clear. Here are a few samples.

ACTION VERB + OBJECT ACTED UPON + QUALIFIER

Read	Miranda warnings	to suspects.
Compute	vehicle speed	from skidmarks.
Use	the police baton	in self-defense.
Write	incident reports.	
Direct	vehicle traffic.	
Counsel	juveniles.	

Note that the sample task statements tell what work is done, not how or why it is done. The statements are short, to the point, and leave little room for guesswork as to what they mean. Most importantly, note the strength of the action verb in each case. Task statements with weak, fuzzy action verbs cause problems to job incumbents who will be asked to rate them, instructors who will be required to teach them, and students who will be required to practice them. Following are some samples of clear and fuzzy verbs.

TASK VERBS

Clear	*Fuzzy*
Name	Understand
State	Appreciate
Identify	Assure
Clean	Arrange for
Load	Establish
Search	Implement
Stop	Initiate
Interview	Insure that
Collect	Participate in
Compute	Plan
Replace	Coordinate
Submit	Maintain
Type	Perceive

A first working draft of a task inventory is prepared from all information obtained. This preliminary document is circulated among the incumbents and knowledgeable persons. They are asked to modify, delete, add, and comment constructively.

• Rating the Tasks

After one or more drafts have been circulated, the list is converted to a task inventory questionnaire (TIQ).[4] The TIQ is the task list plus one or more questions about each task. It has answer blocks or supplementary answer sheets, instructions, and an administrative section for recording information about the respondent and his associated agency.

Rating a task means to apply to it one or more questions for the respondents to answer. Following are some sample questions and their implications to curriculum development.

QUESTION	IMPLICATION
How often is the task performed?	If the task is performed infrequently, the decision may be to not select it for inclusion in the instant case, but to identify it as suitable for on-the-job training (OJT) or other training mode.
How long does it take to perform the task?	If the task requires a great deal of time to perform, the curriculum will need to allow sufficient instructional time.
If an error is made in performing the task, how damaging will the consequences be?	If poor performance of the task poses serious consequences, the curriculum will need to place emphasis on mastery of the task.

How difficult is the task to learn?	If the task is difficult to learn, the curriculum might specify learning of the task in small segments in which complexities are reduced to simpler concepts.
Must the task be learned prior to entering the course?	If yes, the decision may be to require the prospective trainee to prove task competency (e.g., show a license or certificate) as part of the application process.
Is the overall job dependent upon performance of the task?	If yes, the curriculum must place emphasis on mastery of the task.
Is the task hazardous to perform?	If yes, the curriculum must organize the instruction with safety in mind and require task mastery.
How much delay can be tolerated before the task must be performed?	If the task must be performed quickly, the curriculum must specify speed as a condition of passing the performance test.

The design of the TIQ will be influenced by the response-format appropriate for each question. Following are some other possible questions and their response-formats.

How difficult is it to perform this task?

Response-format:

1. Easy.
2. Easy-to-moderate.
3. Moderately difficult.
4. Difficult.
5. Very difficult.

How soon is the task performed after the training course has ended?

Response-format:

0   In the first month.
1   1 to 3 months.
3   3 to 6 months.
6   6 to 12 months.
12 After 12 months.

What is the best method for learning this task?

Response-format:

FTP Formal training program.

OJT   On-the-job training.
SSP   Self-study program.
NST   No study or training needed.

Have you performed this task in the past year?
Response-format:

Y   Yes.
N   No.

Other response-formats might use blocks and circles to be blacked-in or cards with perforated holes to be punched out.

The design of the TIQ will also conform to the ways in which the answers will be scored. The scoring method, whether dependent on machine, computer, or human intelligence, will pretty much dictate the shape, length, and format of the TIQ. The final form in most cases will be a booklet or packet of materials arranged in a logical order.

The main portion of the TIQ is the list of job tasks. In most analysis projects, the list is repeated for every separate question. If many questions are asked and the list is long, the TIQ will be quite thick, time consuming for respondents to complete, and problem prone for project staffers to administer, score, and analyze.

Figure 3 is a sample task list page from a task inventory questionnaire. The page is marked with explanatory notes.

● Analyzing the Ratings

After the TIQs have been administered and the responses collected, the next step is to analyze. In a general discussion of this type, it helps to avoid rigorous explanations of factor analysis, regression analysis, frequency distributions, percentages, means, modes, medians, and measures of dispersion. Even a brief discussion of these statistical techniques takes us from the main point and is likely to be counterproductive. Let it simply be said that "off-the-shelf" computer programs and statistical packages are widely available for producing summary views from task data.

● Selecting the Tasks

At this point, the responses have been tabulated and the summary data have been interpreted. The next step is to review each task for the purpose of selecting those that warrant inclusion in the curriculum. There are at least three selection criteria to be considered:

- relevance of the task to the job
- significance of the task within the overall scheme of the job
- judgment as to whether formal training is the appropriate medium for teaching the task

Mindful of these considerations, the curriculum designer might regard a task as nonrelevant (and therefore reject it) if the summary

TASK LIST	CODE	PAGE __ OF __ PAGES
Rate each task based on how difficult the task is to perform: *The respondent checks this column if he or she has performed the task.*	**C** **H** **E** **C** **K** ✔	**TASK DIFFICULTY** 1. Extremely Low 2. Very Low 3. Low 4. Below Average 5. Average 6. Above Average 7. High 8. Very High 9. Extremely High
1. Arrest violators.		*In this column, the respondent places a value from the above scale.*
2. Search arrested persons.		
3. Place handcuffs on arrested persons.		
4. Interview witnesses.		
5. Read the Miranda warning to suspects.		
6. Interrogate suspects.		
7. Obtain fingerprints from suspects.		
8. Write an affidavit.		
9. Write field notes.		
10. Draw crime scene sketches.		
11. Take photographs at a crime scene.		
12. Lift fingerprints at a crime scene.		
13. Make field tests of suspected drugs.		
14. Mark evidence.		
15. Prepare evidence tags/receipts.		

FIGURE 3: Sample Task List Page

data reflect low likelihood of task performance on the job or a general absence of significance to the job. The designer might also reject as unimportant for training any task showing a low or moderately low percentage of responses indicating that the task should be learned prior to training or could be better learned on the job.

●Assigning Performance Criteria

A task can be viewed as being based on knowledge or on a skill.

EXAMPLES OF KNOWLEDGE-BASED TASKS

Define probable cause.

State the elements of proof for burglary.

Identify behavior signals associated with mental retardation.

Name the immediate actions to be taken upon arrival at the scene of a motor vehicle accident involving injuries.

EXAMPLES OF SKILL-BASED TASKS

Apply handcuffs to an arrested person.

Collect fingerprint evidence at a crime scene.

Make a wall search of a person incidental to arrest.

Draw a diagram of a motor vehicle accident scene.

The curriculum designer realizes the differences between knowledge-based and skill-based tasks. The designer realizes also that skill-based tasks are not entirely physical or motor activities but depend on knowledge to some extent. For instance, the task to "draw a diagram of a motor vehicle accident scene" depends upon knowledge relating to coordinates, compass directions, scale, legend, and triangulation.

The skills that support a task are either manipulative or mental. The action verb of the task reveals this fact.

Manipulative Skills	*Mental Skills*
Operate	Discriminate
Repair	Choose
Adjust	Select
Turn	Classify
Prepare	Solve
Replace	Analyze

Most adult learners possess a sufficient range of manipulative skills before they enter training, and will sharpen them through practice during the course. The mental skills may be more difficult to develop because the knowledge which supports them is likely to be new to the learner.

Knowledge-based tasks are generally tested by written examination, and skill-based tasks are always tested by performance examination. In both the written and performance examinations, the student performs a visible and measurable behavior for each task tested. The written examination asks a question; the student writes in a response; the response is evaluated. The performance examination puts the student in a simulation of the job: a stimulus or cue for action is initiated; the student responds by performing the appropriate task; the performance is evaluated.

Performance criteria. However, for an evaluation to be made of the student's performance there must be some yardstick or measurement. We call such measurements "performance criteria." Each task has its own set of performance criteria. The criteria consist of two elements: conditions and standards.

The *conditions* element identifies the supplies, tools, equipment, and major features of the environment in which a task is typically done. For example, the conditions of the task, "Draw a diagram of a motor vehicle accident scene," would specify that the student be given a clipboard, paper, pencil, template, compass, tape measure, and a simulated motor vehicle accident scene.

The *standards* element identifies the extent of precision the student will be expected to demonstrate in doing the task. Accuracy is always a measure of precision, and speed is sometimes important. The standards of the task, "Draw a diagram of a motor vehicle accident scene," might require that the diagram be free of any errors associated with direction of travel, point of impact, or major contributing cause.

When we apply performance criteria (i.e., conditions and standards) to a task, we create what is called a student performance objective, or SPO. The format of an SPO for a skill-based task looks like this:

CONDITIONS: Given a clipboard, paper, pencil, template, compass, tape measure, and a simulated motor vehicle accident scene, the student will

TASK: Draw a diagram of the scene

STANDARDS: With no mistakes of fact relating to direction of travel, point of impact, or major contributing cause.

A task based on knowledge is simpler to construct. Here is a sample.

CONDITIONS: Given a written examination, the student will

TASK: Name the procedure for placing a juvenile offender in temporary detention

STANDARDS: With 90 percent accuracy.

The accuracy standard will vary from task to task. Critical tasks, such as those that relate to deadly force, safety, and citizen rights, might carry a 100 percent accuracy standard. If improper task performance on the job has a potential for adverse consequences (as revealed by task analysis), the accuracy standard must be high.

After the performance criteria have been assigned, the tasks (now in the form of SPOs) are made a part of the curriculum.

CONCLUSION

Curriculum development is at the very core of the training enterprise. Those who regard themselves as training professionals should obtain an understanding of how a curriculum is researched, designed, and finally constructed. A principal tool in this process is task analysis.

Task analysis techniques come in many varieties. Conceptually, they have one thing in common, namely, the analysis of work activities in terms of tasks and subdivisions thereof. In this regard, task analysis represents an approach to curriculum development that is objective, in some ways quantitative, and in every case an improvement over no analysis at all.

NOTES

1. *Performance Content for Job Training* (Columbus, Ohio: The Center for Vocational Education, Ohio State University, 1977), p. 14.
2. Ernest J. McCormick, *Job Analysis: Methods and Applications* (New York: American Management Association, 1979), p. 91.
3. John Fay, *A Task Analysis of the Special Agent Job in the Georgia Bureau of Investigation*, a paper presented at the Job Task Analysis Symposium, sponsored by the Law Enforcement Assistance Administration, in Dallas, Texas, November 1978.
4. A term used in *Identifying Relevant Job Performance* (Columbus, Ohio: The Center for Vocational Education, Ohio State University, 1977).

9

EVALUATING STUDENTS THROUGH TESTING

Types of Test Items • Conclusion

In an earlier chapter, the practical exercise is discussed as a medium for testing psychomotor objectives. The point is made that a "doing" activity, such as learning to fire a gun, is best evaluated by observing the student perform the activity. Initially, the practical exercise acquaints the student with the task (objective). It then provides practice for the fullest development of the student's skill, and finally serves as a scenario for determining if the student has sufficiently mastered the skill. Mastery in this sense means to perform the task according to certain well-defined standards that serve as a measuring stick for both the student and the instructor. For guidance as to how psychomotor objectives are tested, you should turn to the chapter dealing with practical exercises.

Cognitive objectives are almost always tested through written examinations. This chapter will acquaint you with a variety of test items that can be used to measure a student's attainment of knowledge.

Testing sometimes comes as an afterthought. Because formal testing usually occurs at the end of a module or at the end of a course, it is put on the instructor's mental back burner. The rationale is: "I'll take care of testing when I get there. Right now I'm too busy teaching." The fact is, testing is a major consideration at the beginning, in the middle, and at the end of training. At the beginning, we decide what knowledge the student will be required to learn. A corollary of this proposition is to decide how we will know if the student has in fact learned the required knowledge. In the middle, we need to see how well we are progressing and to make changes to improve progress. At the conclusion of training, we measure in a formal way the student's extent of learning. What we have, then, is an interweaving of evaluation with instruction from start to finish.

Good tests have six characteristics:

- *Validity*. A good test will accurately measure what it is intended to measure and nothing else.
- *Reliability*. A good test will yield consistent results.
- *Objectivity*. A good test can be scored without intrusion of the scorer's personal views.
- *Comprehensiveness*. A good test will cover all the objectives needing to be measured.
- *Differentiation*. A good test will detect small differences in the achievements of students.
- *Usability*. A good test can be administered and scored with a reasonable expenditure of time and effort.

TYPES OF TEST ITEMS

Test items used to measure cognitive objectives are of two types: selection and supply. A selection type item offers choices for a student to select from, and is based on a principle of recognition. In this category are multiple-choice, true-false, and matching test items. A supply type item calls for the student to provide the answer, and is based on a principle of recall. Recall is at a higher level of cognitive behavior than recognition. Fill-in and essay test items fall into this category.

• Multiple-choice Items

Multiple-choice items tend to be favored by training administrators over other types of test items. Why? For one thing, they are relatively easy to score. Scoring can be done manually with a key or by means of electromechanical and computer devices. Scoring of multiple-choice tests does not involve the tedious process of reading and interpreting written answers. Only the true/false testing technique comes near to multiple-choice in ease of scoring, but true/false is flawed by its susceptibility to student guessing.

Many students in vocational training programs seem to prefer the multiple-choice test. Two reasons are frequently given: there is very little writing required of the student, and the scoring method is highly objective. The latter reason is perhaps the best overall qualification of multiple-choice testing.

From a measurement point of view, multiple-choice offers these advantages:

- A wide range of topics can be covered in a single test.
- The technique can measure a student's ability to make judgments and apply knowledge.
- Multiple-choice does not assess a student's ability to memorize discrete facts, but assesses reasoning and situational thinking.

— Measurements can be made at several levels of difficulty, e.g., grasp of fundamentals, application of principles, and formation of judgments.

A multiple-choice item begins with a premise, also called a stem. The premise is followed by several choices (usually four or five), only one of which is the correct answer. The other choices are incorrect and are called distractors. The student selects the answer from the choices presented.

The premise can take the form of a question or an incomplete statement.

The premise as a question

What is the main purpose of searching an arrested person?

    a. To recover stolen property.
    b. To obtain incriminating evidence.
    c. To look for weapons.
    d. To seize contraband.

The premise as an incomplete statement

The main purpose of searching an arrested person is to

    a. recover stolen property.
    b. obtain incriminating evidence.
    c. look for weapons.
    d. seize contraband.

A premise can be supplemented by an illustration. For example:

The picture at the right depicts fractured glass. The arrows are pointing to

    a. primary fractures.
    b. secondary fractures.
    c. concave fractures.
    d. convex fractures.

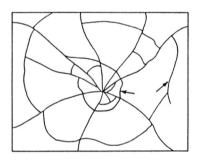

Writing multiple-choice items. When thinking about a starting point, keep in mind that the premise of an item states a problem. The problem needs to be expressed so explicitly that the average, informed student will have no trouble in grasping the meaning of the problem. In fact, the premise should be so clear that any knowledgeable person would be able to give the correct answer without even being offered some choices to select from.

The premise's central issue can get obscured if the writer follows a compulsion to include extraneous and trivial details. If the problem to be answered is hidden among unnecessary information, the student may lose the trail as well as valuable time. A long and complicated premise might be appropriate if reading skills were being tested, but if the purpose is to measure knowledge, as is the case in many criminal justice programs, the language needs to be simple and straightforward.

Each item stands alone, poses just one problem, and the answer does not reveal the answer to any other item in the test. Because many job tasks consist of steps in a process, test items about the job will very likely follow the same sequence. From the point of view that a test is an added opportunity for teaching and learning, the items should reinforce what the student already knows. If the items are jumbled about with no order, the student's thinking may take on an equally jumbled pattern.

A student should not have to guess at what the premise is saying. Without even getting to the choices, the student should be able to figure out what kind of response is demanded. The student is helped if the item writer employs simple and direct language. Using two short sentences is often better than using one long, complex sentence.

When a premise contains a negative word, such as not, never, or except, underline and/or capitalize to emphasize its presence. If you use a negative in the premise, be sure that none of the choices contains a negative. Better still, avoid using negatives altogether. Other words to avoid are all, always, and none. Very few things are absolute, and the presence of an absolute in a choice is a tip-off that the choice is incorrect. Another inadvertent tip-off is to place at the end of an incomplete statement the words "a" or "an," which may serve as a clue to the correct choice. Put the correct indefinite articles at the beginning of the choices instead of at the end of the premise.

When writing choices, start with the correct answer.[1] You can change the order of your choices at a later time. By beginning with the correct choice, you are setting the tone for the distractors. You are also creating in the correct choice a model of structure, form, and terminology to be followed in writing plausible distractors.

Each choice should be a logical and grammatically correct extension of the premise. If the premise is a question, the offered choices should make sense in relation to the idea and the words used. If the premise is an incomplete sentence, each choice must pick up at the end of the premise and complete the sentence without violating the rules of grammar. A common mistake is to switch tenses when moving from the premise to a choice.

The correct answer and the distractors should be similar in length, composition, and in the use of key words and technical terms. There is a tendency, born out of a writer's natural desire to be exact, for the correct answer to be longer than the distractors. If the correct answer cannot be shortened, the distractors can be lengthened. It is not mandatory that all choices be of the same length all of the time, only that correct answers are not apparent by consistent variances in size.

A correct answer is sometimes copied directly from a course reference, such as a law book or medical journal. The particular style and structure of the correct answer should also appear in the distractors. Otherwise, the correct choice will stand out like a sore thumb.

Distractors are not intended to trick or confuse. The idea is not to fool the examinees but to determine fairly if they have attained certain required knowledge. To lead them away from the correct answer may also lead them to accept incorrect information.

The use of "none of the above" or "all of the above" may weaken an item. They can make the item easy, guessable, or confusing. A test writer can usually find a way to rephrase the premise and/or think of a full set of acceptable choices.

An item's answer can be given away if more than one of the distractors means the same thing. Since there can be only one correct answer, the student can eliminate from consideration any distractors that are essentially similar. The following item illustrates:

In making a tire print impression, the amount of water to be mixed with one pound of plaster is
   a. one quart.
   b. one fourth of a gallon.
   c. 8 ounces.

The student may not possess the required knowledge, but he can deduce the correct answer by recognizing that one quart equals one fourth of a gallon. Since responses *a* and *b* cannot both be the one correct answer, the student selects response *c*. This would be a good question only if the teaching point had something to do with logic or deductive reasoning.

A delicate balance exists between a correct answer and its corresponding distractors. They must all be similar in structure, length, terminology, and readability. The correct answer is plausible because it is undeniably correct. The distractors are written so as to be plausible (at least to the student who has not learned the material being tested), but the distractors must also be absolutely incorrect.

A writer or approver of multiple-choice items should be satisfied that every correct answer is in fact correct without qualification. A right answer needs to be founded on some well-established authority and be regarded by experts as universally correct. Not only should the correct answer be factually correct, but to the informed person it should also be a clearly better choice than any of its distractors. If a persuasive argument can be made that a distractor is at least as good a choice as the correct answer, the item needs to be reworked or discarded.

Multiple-choice items are not terribly difficult to write, but they are sensitive to small errors in construction. Following is a reviewer's checklist.

A CHECKLIST FOR
MULTIPLE-CHOICE ITEMS

✔ Does the item test an objective or task?

✔ Does the item reflect current doctrine and good practice in the field?

✔ Will the knowledgeable student be able to select the correct answer without hesitation?

✔ Is the premise easy to read?

✔ Is the premise free of ambiguous words or terms that can be interpreted in more than one way?

___ Is the premise explicit and free of over-generalizations?

___ Is the premise free of extraneous and trivial details?

___ Does the premise pose just one problem?

___ Does the premise stand alone, independent of other items?

___ Is the premise free of an inadvertent use of "a" or "an" as a tip-off to the answer?

___ Is the premise free of absolute terms like "always" and "never"?

___ If a technical term is used, is it the most generally accepted one?

___ If negative wording is necessary, have the words been emphasized in some way?

___ Is the item free of double negatives?

___ Do the choices follow grammatically and logically from the premise?

___ Are the distractors and correct answer parallel in structure, length, and terminology?

___ Is there clearly only one correct choice?

___ Is each distractor clearly incorrect?

___ Is each distractor plausible to the uninformed student even though incorrect?

___ Are the choices free of "all of the above" and "none of the above"?

___ Is the item free of any hints that might reveal the answer to another item?

___ Are the distractors free of identical or essentially similar choices?

___ Do the items follow a logical order?

   If all of the above questions are answered with a yes, you have written a good multiple-choice item.

• True-False Items

The true-false, or binary choice, item asks the student to agree or disagree with a statement. In the rules of its construction and appearance, the true-false item is similar to multiple choice. A premise is given and the student is provided some choices to select from. Here are some examples:

An item with a true-false ending

If an emergency search is not necessary, there is probably time to obtain a search warrant. If it appears while the search warrant is being requested that the criminal goods are about to be removed, an emergency search can be conducted.

a. True   b. False

An item with a yes-no ending

An officer believes that criminal goods are being prepared for transport to an unknown location. He knows there is no time to obtain a search warrant. He decides to make a search. Has the officer conducted an illegal search?

a. Yes   b. No

An item with a composite ending

A low-frequency channel will be found on a band of the radio spectrum operating at 30-300 megahertz.

a. True   b. False   c. _____

In the composite true-false item, the student is required to fill in the correct word or term if he identifies an error in the premise. The informed student would identify the premise as false and insert kilohertz in place of megahertz.

An advantage of the true-false item is its use in testing knowledge of facts. This is also one of its faults because it promotes memorization activity on the part of the student. In a factual question, it is difficult to build in relative degrees of truth or falsity. This characteristic operates to limit the true-false method as an appropriate medium for measuring a student's ability to synthesize information.

A major weakness of the true-false item is the difficulty of writing meaningful premises that aren't excessively obvious. When the premise is overly precise, the correct answer tends in most cases to be true. If the premise is made too general, the correct answer is subject to differences of opinion. Statements that contain absolutes (e.g., always or only) lead the test-wise student to mark the answer as false, and when less extreme modifiers are used or possible exceptions cited, the guessing student will favor the true option.

In any type of binary choice item, guessing will be a major problem. A student's chances of guessing right are very good when a test is short. The odds against guessing right rise rapidly as the test gets longer.[2]

Number of true-false items	Chance of getting a 70% by wild guessing
10	1 out of 6
25	1 out of 50
50	1 out of 350
100	1 out of 10,000
200	less than 1 out of 1 million

The true-false approach encourages an instructor to lift statements from the reference text or lesson plan. This will cause most of the questions to be correctly answered as true. The student who finds it necessary to guess will generally go with the true option because he knows that the odds favor that selection. To cut down on this form of guessing, the instructor can either develop additional questions which have false as the correct answer, or convert some of the true options to false options. When converting, a possibility exists for unintentional booby-trapping.

A true statement made false might turn out like this:

The Miranda decision applies to non-custodial interrogation.
   T F

Unless the question is read carefully, the student may miss the "non" buried in the statement. Here's another tricky one:

The Miranda decision, issued by the Supreme Court in 1974, applies to custodial interrogation.   T   F

The statement is false because the Supreme Court issued its decision on Miranda in 1964. The major element of the premise is correct but a minor false element makes the whole statement false.

Questions like these have no place in a professionally constructed examination.

True-false tests are useful but limited. They can be useful in non-graded spot quizzes and in provoking student discussions. As a formal measuring tool, they are ineffective in gauging the upper levels of cognitive behavior. In the lower levels of thinking, where the possible choices are few and there are no gray areas to be considered, the true-false item can be valuable.

● **Matching Items**

A matching item usually consists of two columns of items that have to be paired. One column may consist of terms, numbers, or principles. The other contains definitions, computations, or applications.

On the following page, match the terms on the left with the terms on the right.

1. Contraband   [ ] Jimmied lock
2. Fruits of the crime   [ ] Heroin
3. Tools of the crime   [ ] Military explosives
4. Evidence   [ ] Fingerprints
                          [ ] Car used for bootlegging
                          [ ] Pornographic photos
                          [ ] Stolen whiskey

The matching process can be varied. The item may call for the student to match

— words with definitions.
— mathematical equations with their answers.
— symbols with their names.
— principles with situations.
— causes with effects.

Matching items are really multiple-choice items in disguise. Both approaches allow for objectivity, scoring is simple, little writing is demanded of the student, and some higher regions of cognition can be assessed.

The matching item, however, is very susceptible to logical and verbal clues. How many clues can you find in this example?

Column A	Column B
1. Miranda	place where convicted
2. June 13, 1966	an element of the ruling
3. Arizona	year offense was committed
4. 1964	date of the decision
5. right to remain silent	plaintiff
	a Fifth Amendment protection
	defendant

Did you notice in the above item that

— "date of the decision" has to match "June 13, 1966" because it is the only date given?
— "year offense was committed" has to match "1964" because it is the only year given?
— "place where convicted" has to match "Arizona" because it is the only place given?
— "an element of the ruling" has to be "right to remain silent" because all other choices relate to either a person, place, or time and that the same reasoning applies to "a Fifth Amendment protection"?
— after you made two or three matches the remaining matches were easy to guess?

Some of the problems that appear in this matching item can be corrected by allowing any single item in Column A to be matched more than once in Column B. Column B should be at least three items longer than Column A. Doing this will cut back on guessing and deduction by process of elimination. The item would also be improved by placing like or homogeneous items in each column. The following is an example of homogeneity.

Match these two sets of items by placing numbers from Column A into the blocks of Column B.

Column A
1. lens
2. mercury
3. transistor
4. electromagnet
5. filament

Column B
[ ] barometer
[ ] electric light bulb
[ ] automobile engine
[ ] microscope
[ ] periscope
[ ] radio
[ ] computer
[ ] telephone

● **Fill-in Items**

A fill-in item requires the test taker to supply one or more omitted key words/terms. Fill-ins work very well in testing recall ability and can be constructed to sample a broad range of topics. They have strong discriminating value and challenge a student's remembrance of specific facts. (Discriminating value means the benefit derived from being able to identify those who don't know, those who are somewhat knowledgeable, and those who are acceptably knowledgeable.) This feature happens also to be a limitation since fill-ins tend to assess memory and verbal facility rather than application. Fill-ins additionally present a problem to the test grader who must accept or reject words and terms that are close but not absolutely correct.

A fill-in is generally found in three forms: the completion item, enumeration item, and identification item.

Completion item. This is a sentence or short paragraph in which key words have been replaced by blank spaces or empty lines. If the item is a short sentence, one blank line is appropriate. A long sentence or paragraph may have several blank spaces but usually three or four at most.

The student is led into the teaching point before being asked to contribute to it. This requires that the blank spaces appear toward the end of the item. Grammatical construction is important. When the missing words have been inserted, the entire statement should read clearly, and where possible, the statement will read clearly only when the correct words have been supplied.

Here are some samples of completion items:

SPO is a term familiar to criminal justice instructors. SPO stands for _____ .

Something which is illegal to possess is called _____.

An affidavit is a _____, written statement.

Enumeration item. In this item form, the student is asked to name or list a number of homogeneous items. For example:

Name the three parts of an SPO and place them in the order in which they appear.

1. _____
2. _____
3. _____

Note that an enumeration question can also require the student to place answers in a particular order—in this case, by order of appearance. In other cases, the order might conform to importance or sequence.

A common mistake with an enumeration question is to make the list too long. A poor question would be as follows:

List 15 items needed to make a plaster of paris cast of a tire print.

Here is an alternate way to test the same teaching point:

List 5 items that are needed during the surface preparation phase when making a plaster of paris cast of a tireprint.

List 5 items . . . . during the mixing and pouring phase when . . . . a tireprint.

List 5 items . . . . during the lifting and cleaning phase when . . . . of a tireprint.

A question that asks for a relatively long list tests recall ability. Note that the alternate approach in the above example tests both recall and application.

Another common error in the construction of an enumeration question is to ask for an incomplete list. For example:

List 5 of the 15 items needed to make a plaster of paris tireprint.

The problem with this question is that most students will be able to recall 5 of 15 items, but only a few students will be able to identify them all. The question is inherently unfair to those having greater recall.

About 5 items are sufficient for a single enumeration question, and it helps if they are linked to a relevant factor such as a step in a process or in the order of use.

Identification item. This item form uses a pictorial representation such as a sketch, map, drawing, diagram, or photo, and sometimes a three-dimensional object. The student is required to provide the names of things shown or to find problems, as in trouble-shooting for equipment malfunctions.

This is an example of an identification item:

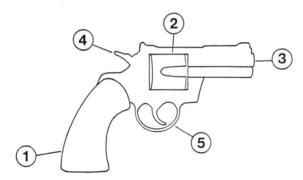

Fill-in items can be scored by hand rather quickly and marked reliably, provided the scoring key is thoughtfully put together. The key should contain, in addition to the purely correct answers, any permitted synonyms, substitute terms, or reasonably acceptable answers.

• Situational Items

Test questions can be presented through hypothetical situations. The situation is simply a vehicle for presenting questions. The questions can be multiple-choice, true-false, matching, fill-in, or essay.

A desirable feature of the situational item is that it imparts to students the feeling of reality. Even when short, a situational item tells a story in which the student becomes vicariously involved. Students are already thinking about the jobs they are being trained to fill and are naturally motivated to apply their thinking processes to situations they may someday face when on their own without an instructor's guidance. For this reason, a situational item must be highly job relevant and realistic.

Perhaps the most desirable feature of the situational item is the opportunity it presents for measuring application of knowledge attained. Although situational items can be used effectively to measure recall and recognition, they are at their best in requiring application.

Because they are difficult to construct, situational items tend not to be used to their full potential. They also consume more time during test administration, and usually automatic equipment is not useful in scoring.

Following are some examples of situational items:

Officer Brown's first assignment out of the police academy is to ride patrol with Sergeant Green. While on patrol, Sergeant Green boasts of the fine meals he obtains as "gifts" from several restaurants in his patrol sector.

In 50 words or less, state what you think Officer Brown should say or do.

Assume you are the first officer to arrive at the scene of a two-car collision involving serious personal injury. On the lines below, state the major actions you should take, in the order they should be taken.

1. _____
2. _____
3. _____
4. _____

While interviewing a person you believe to be a witness to a felony, the person says something that causes you to believe the person is a suspect. At this point you should

    a. continue the interview as if nothing happened.

    b. discontinue the interview and give a Miranda warning.

    c. stop asking questions but allow the person to continue talking if he wishes.

    d. administer a Miranda warning at the conclusion of the interview.

● Essay Items

Essay questions work well in measuring a student's ability to organize facts, create solutions, and exercise judgment. Essay items are not appropriate if the instructor intends to test only lower level cognitive behavior, such as recall and recognition.

It is a good practice to use several short essay items in place of one long one. A common problem in constructing an essay question is being too general. This can be overcome by using the training objective as a guide. For example, if a training objective calls for the student to describe the procedures for referring a juvenile offender to a social service agency, the question might look like this:

Describe in 200 words or less the procedures for referring a juvenile offender to a social service agency.

Your answer should discuss

    1. the rights of juveniles as established by law.

    2. the manner of treatment of a juvenile while in police custody.

    3. the mechanics of transporting/transferring a juvenile to a social service agency.

    4. juvenile court procedures.

The four criteria tacked onto the end of the question should have been key teaching points made by the instructor in the classroom. They are added not to surprise the students but to determine if they have acquired the certain specific pieces of knowledge that are comprised in the training objective. Their presence also serves to reinforce learning.

When an essay item is derived in this manner from a clearly stated objective and is further explicated with rating criteria, the student knows what is expected and the instructor has the basis for scoring the answer. Those students who are able to bluff answers because of superior writing skills lose their advantage over others who do not write as well but have the knowledge.

Even with the inclusion of scoring criteria, an essay answer is difficult to evaluate. Scoring cannot be done by machine nor can it be done effectively by anyone other than the instructor. More seriously, there is the danger that the instructor will, consciously or unconsciously, assign grades which coincide with personal views and experiences.[3]

CONCLUSION

If we are committed to the delivery of quality instruction, we must at the same time be committed to quality testing. Two critical observations can be made from testing: we can observe if students are learning, and we can observe if instructors are teaching. From these observations we can determine where modifications need to be made to improve the instructional process. Inherent to this proposition is the idea that instructors are rated primarily on the record of achievements produced by their students. This being the case, instructors owe it to themselves as well as to their students to construct test items that properly measure the training objectives they have been charged to attain.

NOTES

1. *Instructions for Writing Good Multiple-Choice Items* (New York: Professional Examination Service, 1982), p. 3.
2. Bernard Feder, *The Complete Guide to Taking Tests* (Englewood Cliffs, N.J.: Prentice-Hall, Inc., 1979), p. 57.
3. W. James Popham and Eva L. Baker, *Systematic Instruction* (Englewood Cliffs, N.J.: Prentice-Hall, Inc., 1970), p. 143.

10

CIVIL LIABILITY FOR IMPROPER TRAINING,

AND HOW TO AVOID IT

The Theory of Negligence • What Can Be Done? • Conclusion

In the last two decades criminal justice agencies and their representatives have been engulfed in a continuing and rising tidal wave of lawsuits. Most of the cases filed have been directed against law enforcement officers and correctional specialists. Two factors appear to be at work in this trend: first, the increasingly litigious nature of our society, and second, an expanding social conscience operating in support of citizens injured by government employees. To be sure, persons and organizations other than those involved in the processes of criminal justice are being sued with greater frequency and success. But the pattern that emerges from these actions reveals a pronounced targeting of law enforcement and corrections employees.

A particularly disturbing aspect is a fresh sophistication by plaintiffs in pursuing their cases. Previously unused and sometimes innovative tactics are being staged through old and recent laws. Plaintiffs' attorneys are articulate and intelligent, and they aggressively exploit every advantage.

Furthermore, because misconduct litigation is fast becoming a prominent and highly profitable specialty, there are others who exploit it; some lawyers, for example, charge fees to teach their peers the ins and outs of suing criminal justice agencies for negligence. Seminars on the subject are offered around the country, and a how-to manual is available to guide the novices. Also, expert witnesses, many of them former police and correctional officers, are paid to testify for plaintiffs.

The frequency of cases and the amount of awards follow no particular pattern with respect to geographic location, size of department, or type of injury alleged. Suits are being brought and won at all levels, in organizations and communities large and small, in all locations of the country, and for a wide range of grievances. If one common thread runs through this proliferation of suits, it is the consistently recurring complaint of negligent training.

The trend is not likely to slacken at any time in the foreseeable future. Rather, it will most likely continue to rise and not even begin to level off in this decade.

Clearly, a warning has been sounded by unhappy citizens and sympathetic juries. The time is long past for decrying the situation; there is only time to assess the dimensions of the problem and take corrective action. A first step is to understand the major concepts of law pertaining to civil litigation, especially as they relate to training.

THE THEORY OF NEGLIGENCE

The most common path of pursuit in civil litigation is the negligence theory. In this approach the argument is not that the injurious conduct was malicious in nature, but that the injury and damages resulted from a failure to perform a duty with due care.

A basis for legal liability resulting from the failure of supervisors to fully and properly discharge responsibilities of office can be found in Title 42, Section 1983, of the Civil Rights Act of 1871. This early civil rights law provides that

> [e]very person who, under color of any statute, ordinance, regulation, custom, or usage, of any State or Territory or the District of Columbia, subjects, or causes to be subjected, any citizen of the United States or other person within the jurisdiction thereof the deprivation of any rights, privileges, or immunities secured by the Constitution and laws, shall be liable to the party injured in an action at law, suit in equity, or other proper proceeding for redress . . . .

Liability is the result of negligence or failure to give proper attention or care to one's duty. For the liability to be recognized, it must be the cause of a deprivation of rights secured by the Constitution.

Within the negligence theory, there is a particular vulnerability to accusations of improper training. The courts have consistently ruled in favor of plaintiffs who can show injury caused by negligence resulting from the absence of training or the administration of faulty training. The citizenry and the law impose upon governmental agencies an affirmative duty to provide their employees with requisite knowledge and skills. When jobs contain the potential for abuse and injury, as is the case with many jobs in law enforcement and corrections, the affirmative duty to provide training is expected to be met without qualification.

More often than not, the injured party will file suit against the offending officer as well as the officer's superiors. The plaintiff's charge will frequently allege that the officer acted intentionally to cause injury and that the superiors should also be held accountable for being negligent in failing to take preventive action.

When a suit is pursued along these lines, the officer and superiors are very apt to come into sharp and bitter disagreement. The officer will argue that his or her actions conformed with policy, procedures, and the training provided by superiors. The superiors will argue that their subordinate's actions were inconsistent with the standards established for the department. The conflict is certain to weaken their separate defenses and cast a shadow of doubt in the minds of jurors.

The damages which may be assessed in a negligence case are of three types: direct, punitive, and nominal. Direct damages may include such things as medical expenses, lost wages, and the costs of replacing or repairing property. Punitive damages are usually assessed when an element of fraud, malice, or oppression is present. The third type is called nominal damages. If assessed, the amount is usually set at one dollar, hence the term nominal.

• The Concept of Proximate Cause

In this concept, a single wrongful act may be caused by two or more persons acting at different points in time. For example, a police officer might make an unlawful arrest. The officer says his action was based on knowledge imparted to him in a departmental training session. The concept of proximate cause supports the plaintiff's charge against the officer and any other persons who contributed to the unlawful arrest. In this example, the contributing persons could be the departmental instructor, his superior, and so on right up to the chief of the department or the mayor.

A good illustration of proximate cause is found in *Sager v. City of Woodland Park*, 543 F. Supp. 282 (D. Colo. 1982). A-3, D/PS. A Woodland Park officer accidentally killed a person he was arresting when a shotgun he was pointing at the suspect's head discharged while the officer was trying to hold the shotgun with one hand and handcuff the arrestee with the other hand. This technique of handling dangerous prisoners was shown in a training film seen by the officer while in rookie school. The rookie school was run by the City of Colorado Springs. The City of Woodland Park sent its officers to Colorado Springs for basic certification training.

When the administrator of the estate of the deceased arrestee brought a lawsuit against the officer and the City of Woodland Park, that city in turn sued the City of Colorado Springs. At trial, the training officer in charge of the Colorado Springs Training Academy testified the film in question was supposed to illustrate how NOT to handcuff a prisoner, but someone forgot to tell the class it illustrated improper technique. The trial court rejected an argument that the death was not "caused" by the negligent teaching. The chain of causation was sufficiently clear and the death was reasonably foreseeable.[1]

This case is of particular importance to agencies that provide training for individuals from other jurisdictions because improper training could result in liability to the training agency.

Lawsuits that allege insufficient instruction serve as reminders that the days of training by the "seat of the pants" are over. Today the techniques of quality control have as much meaning in the classroom as in any work environment where excellence is prized.

The general public holds high expectations concerning training. The media have helped to shape (and sometimes distort) public perceptions, none more so than in the law enforcement area. When training expectations fall short and tortious wrongs ensue, the community is angered and the injured parties seek justice through the courts.

WHAT CAN BE DONE?

Any response strategy to counter the civil litigation movement should be aimed at eliminating in the training domain any and all conditions that might contribute, or could be construed to contribute, to charges of improper instruction. Even the finest training operation must anticipate that negligent training lawsuits will be filed, and be prepared to answer those charges with a positive defense based on accurate and detailed documentation.

Five tactics should be included within the strategy:

— validate training

— administer training to specifications

— evaluate the trainees

— maintain good records

— establish instructor standards

● Validate Training

In the sense used here, validation means to ensure through an objective process that the training provided corresponds to duties associated with the job. The key objectives of validation are to verify that—

1. doctrinal content and skills development are correct,
2. instructional methods are appropriate and effective, and
3. training is relevant to the workplace and answers the day-to-day needs of job incumbents.

One of the more objective and commonly used techniques of validation is task analysis. Information drawn from task analysis gives to the curriculum designer a wealth of facts obtained from incumbents and others close to the job. The data reveal with high accuracy and specificity the nature and conditions of the trainees' future work environment.

A curriculum constructed from task analysis data will establish the baseline tasks of the job and will highlight tasks which if not performed or if performed incorrectly could lead to litigation. Further, the task analysis approach uncovers the knowledges and skills which support each task. For example, if a task requires a police officer to use his revolver in defense of human life, the officer must be taught how to handle and fire the revolver (skills), and he must know the deadly force law and be able to differentiate between threatening and nonthreatening situations (knowledges). The curriculum will require each officer-trainee to perform the skill part of the task, demonstrating a competency to predetermined standards. The knowledges part of the task might be tested by written examination, again in accordance with high standards.

A curriculum is analagous to a movie script which guides the film director (instructor) as he cues and maneuvers the actors (trainees) through complex scenarios (hands-on exercises) that simulate some aspect of reality (the job). The training is valid when the script is well written and the actors give credible performances. These are the usual specifications comprised in a curriculum:

- tasks (also called actions or training objectives)
- task standards
- task conditions
- time allocations
- scopes (also called unit descriptions)
- sequencing
- testing modes
- instructional methods and media
- instructor qualifications
- lesson plans or instructor guides
- student handouts or study guides

By far, the most important specification is the task. Tasks serve as the focal points and basic framework of the curriculum. All other specifications are derived from and influenced by them. The influence of the task is most apparent in the two curriculum excerpts on pages 200-201.

When a curriculum has been validated (i.e., determined objectively to be job relevant) and when instructional activities have been executed according to plan, the opportunities for negligence are largely, if not entirely, removed and a strong defense is constructed against accusations of improper training.

● Administer Training to Specifications

For a training course to be made resistant to charges of negligence, a minimum of logic must prevail. Logic tells us that the success of a training operation cannot exceed the combined capacity of its component parts. The instructors, the logistics, and the students might all be top notch, but the training will be less than successful if the program is poorly conceived or carried out haphazardly.

Curriculum Excerpt 1

Task Number: 45
Unit: Firearms

TASK: Apply deadly force in defense of life.
SUPPORTING KNOWLEDGES (SK):

T45.SK1	Know the departmental policy concerning deadly force.
Conditions:	Written exam in classroom.
Standards:	Error free.
T45.SK2	Know the state firearms law concerning deadly force.
Conditions:	Written exam in classroom.
Standards:	Error free.

SUPPORTING SKILLS (SS):

T45.SS1	Fire, load and unload the service revolver.
Conditions:	Firing range; night firing desirable.
Standards:	Score at least 165 of 250 points on the NRA Police Combat Course.
T45.SS2	Handle, clean, transport, transfer and store the service revolver.
Conditions:	Firing range; cleaning equipment.
Standards:	To the satisfaction of the instructor.

Curriculum Excerpt 2

SK Number: T45.SK1
Unit: Firearms

SUPPORTING KNOWLEDGE TO BE TAUGHT:

Know the departmental policy concerning deadly force.

TASK SUPPORTED:

Apply deadly force in defense of life.

TIME ALLOCATIONS:

Pre-class preparation:	20 min.
Classroom discussion:	15 min.
Classroom practical exercise:	15 min.
Post-class/pre-test study:	20 min.

INSTRUCTIONAL METHODS AND MEDIA:

Discussion; written exercise, graded and critiqued.
Viewgraph transparencies; chalkboard.

TESTING MODE:

   Conditions: Written examination using a problem situation; answer
                  sheet.

   Standards: No errors.

INSTRUCTOR:

   Certified; attorney desirable.

LESSON PLAN AND STUDENT HANDOUTS:

   Lesson plan is on file and current.
   Student handouts consist of pre-classroom study assignment sheet; in-class
   problem exercise sheet; summary sheet; post-class and pre-test study.

SEQUENCE:

   This SK is founded on the Constitutional Law unit and the Police Civil Liability
   unit which precede Firearms.

(Note to reader: This hypothetical curriculum excerpt gives details of only one supporting knowledge. Each SK and SS of every task would be described separately.)

The curriculum can be the training supervisor's most valuable
tool for planning, organizing, and controlling. If the tool is ignored
or used without skill or vigor, the training will suffer as a consequence. Sadly, some training supervisors regard a curriculum as something to be merely tolerated, deserving not much more than lip service, and certainly not something meant to be fully implemented.
After all, they will argue, the curriculum was put together by people
who have no real appreciation of the problems that confront trainers.
This line of reasoning may very well come from the same source that
produced the statement, "Forget what you learned in the academy,
kid. Now you're gonna learn how to do it my way."

Where this attitude prevails, the curriculum is likely to find a
permanent place in file thirteen; if followed at all, it is in the general
sense—as a guide, not as a controlling standard. Instead of being
applied as the working instrument it was designed to be, the curriculum collects dust in some dark recess where it can't get in the way of
"business as usual."

If this sounds cynical, it is only to underscore the serious implications present in a situation where control over what is being taught
and learned is lacking. When a training supervisor ignores a curriculum, so will the instructors. It does not take much imagination to
speculate on the variety of civil liability risks that are created when
instructors and their supervisors are allowed to teach according to
their own dictates. The appropriate remedy is for the program director to make clear that curriculum specifications are not negotiable
items and that any curriculum change will be done through an estab-

lished process. Once a course has been approved and is in progress, instructors simply cannot be permitted to modify or disregard specifications.

The program director can monitor training in several ways to ensure that the curriculum is being implemented. The director can—

- ask students in person or by written survey if they personally participated in certain programmed activities. (A sample survey form is shown on the following page.)
- visit classrooms/training areas to verify that students are engaged in activities that support the training objectives.
- read the written examinations and performance test guides to ensure that the objectives are being measured.
- look at test scores, critique sheets and other written materials that reflect the details of daily activities.

Far better to discover training imperfections as they occur than to wait until they produce undesirable consequences on the job. Mistakes noted as they happen are easier to correct and are free of the potential for citizen complaints and redress in the courts.

• Evaluate the Trainees

Students are evaluated in two dimensions, general and specific. Generally, they are appraised in terms of personal appearance, demeanor, attitude, motivation, and similar characteristics. In the specific dimension, students are evaluated in objective terms, that is, by the administration of tests. Our concern in this unit is with evaluation by testing.

Two types of tests are common to criminal justice training programs. Written examinations measure knowledge attainment and performance examinations measure skill development.

Since every task or training objective is either knowledge oriented or skill oriented, determining the appropriate type of test is not a problem. If the task is to "name the elements of proof of burglary," the test is by written examination, and if the task is to "collect fingerprint evidence," the test is by performance or doing.

Written examinations. A written examination may contain one or more classes of questions such as essay, write-in, matching, true/false, and multiple choice. The questions can range from subjective to objective, and operate from the principles of discrimination, recall, and recognition. Subjective questions have a lesser value in entry-level training programs because most knowledge-oriented tasks are either performed correctly or incorrectly, with no tolerance for "in-between" responses. Subjective questions are also difficult to grade and depend on the interpretations and judgments of the grader. By contrast, objective questions do not have these limitations and lend readily to task-centered training. Here are some samples of different types of objective questions.

STUDENT SURVEY NUMBER 2

Dear Student:

You have just completed the second module of the basic law enforcement training course. Please answer the following questions concerning selected elements of the module.

1. In the unit entitled "Vehicle Stops" did you personally
    a. view the film "How to Approach a Stopped Vehicle"?   Yes [ ]   No [ ]
    b. practice approaching a stopped vehicle in a simulated situation?   Yes [ ] No [ ]   How many times? _____
    c. receive the student handout covering how to pull over and approach a stopped vehicle?   Yes [ ] No [ ]

2. In the unit entitled "Arrest Procedures" did you personally
    a. view the slide presentation on how to make a felony arrest?   Yes [ ] No [ ]
    b. practice the approach technique for making an arrest?   Yes [ ] No [ ] How many times? _____
    c. receive a critique sheet that constructively commented on your approach technique?   Yes [ ] No [ ]
    d. practice applying handcuffs in simulated arrest situations?   Yes [ ] No [ ]   How many times? _____
    e. practice making three types of body searches in simulated arrest situations?   Yes [ ] No [ ]

3. In the unit entitled "Police Community Relations" did you personally
    a. perform the written classroom exercise concerning citizen perceptions of police performance?   Yes [ ] No [ ]   Was the exercise graded and returned? Yes [ ] No [ ]
    b. receive the pre-class study assignment collected, graded, and returned to you with comments?   Yes [ ] No [ ]
    c. receive the pre-test study guide?   Yes [ ] No [ ]

4. For each of the 8 units comprising Module II,
    a. were the training objectives explained to you? If no, which unit or units were not explained? _____
    _____
    b. were there any task skills you feel you did not sufficiently learn? If yes, which skills?_____
    _____
    c. were there any task knowledges you feel you did not sufficiently learn? If yes, which knowledges? _____
    _____

On the lines below, write in the four elements of proof for burglary.

1. _____

2. _____

3. _____

4. _____

The left column names three offenses. Below each offense are blank lines. The right column contains terms that relate to elements of proof. Match the terms in the right column with the offenses in the left column.

Burglary   a. Unlawful taking.

——   b. With intent to commit a felony or larceny
——   therein.
——   c. From the possession of another.

Larceny   d. Unlawful intentional inflicting.

——   e. With intent to permanently deprive.

——   f. Unlawful entry.

Assault   g. To a fixed structure.

——   h. Upon the person of another.
——
                    i. With or without force.

All the following are terms that relate to the elements of proof for the offense of burglary EXCEPT:

    a. Unlawful entry.
    b. Of a fixed structure.
    c. In the nighttime.
    d. With or without force.
    e. With intent to commit a felony therein.

In testing for an important knowledge, more than one question needs to be asked—not just to convey importance to the student, but also to obtain assurance that the student really possesses the knowledge and did not guess the answer.

Everything that is taught should be tested. Testing some tasks and forgetting about others is not an acceptable practice. Neither is testing extraneous information or information not included in the curriculum. Testing fully only what has been taught is a direct, no-frills, no-nonsense approach.

In many training operations, the types of questions appearing on a written examination are determined by the grading technique. Administrative expediency may count for more than the discriminating power of question style. If a school or academy has a machine that automatically grades tests using answer sheets corresponding to multiple-choice questions, tests will probably be constructed of multiple-choice questions. This is not necessarily bad, but it does require the test writers to work harder in developing questions that are not repetitive but are still within the style dictated by the grading technique.

To assure that written examinations are varied but still directly address curriculum requirements, some instructors prepare a master question bank. An MQB consists of a large number of questions, all written in the same style, for a single course. A supporting knowledge for each task taught in the course will have about 5 to 20 questions in the bank. The questions are coded to the tasks. When a written examination comes due during a course, questions are drawn from the MQB.

For tasks tested by written questions, the conditions are limited to the circumstances of the test itself, and the standards are accuracy and time, or accuracy alone. A student performance objective (SPO) might look like this:

Conditions: Given a written examination, the student will

Action: Name the four elements of proof for the offense of burglary

Standards: With 85 percent accuracy.

Performance examinations. The testing concept is the same for the skill-oriented task, but the conditions and standards are more detailed. Here is an example:

Conditions: Given a set of handcuffs with a key and a fellow student to role-play as an arrested felon, the student will

Action: Apply handcuffs

Standards: In accordance with procedures contained in Departmental SOP 12, ensuring that cuffs are double-locked and that palms face outward, in 90 seconds.

An SPO for a skill-oriented task is especially demanding of an instructor's time, energy, and resourcefulness. The instructor has to find a testing location and furnish it with the required equipment, recruit assistants, organize the students and get them to the testing location, and conduct the tests.

Instances of instructors allowing some students to pass without being tested or without achieving the minimum competency levels, if they happen at all, are most likely to happen in the performance examinations. The program director needs to be aware of this possibility and take preventive steps, such as ensuring that—

- sufficient time is made available for testing so that an instructor won't be rushed to finish.
- sufficient practice has preceded the testing so that students will have little difficulty adjusting to the testing mode and showcasing their skills for evaluation.
- the primary instructor has plenty of help (from other instructors and perhaps the students themselves) in setting up, conducting, and evaluating.
- slower learners receive special attention prior to and during the testing.

Establishing a spread among learners or comparing learners against each other should not concern the instructor. The idea is to find out if the student has reached an acceptable level of competence. It is strictly a pass/fail situation. It is therefore pointless, and misleading to the student, for a grade to be assigned to a task. Why even try to compute a task grade or even a composite grade when the only measurement that counts is whether or not the student satisfactorily performed the task?

●Maintain Training Records

Because documentation can serve as a strong defense to a charge of negligent training, keeping records of every aspect of a student's progress from start to finish makes very good sense. At the front end are documents which reflect the qualifications that a student brings to the course. Licenses, entrance examination scores, aptitude and psychological test scores, high school and college transcripts, and certificates of prior training are examples. These items are indicators of the student's entering abilities and predictors of his or her course performance.

If a course applicant does not meet prerequisites but is nonetheless allowed to enter, a record should be made of who granted the waiver and why. This should serve as a red flag, not to stigmatize the student but to alert the staff to a need for special teaching attention. And whatever extra efforts are expended by the staff and the student to overcome the deficiency should be made a matter of record.

Organizing the documents. Documents associated with course administration run the gamut from the opening day schedule to the graduation agenda. Within this large collection of written materials are two broad classes: documents that relate to training activities generally and documents that relate to students individually. One way to organize what can surely be a very large mass of paperwork is to place the general documents in a single, large file and the student documents in separate dossiers.

The general file is for documents from one single course offering, not all offerings of the same course. The general file can be broken down into subcategories such as correspondence and memoranda, course announcement and schedule, curriculum or program of instruction, lesson plans, student handouts, class roster, attendance sheets, etc. Related to the file, but maintained apart from it for security reasons, are the written examinations.

Lesson plans and handouts are excellent documents for refuting negligent training claims. They reflect what the instructors taught and what the students were expected to learn. For example, a lesson plan on self-defense tactics would require an instructor to emphasize the risk of injury to a person being restrained by a choke hold. The student handout would reinforce that important teaching point. The lesson plan and handout would directly rebut a claim of improper training of the choke hold. One note of advice: put preparation/revision dates on lesson plans and handouts.

The attendance sheets can also be important. If the officer in the example just given falsely represents that he was not in class on the day the lesson was taught and the handout distributed, thereby imputing negligence to the training agency, the attendance sheets provide an opportunity for refutation.

A student's dossier contains items that reflect entry into the course, participation in it, and departure from it. There might be evidence of registration, tuition fees paid, issuance of supplies, disciplining, counseling, academic problems, absences, make-up and remedial training/re-testing, special honors earned, and test results.

From the standpoint of potential civil liability, test results are extremely significant because they substantiate that important, job-related tasks were learned by the trainee. It also helps when the test results are recorded in a format that describes the tasks tested, the names of the evaluator and approving official, whether re-teaching and re-testing were needed, and the initials or signature of the trainee in acknowledgement of the record's entries. The Task Performance Checklist on page 208 presents a format suitable for these purposes.

●Establish Instructor Standards

Instructional staff is unquestionably the backbone of the training organization. It will not matter if students are bright and eager, facilities first-rate, and the administration efficient. All these elements are important, but the controlling element will certainly be the competency of instructors.

In states where mandated training programs are well established, a strong movement toward the adoption of instructor standards is under way. A certification process will accompany enforcement in

TASK PERFORMANCE CHECKLIST

NAME	DEPARTMENT	EVALUATION DATE	EVALUATION ☐ SATFY ☐ UNSATFY	TRAINEES INITIALS
COURSE TITLE	EVALUATOR		APPROVING OFFICIAL	

SCORING INSTRUCTIONS

Indicate task performance by (✓) in "YES" or "NO" column. Explain all "NO" ratings in REMARKS column and schedule Review Training, followed by re-evaluation. Individuals must successfully complete ALL items.

SUBJECT OR UNIT TITLE   APPLICABLE SS AND SK CODE NUMBERS

STUDENT PERFORMANCE OBJECTIVES	YES	NO	REMARKS	DATE OF RE-EVALUATION	YES	NO	REMARKS

almost every case. Instructor certification may specify minimums that relate to—

- education and training accomplishments,
- field experience in the subject area to be taught,
- familiarity with and acceptance of course curriculum, specifications relating to the subject to be taught, and
- successful completion of an approved instructor training course.

An instructor's competency can be judged in two areas: knowledge of subject and ability to teach. If either area is deficient, the instructor's performance will be correspondingly deficient.

Each of us at one time or another has been the victim of the knowledgeable instructor who, despite good intentions and best effort, was just not able to get his message across. By contrast, the instructor who is weak in the subject area but strong as a teacher is apt to be less noticeable. Through superior communications, a small amount of information can be stretched a long way.

The exceptional instructor will be solidly proficient in both subject matter knowledge and teaching abilities. The average instructor will have a combination of strengths and weaknesses in each area, and the below-average instructor will be significantly weak in at least one area. If circumstances require the selection of a below-average instructor, a training director would want to avoid selecting the instructor who is weak in topic knowledge, a problem that cannot be corrected easily or quickly. An instructor who lacks a solid command of his or her subject needs to return to the field and gain more knowledge through job experience and self-development.

The instructor who knows the topic to be taught but cannot teach very well can improve with much less difficulty and in a reasonable period of time. A certain amount of improvement will inevitably result from the teaching experience itself and from the process of instructors interacting and learning from one another. But surely the most dramatic improvement can result from attendance at an instructor training course.

A training course for criminal justice instructors is typically one or two weeks long and covers topics such as learning theory, instructional strategies and methods, learning aids, lesson plan writing, and development of practical exercises. The one-week course has only enough time to explain basic teaching concepts; the two-week course will additionally allow the attendee to make one or more graded presentations using lesson plan materials, learning aids, and handouts developed while in the course.

Where instructor training is required as a condition of certification, the certifying agency will most likely conduct or make available a range of approved courses. In addition to a course that prepares an instructor to teach generally, specialized instructor training courses in firearms, pursuit driving, and self-defense may be provided.

The certifying agency might require periodic re-certification and publish a directory of certified instructors. Training administrators who offer courses that fall within the oversight responsibility of the certifying agency could use the directory as an information source in acquiring the services of guest instructors.

A major assumption in this discussion of standards for instructors is the existence of laws or rules that prescribe minimum qualifying criteria. The absence of formal requirements should not be seen as a rationale for not upgrading instructors, and under no circumstances should it be seen as a legal defense to complaints of incompetent instruction. Even where minimum standards prevail, a very persuasive argument can be made that such standards are, after all, only minimums, and that taxpayers have a right to expect more.

Nothing prevents a training administrator from establishing instructor standards where none exist or in setting higher standards where minimums are demanded. An administrator who is satisfied with having no instructor standards or chooses to operate with minimums has his sights set downward and will achieve mediocrity at best.

CONCLUSION

This chapter illustrates the need to reduce risks associated with inadequate and poorly managed training programs. A question to be asked by training administrators is not whether they can afford to have quality programs but whether they can afford not to have them. As each new action is brought in civil court, the stakes grow higher.

We have looked at four broad areas where improvements can be made to reduce the exposure to liability. We examined training validation as a process of ensuring that what is being taught is relevant to actual needs in the working environment, and we looked at the curriculum as an organizing and controlling instrument of management. The values of quality control and documentation were discussed in relation to trainee evaluations and accurate record keeping. Finally, we looked at instructor standards as a means for improving the quality of training operations.

NOTES
1. Loyd Reece Trimmer, *Fundamentals of Professional Liability for Law Enforcement Trainers* (Salemburg, N.C.: Department of Justice, State of North Carolina, 1984), p. 2.

PART II

THE INSTRUCTOR

IN VARIED ROLES

11

THE INSTRUCTOR AS COMMUNICATOR

How Does Communication Happen? • Preparing the Topic • Improving Delivery • Conclusion

How well an instructor conveys ideas to his students depends to a great extent on the process through which humans communicate. Because human communication consumes such a large chunk of everyday life, we tend to take it for granted. We assume that what we say is picked up exactly as we mean it, and that what we understand is exactly what is said to us. Talking and listening are activities so common and ordinary that we don't think of them as being complex and uncertain. Our everyday experiences prove to us that human communication is imperfect, yet we seldom stop to consider what causes the frequent breakdowns in the transfer of information among people.

It is appropriate now—now that we are entering a discussion of speaking techniques—to first examine the basic elements that make up the communicative process. [1]

HOW DOES COMMUNICATION HAPPEN?

Communication occurs when one person transmits ideas or feelings to another person or to a group of persons. The effectiveness of the communication is measured by the closeness or similarity between the idea that was transmitted and the idea that was actually received.

The process of communication consists of three elements: the source, the symbols, and the receiver. The source can be thought of as a sender, a speaker, a writer, an instructor, or a transmitter. The symbol elements in the communication process are the words, signs, or other language that contain the message transmitted from the source to the receiver. The receiver is the listener, reader, student, or audience. The three elements of the communicative process are dynamically interrelated; that is to say, each element influences the other and is in turn influenced itself. For example, if a listener (receiver) has difficulty in understanding the message (symbols) of an instructor (sender), the listener is likely to indicate his confusion, thus causing the instructor to become uncertain and lose control of his ideas. The result is that communication effectiveness is reduced. On the other hand, when a listener reacts favorably, the instructor is encouraged and the flow of ideas is facilitated. As the example indicates, the relationship between the communicative elements is reciprocal.

●Source (Instructor)

The effectiveness of an instructor (source) to communicate is conditioned by at least three factors. First, his personal language abilities will influence the selection of words or phrases (symbols) that are meaningful to students (receivers). Second, he will reveal, consciously or subconsciously, certain personal attitudes that reflect upon the ideas being transmitted and the persons receiving those ideas. If the ideas are to be communicated effectively, these personal attitudes must be positive. He must be confident and must demonstrate a belief that the ideas are important to his listeners. The third factor that conditions successful communication is the quality of the message. To be a successful communicator, the instructor needs to teach from a broad background of accurate, current, and stimulating material.

●Symbols (Language)

At its most fundamental level, communication is established through the use of simple oral and visual codes. The letters of the alphabet constitute a simple code. Body movements, hand gestures, and facial expressions are a type of code. Words, made up of letters from the alphabet, are used in combinations to form a language, which is a code. Codes are seldom used alone. Ideas are communicated best when codes are combined in patterns. Ideas must be prepared carefully if they are to reach the receiver in a form that is understandable. Ideas must be analyzed to determine which are most suited to starting and concluding the communication and which should be used to clarify, define, limit, amplify, or explain. The successful transfer of information from source to receiver is dependent upon the codes or symbols that comprise the message.

The nature of language and the variety of ways in which language is used naturally lead to misunderstandings. These misunderstandings arise primarily from (1) a lack of common core of experience; (2) a confusion between the symbol and the idea symbolized; and (3) the unnecessary use of abstractions.

Common core of experience. Probably the greatest single barrier to communication is the absence of a common core of experience between the source (instructor) and the receiver (students). Communication is effective only to the extent that the experiences of the communicator and the receptor are similar.

Many people think that words convey meanings from speaker to listener in the same way that a truck carries vegetables from a farm to the marketplace. Unfortunately this is not true because words never carry exactly the same meaning from the mind of the speaker to that of the listener. In fact, words fail to transfer meaning at all. Words are simply stimuli that the communicator sends out to arouse a response of some type on the part of the receptor. The nature of the receptor's response is a function of the receptor's past experiences with the words and the things or concepts to which they refer. These past experiences on the part of the receptor give meaning, not in the words themselves, but in the mind of the receptor. Without a common core of experience there can be no effective communication between the source and the receiver.

Confusing symbols and things symbolized. Language has a function similar to that of a map. As a map represents some specific territory, language corresponds to certain objects or concepts that it represents. A map that contains errors in measurement is like a statement that contains inaccurate facts. When humans, the users of words, fail to make accurate descriptions, the result is confusion between the symbols and the thing symbolized.

Unnecessary use of abstractions. Words can be thought of as either concrete or abstract. A concrete word refers to an object that a human being can experience directly. Abstract words represent ideas that cannot be directly experienced. For example, suppose that you have a Ford automobile you have named "Sweet Sally." To you and to people who have seen your automobile, "Sweet Sally" is concrete because the name represents a reality that can be touched and seen. If, however, you refer to the automobile as a Ford, your listener cannot form a mental image that is concrete because there are many Ford automobiles. At an even higher level of abstraction, you could refer to your automobile as a motor vehicle. The phrase "motor vehicle" is so abstract that your listeners are likely to form a mental image that does not resemble "Sweet Sally" in any meaningful way.

This is not to say that abstract words are undesirable. Their purpose is not to bring forth specific items of experience in the mind of the receiver, but to serve as symbols that describe wide areas of experience. If an instructor were forced to use only concrete words, he would soon find himself constrained by details. Abstractions are therefore convenient and useful, but they can lead to misunderstanding. Abstractions may not evoke in the student's mind the specific objects of experience that the instructor intends.

● **The Receiver (Student)**

Communication succeeds relative to the reaction of the receiver. When the receiver reacts with understanding or, better still, changes his behavior according to the message transmitted, then it can be said that effective communication has occurred.

Readiness. The likelihood that a message will be received depends upon the readiness of the receiver to accept the message. The receiver may not be prepared to listen; he may not be capable of comprehending the message; or he may exercise his intellectual right to question the validity of the message. When the listener's attention is obtained, the first impediment is eliminated. And if symbols are selected that have meaning to the student, the second impediment is eliminated. The third impediment can be made to work to the instructor's advantage. The student who questions the validity of an idea is a student who is ready for a healthy teaching-learning dialogue. An instructor can capitalize on the student's desire to question an idea by providing a classroom atmosphere which encourages questioning.

Attitudes. The major barriers to successful communication are most often found in the area of student attitude. A receiver's attitude may be one of resistance, of willingness, or of passivity. To discover the nature of the receptor's attitude, it is necessary to obtain some reaction reflective of his or her attitude. The more the communicative approach is varied, the greater the chance of promoting a reaction. An obligation exists for an instructor to assess student attitudes and to use the assessment as a basic guide for the selection and transmittal of ideas.

PREPARING THE TOPIC

Many an experienced instructor will equate teaching effectiveness with mastery of the topic, and will also observe that most students in a training program are there to learn, so they are as interested in the topic as is the instructor.

●Sources of Information

Gathering materials on the subject to be taught is the starting point for topic preparation. The sources for topic material include authoritative written references, ideas obtained from other knowledgeable persons, and personal experience. An instructor concerned with making a good presentation will probably draw his topic material from all of these sources.

The instructor might begin by assembling all the personal knowledge he has concerning the topic.[2] By writing this down on paper, the instructor has made a preliminary organization of material. This tentative grouping of ideas will help to reveal the major gaps that exist in the body of knowledge that needs to be gathered. Through this process the instructor becomes aware of areas within the topic that require further research and collection of reference materials.

A next move in collecting pertinent information might be to draw on the experiences of others. A fruitful source is the subject matter specialist or expert who can provide new facts and first-hand testimony. Information obtained from knowledgeable persons will help to clarify concepts and lead toward the exploration of new sources of materials.

The most abundant source is the modern library. Books, magazines, periodicals, journals, abstracts, microfilm and similar references can potentially provide a large quantity of information. It should be remembered, however, that the quality of information obtained is more important than the quantity. Primary concerns are accuracy and relevancy of the material. Once information has been assembled, the next step is to evaluate it. Some ideas will need to be combined, while others can be eliminated. Ideas that are developed on the basis of personal experience or from information obtained from other persons can be combined with ideas contained in written references. Writing, editing, and rewriting will begin to shape various ideas into a logical pattern. (See Chapter 15, "The Instructor as Writer.")

A rule worth following is to avoid making excuses for a presentation. Never make a comment that can be interpreted as an excuse for lack of preparation, lack of instructor knowledge, or an inability to teach under adverse conditions.[3] An excuse only underscores a weakness and emphasizes to students a problem that may be minor, or might not exist at all except in the mind of the instructor. When an instructor reflects an apologetic attitude, student confidence in the training program will be undermined. Thorough topic preparation is a dependable safeguard against a poor teaching performance.

●The Lesson Plan

Topic preparation cannot be considered complete until the pattern of ideas has been placed into writing. A lesson plan is the usual format for recording information that is intended to be taught. A well-constructed lesson plan helps to assure a good speaking presentation. By providing a structural form for the delivery of ideas, the lesson plan also helps the instructor evaluate his material. He can be assured of the answers to basic questions: Is the overall thinking clear? Is each idea or teaching point treated according to its importance in the general scheme of the topic? Is there a natural flow of ideas? Are ideas arranged in an intelligent sequence? Do the teaching points directly support training objectives that are established for the topic? Can the ideas be presented within time limits established for teaching of the topic? Such questions when answered in the affirmative give assurance that the topic has been adequately prepared. (See Chapter 6, "Writing a Lesson Plan.")

IMPROVING DELIVERY

How well a speaker succeeds depends to a very large extent on the fashion in which he presents his material. In much the same way an artist uses his paints and canvas, the instructor uses the tools at his disposal to get his ideas into the minds of students. A lively presentation is hard to resist.

The dynamic and genuinely enthusiastic instructor can bring life into the dullest subject matter. He has such an interesting manner of delivery that his teaching is infectious and not easily resisted. He has discovered the joy of teaching and transmits that pleasure to his audience.

People can be talked with or they can be talked at.[4] Good delivery is talking with people and poor delivery is talking at people. Successful communication is dependent upon good delivery. When people are talked at they can be as unresponsive as inanimate items. An instructor can talk at an empty chair, but the chair can't respond. A lifeless object has no way of showing interest or returning communication. For effective communication to take place there needs to be an interaction between the transmitter and the receiver. An instructor may know his topic thoroughly and may have prepared an outstanding lesson plan, but unless he has developed good speaking habits the quality of his instruction will likely suffer.

●Directness

Both the instructor and the student should feel that they are in touch with each other. The instructor should work hard to achieve the direct type of communication that is typically found in the friendly conversation between two persons. Each person in a conversation listens with concentration to the other, and both are sensitive to feedback that is stimulated by their expressed ideas. If one person in the conversation does not understand something, the other is usually quick to explain it. Speaking to a group of students is merely an enlarged conversation—with frowns, smiles, affirmative or negative head movements, impassiveness, and other feedback signals. The instructor interprets this feedback and modifies his delivery accordingly.

In a sense, directness in delivery means using a style of straightforward talking that features such pronouns as "we" and "you." Looking directly at individuals and addressing them by name is a form of intimate classroom dialogue that promotes sensitive communication.

Directness also means being alert to student reactions. Facial expressions, laughter, applause, changes in posture, and other observable signs indicate successful communication. By watching individuals the instructor can detect doubt, interest, agreement, misunderstanding, enjoyment, and other observable reactions. He can then adjust his delivery accordingly.

When sensitive to student reactions, the instructor will find it easier to convey a feeling that he is talking to each student individually. Sincerity and conviction are subtle qualities that are expressed in simple ways. Eye contact is one of those ways. The effective speaker maintains eye contact with students just as if he were engaged in conversation with friends. Catching and holding eye contact with individual students—not skipping superficially from face to face—will create a feeling of personal contact. The accomplished speaker avoids looking down at the floor, up at the ceiling, or out the window because he knows these actions interrupt the communication flow.

●Appearance and Body Language

Students react to what they see. Personal appearance strongly influences the acceptability of an instructor. The average student expects an instructor to be above reproach in personal appearance and is disappointed when such is not the case.

The instructor needs to see and be seen by all students. He takes a position from which the full class can observe him and from which he can see all of the class. He adopts an attitude of physical and mental readiness, but does not stand rigidly. He stands erect, with weight evenly balanced on both feet, and hands and arms freely suspended.

Motion attracts attention and the skilled instructor will use this fact to full advantage. Physical vitality is movement with a purpose.[5] Aimless, random movement has little or no purpose in instruction.

Movements of the hands and arms can serve to clarify and emphasize spoken language. Because they convey ideas or emotions, gestures ought to be employed as teaching tools. The body should move naturally and spontaneously during instruction. Some persons are unable to adequately express themselves without extensive use of gestures. On the other hand, some persons find gestures to be a problem.

The beginning instructor will feel that his hands are awkward and useless. An easy way to overcome that feeling is to simply let the hands hang loosely.[6] Without trying to appear nonchalant or disinterested, it might help to temporarily rest one or both hands on the speaker's stand. Wringing and twisting of the hands is an outward signal of inner tension. Such signs can cause students to become tense, thus diverting them from learning.

Although specific gestures can be used to emphasize certain ideas, artificial or contrived gestures are easily detected. Gestures that are clearly uncharacteristic of an instructor's personality should be avoided. The effective gesture will arise from genuine enthusiasm. It is not desirable to underline every statement with a gesture—this would defeat the overall purpose of using body movements to amplify important teaching points.

There is a natural tendency for students to focus upon an instructor's mannerisms rather than the ideas he presents. Many an instructor is not aware of a peculiar mannerism he displays. Every instructor needs to frequently examine and constructively criticize his teaching style so that negative mannerisms can be identified and eliminated.[7]

A basic rule to follow with regard to posture and body movement is moderation. An instructor should not remain glued to one spot with hands out of sight. Conversely, continual movement without purpose is distracting. As an instructor's skill and experience increase, his movements become less obvious, more natural, and supportive of learning activities.

●Controlling Nervousness

Nearly every instructor will experience nervousness to some degree during his initial appearance before a class. Nervousness is a normal condition which simply indicates that the instructor is concerned, and properly so, about student reaction to his instruction. An instructor who is completely without nervousness is likely to be an uncaring or unimaginative individual who is willing to settle for a mediocre performance. Natural nervousness can result in a more enthusiastic and expressive delivery. A good instructor can usually develop a particular method for getting his "butterflies" in formation. Under control, nervousness will work for the speaker instead of against him.

To achieve control over nervousness, it helps to understand it. Unpleasant mental and physical reactions usually result from a natural fear of student reaction.

Because there is little that can be done to prevent nervousness, a good procedure is to simply make the best of it by trying to put it to work. Most people find that speaking louder, using greater lung strength, and moving with deliberate bodily gestures will expend nervous energy in useful ways. Increases in heart rate, blood pressure, and breathing are physical reactions that can be controlled with a little concentration. A mixture of concentration, practice, and experience will help the instructor to quickly pass the early onset of stage fright that is so commonly associated with the introductory phase of instruction.

●Speech Technique

There is nothing mysterious about developing an efficient speaking manner. Any person, provided he has no serious speech impediment, can easily and significantly improve upon his natural ability to communicate orally. The prerequisites are a determination to learn the basics of good speech and to practice, practice, practice.

Voice. Humans have developed a highly sophisticated system of vocal sounds to convey ideas. The quality of vocal sounds will either attract, repel, or leave the listener indifferent. The best teaching tool in the personal inventory of an instructor is his voice. The most direct means of communication between the instructor and his student is voice contact. Most persons have speaking voices adequate for instruction. Even a below-average speaking voice can be developed if a few basic fundamentals are learned.

Variety in voice is an important key to good speech delivery. The instructor may vary his pitch, speech rate, and loudness, but these variations must remain in harmony with the meaning and emphasis of the subject matter. Changes in pitch up from the instructor's natural pitch level may suggest anger, excitement, or uncertainty. At lower ranges, the pitch level will suggest confidence, assurance, and relaxation. A slower speaking rate may be used to clarify or add importance to words or phrases. Raising or lowering the loudness of the voice will add emphasis and convey emotion. The voice of an instructor can reveal his emotional and physical state. An audience can detect when the instructor is nervous, angry, happy, or fatigued.

Voice *quality* is a characteristic which distinguishes one voice from another. Some voices have agreeable qualities while others do not. The average individual has a voice that can be made pleasing to the ear. Those few individuals not blessed with pleasant voices can usually overcome such common voice deficiencies as nasality, hollowness, or monotone. By experimenting with changes in pitch, loudness, rate of speech, inflection, and breathing rhythm, a person is capable of at least reducing unpleasant voice qualities.

The *pitch* of the voice should be natural. Voice pitch in a classroom should be equivalent to that which the instructor uses in normal conversation. The instructor should determine the pitch level at which he is able to speak with greatest clarity and then learn to vary this pitch to produce emphasis where needed. Inflection, or variation of pitch, adds a subtly expressive dimension to the voice. It combats monotony and adds interest to the delivery.

The loudness or *volume* of the voice should be sufficient for all students to hear without difficulty. Inadequate volume will practically guarantee a decline in student attentiveness. At the other extreme, excessive loudness can cause a student to tune the instructor out, if only in self-defense. The size of the class and the conditions under which instruction is presented will determine what volume level is needed. Voice volume is especially important outdoors or in areas with poor acoustics. By watching student reactions, an instructor is able to tell how well the students can hear him.

If class size, acoustics, or other factors require a constantly strong level of voice volume, it will not be long before the instructor is physically exhausted. A speaking session that places a strain on the voice should be kept as short as possible. Apart from the consideration of fatigue, an unnaturally strong voice volume does not permit the voice to accentuate words for emphasis.

The *rate of speed* used in speaking should be governed by the information being delivered. Simple concepts can sometimes be covered quickly (but never superficially). Complicated information should be articulated slowly and deliberately. Also associated with speaking speed is the collective listening capacity of the class. Speech rate is dependent upon the speed at which the listeners can assimilate information. An instructor has to be sensitive to the complexity of ideas and to the ability of students to grasp them.

Expressiveness and pleasing variation can be obtained by *changes in pace*. Quickening and reducing the speech rate, as well as an occasional pause, will lend variety. Practice with the use of audio record and playback will help an instructor check his speech rate. Between 120 and 150 words a minute is a normal rate of speed. If the rate exceeds 160 words a minute, the below-average listener will have difficulty keeping pace. If the rate is less than 90 words per minute, the above-average listener will probably lose interest. Too fast a delivery tends to confuse; a slow delivery tends to irritate.

Use of words. Because language is the primary medium through which most learning takes place, the instructor must acquire a healthy regard for words.

Verbal communication requires application of words that have precise shades of meaning. Words must be carefully chosen, and sentences must be constructed clearly and logically. The right words at the right place keynote effective speech as well as effective writing.

Using words that are common to the vocabulary of the students is helpful in making ideas clear. The purpose of teaching, after all, is to clarify, not confuse. If complex terms cannot be avoided, the instructor should use them, but he should define each new term the first time it is used.

Careful selection of words means that words must be grouped in proper arrangement so that ideas are expressed clearly and accurately. This does not mean that long and complicated sentences are necessary. Short sentences help to isolate key teaching points so that student understanding and attention are enhanced. Non-essential words and phrases should be eliminated, and sentences should be free of unnecessary and trite expressions.

Concepts that are expressed badly indicate faulty or weak thinking on the part of the instructor. The experienced instructor thinks about what he is saying and what must be said next. He creates connective word groupings that help different ideas flow together into a cohesive whole. If the instructor has difficulty in finding the right words to express teaching points, he should try writing the key points of the lesson in short, complete sentences. Although this technique is helpful in preparation, reading to the class from a script is artificial and cumbersome. An outline, rather than a written script, is more suitable for use in the classroom.

Pauses between sentences and between important words in sentences provide the punctuation of verbal communication. A pause will permit an idea to be more thoroughly digested before the mind is required to move on to the next idea, and it will permit the instructor to formulate his next idea. A pause will give added meaning and interpretation to an idea, but it must be clear and decisive. The pause that results from uncertainty is easily detected. When a pause is intentionally employed as an enhancing technique, it is immediately understood.

Diction. Distinct pronunciation and enunciation are characteristics of the skilled instructor. Pronouncing each syllable distinctly helps students understand more readily. When instructing a large group it may be necessary to enunciate in a moderately exaggerated fashion. This helps to minimize learning problems that result when students cannot hear what is said.

Even though good speaking requires good diction, the use of an occasional colloquialism is acceptable. This depends on the student audience. When it is apparent that the students feel more comfortable in using colloquialisms themselves, it might be a mistake for the instructor to insist on using the "King's English."

When introducing students to a new or unfamiliar word, the instructor should be particularly careful to enunciate clearly and deliberately. Slurring, swallowing, and mumbling words are speaking problems that can be eliminated with a little personal effort. Achieving clarity of expression does not necessarily require a major change in a person's speaking style. Just three simple things are necessary: practice, practice, and more practice.

Practice. To develop a good speech technique the instructor should first assess his own speaking weaknesses. This is best achieved by a careful examination of his present ability to speak in a teaching situation. Tape recordings, both audio and video, as well as critiques by fellow instructors, help in making an objective identification of speaking liabilities.

An understanding of why other persons are either good or poor speakers is a prerequisite to self-analysis. When listening to a good speaker, it is useful to analyze the methods being employed. In this way an instructor can become alert to desirable speech qualities and can establish goals with regard to personal speaking abilities. Since the development of a speaking technique is essentially an imitative process, it is important that the instructor watch good speakers perform and experiment with their methods. It would be imprudent, however, to try all methods successfully employed by other speakers. Differences in personality and style do not make it possible for every method to transfer from one speaker to another.

Finally, the instructor is well advised to adopt a program for self-improvement and follow it. Opportunities to speak any place at any time should be seized. Chances to talk in front of people should be accepted as challenges for improvement. By practicing at home and by applying good speaking methods when interacting with people in the general social context, the instructor becomes increasingly proficient in speaking skills.

CONCLUSION

Instruction involves more than making a speech or talking to students. The real proof of successful speaking is the successful transfer of information. Merely saying the words does not guarantee transfer. Simply sending information is insufficient. The instructor with a message to deliver must have an audience that is receptive. And, since receptivity is not a built-in audience characteristic, the instructor must find ways to create listener receptivity.

NOTES

1. There are several theories of communication. The elements of the theory broadly described in this chapter are described in greater detail in Chapter 5, *Principles and Techniques of Instruction* (Washington, D.C.: Department of the Air Force, 1974).
2. Thomas F. Staton, *How to Instruct Successfully* (New York: McGraw-Hill Book Co., 1960), p. 69.
3. *Techniques of Military Instruction* (Washington, D.C.: Department of the Army, 1967), p. 31.
4. *Instructor Training* (Atlanta: Georgia State Merit System of Personnel Administration), p. 4-1.
5. Dugan Laird, *Approaches to Training and Development* (Reading, Mass.: Addison-Wesley Publishing Co., 1978), p. 170.
6. *How to Prepare and Conduct Military Training* (Washington, D.C.: Department of the Army, 1975), p. 102.
7. Allen Z. Gammage, *Police Training in the United States* (Springfield, Ill.: Charles C. Thomas, 1963), p. 216.

12

THE INSTRUCTOR AS LEADER

Leadership Styles • An Approach to Leadership Problems • Charisma: Pros and Cons

A good leader gets the best from his subordinates. He guides, directs, and points the way. It is the instructor, more than any other person, who ensures that the learning goals of the organization are achieved.

Delegation of authority is an essential characteristic of any organization that attempts to direct human activities. Within an organization, instructors are delegated authority by their superiors. For delegation of authority to work, the instructor's authority must be accepted by the students.

If the instructor is to lead, he must be able to demonstrate that the training institution's goals coincide with those of the students. Pampering students will not achieve this, nor will threatening them. The instructor must follow a middle approach that provides positive and decisive direction. If the instructor fails to establish himself as leader, others within the student group or from outside the group will step in and assume the leadership position.

LEADERSHIP STYLES

It is difficult to isolate any single set of qualities that guarantee good leadership. Much research evidence suggests that the qualities of successful leaders are not universal. Instead, they tend to be specific to a situation. The demands of one type of situation will more readily be met by one style of leadership than another. For example, the type of leadership necessary to bring about change and initiate action in a dynamic organization differs from the type of leadership needed to maintain order in a conservative organization. Although research on leadership has not produced a universally accepted list of leadership attributes, most reports include such descriptive terms as moral courage, mature judgment, objectivity, initiative, understanding, emotional stability, problem-solving ability, integrity, intelligence, ability to communicate, and drive. The safest conclusion that can be drawn from extensive research findings is that the concept of leadership is extremely complex.

Leadership styles can range from an approach that uses little control over subordinates to one that utilizes absolute control. The choice of an approach generally reflects the demands of the situation and the personality of the leader. The instructor considers the self-discipline of his students, their degree of understanding, their acceptance of learning obligations, their individual and collective motivation, and the overall goals established by the training organization. He uses these observations to help him select the approach he will use in leading his students. His own background and temperament are also important factors in the selection of a suitable approach.

Leadership approaches are of three types. A leader will tend to combine characteristics of all three leadership styles.

●Democratic

The essential feature of democratic leadership is its orientation toward those led, particularly the group.[1] The democratic instructor acts as a guide, attempting to merge student desires with organizational requirements. Students participate in the arbitration of differences between student desires and organizational demands. Although students may find their participation satisfying, they are sometimes frustrated by the length of time needed to reach collective decisions. Internal conflict may occur within the student group when differing viewpoints cannot be reconciled.

●Authoritarian

The authoritarian style of leadership in the sense used here relates primarily to decisionmaking power being vested in one individual. The authoritarian pattern is clearly one of directing people to do things, rather than soliciting their input. Decisions made by the authoritarian leader do not reflect the compromise found under the democratic style. A chief advantage of the authoritarian style is the speed with which decisions are made. This is particularly helpful at times when delay can damage training.

An authoritarian leader is not a dictator. The nature of the training environment provides cultural, social, and legal strictures which prevent the use of dictatorial leadership.

●Integrated

Integrated leadership is a combination of the democratic and authoritarian styles. It is perhaps the most difficult to accomplish. The instructor stays in touch with the overall temper and mood of the student group, making the students feel that their own wishes are a part of the motivating force, even when they are in fact being led.

The instructor creates or modifies learning activities to correspond with student desires, but always with the established training goals remaining uncompromised. When successful, the integrated approach provides strong support to the instructor, and the training goals are easily met or exceeded. A difficulty with this approach lies in the time required to build a team concept and mold the group into a single functioning unit.

AN APPROACH TO LEADERSHIP PROBLEMS

No single approach to leadership can be recommended as superior. All three approaches can be used successfully, depending on the situation. However, an instructor should not try to affect a style unsuitable to his personality.

When a training course is relatively short, the authoritarian type of leadership might be more productive because of the limited time period. A tight schedule does not permit participative decisionmaking. When training extends over a longer period of time, however, the democratic style of leadership may be the better option. Quality of training tends to improve, often substantially, when students are allowed to participate in decisions that affect the training process.

A first consideration for the instructor is not whether he has an influence upon his student, but the nature of the influence. How an instructor exerts his influence over students will determine the results achieved. The organization of a classroom is built from the top down. Leadership starts with the thinking and behavior of the instructor and is translated into a variety of actions by the student group. If the ideas of the instructor are not correct, the thinking and actions of the student group are likely to be incorrect.

It would be marvelous to have a set of rules for an instructor to follow whenever he is faced with a leadership problem. But no two problems can be solved by precisely the same method. The constantly shifting nature of leadership and the infinite combination of methods or approaches in dealing with problems rule out the probability that a single set of problem-solving rules will ever be developed.

Although there seems to be no surefire method for handling all manner of leadership problems, one factor does stand out above others. That factor is flexibility. To exercise effective leadership, the instructor must discard any notion that every situation can be solved by a predetermined method. He must be willing and able to adapt and modify leadership actions in relation to changing circumstances. Flexibility in this sense requires an accurate perception of a situation and a decisive implementation of actions based on a prediction of consequences. To perform in accordance with this concept, the instructor must have two general skills: diagnostic skills and action skills.

•Diagnosis

The skills of diagnosis include observing, listening, analyzing, and predicting. Adequate diagnosis depends upon an ability to distinguish between relevant and irrelevant elements that operate within a given situation.

Identifying symptoms is not enough; one must uncover the underlying causes. The instructor is more likely to make a sound diagnosis when he is determined to understand the actual problem. To do so, the instructor must cast off unsubstantiated assumptions about people, groups, events, and other elements related to the problem; he must try to see things as they are, rather than as what he thinks they should be.

This realistic attitude helps the instructor accept people as they are. This does not mean that the instructor must tolerate irresponsible actions, inadequate performance, or laziness on the part of students. But he should recognize that people are not perfect and that the assessment of any situation involving people must take that fact into consideration.

Understanding one's own limitations is another important aspect of diagnosis. Sometimes a problem has been created by the instructor's own shortcomings, and he needs a measure of self-understanding in order to recognize where he has erred.

The instructor will find it useful to analyze each specific leadership situation calmly and methodically. He should look at the situation in terms of human attitudes and behaviors. The leader understands that individual facts cannot be interpreted correctly except as components of a larger mosaic. When all the attainable facts are examined, their real significance will usually become more evident.

In most situations requiring a leadership action, the instructor has a number of options. Because each problem is unique, considerable skill is required in selecting and executing those options which, singly or in combination, are most appropriate. Once the instructor has made a realistic appraisal of the situation, he is ready to develop a plan of action. To be successful, the plan should be coherent and at the same time allow the instructor some flexibility.

•Action

It is one thing to select an action but quite another thing to execute it. Deciding what should be done involves diagnosis. Getting it done involves carrying out the selected options or alternatives.

Action skills are very likely the most important skills possessed by an instructor. The accuracy of a diagnosis becomes moot when the instructor lacks the ability to act upon it. Assume, for example, that all or most students in a class failed a performance examination. Diagnosis calls for a new lesson plan, new instructional techniques, and a new practical exercise scenario. The instructor may recognize and accept the reality of what has to be done, but may not be capable of doing it. Action is conditioned by a leader's personality, background, confidence, and grasp of reality. Lack of experience or education, lack of initiative, rigidity, bias, and similar impediments can severely restrict a person's capacity to lead.

Action is also conditioned by forces external to the leader. The competent instructor understands his organization and the forces by which it is moved. External forces might be the influences and constraints of politics, money, or time. Although sometimes powerless, an instructor is usually able to exercise a certain degree of control over the environment in which he operates.

CHARISMA: PROS AND CONS

The word "leadership" frequently suggests a special personal quality that captures the allegiance or devotion of followers in relation to a leader. Leadership does have an aspect of charisma, but to give special prominence to the inspirational influences of leadership diverts attention from the fundamental skills that elicit desired human performance. The final proof of leadership is found in the quality of performance rendered by people, whether as individuals or as a group. Each leadership decision and each leadership act must take into account the probable attainment of desired results.

Capable leadership is not simply a matter of intuition, luck, or native ability. The fundamentals of leadership can be learned by the average individual. The concept of leadership stressed here emphasizes skills and attitudes which can be acquired by individuals who may differ widely in their natural traits and abilities. This concept stresses leadership as an organizational function rather than leadership as a personal quality.

On the other hand, leadership in the personal sense is concerned with the internal characteristics of the leader and the effect of his personality in motivating and inspiring others to follow his direction. Except for a consistently high degree of personal motivation, no single set of inherent abilities are consistent with all successful leaders.[2] It is therefore sensible to think of leadership as a function or process that can be enhanced through the application of basic human relations skills.

NOTES

1. William G. Scott, *Human Relations in Management: A Behavioral Science Approach* (Homewood, Ill.: Richard D. Irwin, Inc., 1962), pp. 392-93.
2. Exception to this statement might be taken by Fred E. Fiedler, whose research studies (see especially *Leadership and Leadership Effectiveness Traits: A Reconceptualization of the Leadership Trait Problem,* [New York: Holt, Rinehart and Winston, Inc., 1961]) indicate the possession of consistent, reliably measurable personality attributes by effective leaders.

13

THE INSTRUCTOR AS MOTIVATOR

Motivation and Needs • Overcoming Individual Obstacles • The Effects of Groups on Motivation • Creating a Climate for Learning

The success of an instructor as the leader of his students lies in his ability to motivate them. To do so, the instructor needs skills far more complex than merely being popular. An effective teacher-learner relationship is not just a matter of accommodation, but of working together cooperatively, productively, and with social satisfactions. The instructor's principal task is to create a climate for learning in which student efforts are organized and directed toward mutual goals. To accomplish this, he must understand the human needs, differences, and emotions of students. And he must possess human relations skills that are founded less on intuition and more on a firm understanding of the behavioral sciences.

MOTIVATION AND NEEDS

Motivation is an extremely important consideration for the instructor. How much a student is motivated is linked to how much value the training activity has for him personally. An instructor can increase the amount of value students will find in a training activity. His job is to discover what "turns students on" and to innovate methods and strategies that evoke student interest without straying from academic objectives.

What is motivation? A motive is a characteristic that impels change or supports human behavior. Motivation can be useful in getting people to do something they have not done before, in getting people to stop doing something they have been doing all along, or in getting people to continue doing what they have been doing.

•Maslow's Hierarchy

A commonly accepted theory of motivation has been advanced by A. H. Maslow.[1] Maslow describes people as having needs in five categories: physiological, safety, love, self-esteem, and self-actualization. According to Maslow's hypothesis, human needs can be ordered into a hierarchy, with physical needs being the most basic and ego needs being highest. In this hierarchy, a higher need does not provide motivation unless all lower, more basic needs are satisfied. When a lower level need is satisfied, it is no longer a motivator of human behavior. (See Figure 8.)

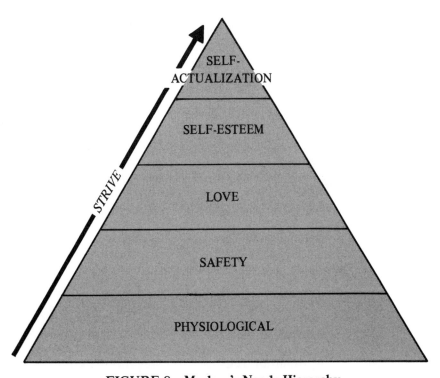

FIGURE 8: Maslow's Needs Hierarchy

In the first class are man's physiological needs: food, water, air, and rest. As long as these needs are wanting, the individual will be occupied with attempts to satisfy them. Once they are satisfied, a higher set of needs will dominate the individual's behavior pattern.

The next level of needs includes safety and security. A desire to remain free from harm or want is the prime motivator for this class of needs.

The natural human needs for belonging and love constitute the next level. When physiological and safety needs are satisfied, the individual strives for human relationships and affection. For the student, social needs include friendship, identification with the student group, teamwork, helping others, and being helped. Many students probably have satisfying relations with other people in and out of the classroom and thus satisfy this level of needs fairly well. When these needs are already satisfied, congeniality may not be an important factor in the training environment. However, when a student's social needs go unsatisfied outside the training environment, he will try to satisfy them in the classroom. The instructor has to recognize this fact and come to grips with it.

The next group of needs is concerned with self-esteem. Self-esteem needs relate to what a person thinks of himself. They include achievement, competence, independence, status, and recognition. Most of us never stop needing reassurance that we are held in high esteem by others. Even if we satisfy our ego needs today, we are certain to seek the same satisfaction tomorrow and for every day thereafter. This factor differentiates ego needs from physiological and social needs which, when satisfied, cease to motivate. For most Americans, physiological and social needs are largely satisfied. Often, the best approach for motivating students is to concentrate on the satisfaction of their ego needs.

The highest order of needs is called self-actualization. At this level, an individual expresses himself through the exercise of his capabilities. He achieves satisfaction through self-fulfillment. The search for knowledge, the development of one's own potentiality, and the creative urge are expressions of self-fulfillment. Satisfaction of this student need offers the greatest opportunity and challenge to the instructor.

The major concepts of Maslow's theory can be summed up by saying:

1. Man is a continuously wanting animal. When he has been satisfied in one need, he develops desires in another.

2. When a person's needs have been satisfied they cease to motivate. A person must feel a need before he is moved to initiate, change, or sustain his behavior.

3. Identical needs may be satisfied in different ways. A person who needs money may be motivated to obtain it through hard work or by stealing.

4. A given style of behavior may satisfy more than one need. There may be several reasons why an individual will work hard to obtain money. He may be trying to obtain social prestige, or power, or he may crave material goods.

5. An individual's attempts at need satisfaction will not always please other persons. Obviously, the person who fulfills a need to obtain money by robbing banks will not make a bank manager happy. Neither will an instructor be happy if a student cheats on an examination because of a need to obtain status among fellow students.

●Maslow in the Classroom

What are the implications of Maslow's ideas in respect to teaching and learning? A look at the hierarchy reveals that the needs most closely related to learning are relatively high. They cannot be expected to operate as motivators of behavior unless the more basic physiological, safety, belonging, and self-esteem needs have been met.

Can it be said that students will automatically strive for learning when all lower level needs have been met? The answer is no. One student, his full range of needs rather fully satisfied, may feel he can coast along. His level of learning may be reduced. A student's determination to study hard is not necessarily correlated with pleasure or happiness. Another student, his needs also largely satisfied, may set for himself a high goal and work toward it, thus improving his learning. This student's determination springs from a desire for self-fulfillment. Continuing satisfaction of needs for many students may not mean a condition of happiness, but a condition of tension that motivates them on to greater accomplishments.

Basic to an understanding of human needs is the recognition that a person responds to other people, situations, or problems as they are perceived, not as they actually are. If a student sees a training objective as a path to the attainment of one or more of his personal goals, he will tend to be a hard-working student. If, however, a student sets his personal goals relatively low, his need may be easily satisfied. The student feels himself successful if he meets or exceeds his own goals, which may be less than what is minimally expected of him by school standards.

This discussion of human needs points up the difficult job that an instructor has in developing student desires for learning. It is not enough for an instructor to simply teach. He must establish conditions in which students can fulfill their ego needs and at the same time achieve learning goals. The essential task of an instructor is to act as middleman between the training organization and the student. Using a variety of teaching methods, the instructor negotiates, arbitrates, and finally produces an arrangement that allows students to meet personal aspirations while still meeting the training organization's academic requirements.

OVERCOMING INDIVIDUAL OBSTACLES

Learning is a process of modification and growth that takes place in the individual. Each student has separate aspirations, anxieties, frustrations, hopes, and potentialities. The instructor's obligation is to challenge each student within his capability to learn and to "grow." The instructor who understands what obstructs learning, as well as what encourages it, increases the chances for success.

To treat a person as just one unit within a group of students is a surefire way of alienating those who need individual assistance.

When human relations are tailored to correspond with the composite personality of the student group, the building of genuinely effective relationships with individuals is compromised. Some adjustment must be made for the differing life experiences and abilities of students as separate persons.

When considering the relative abilities and aspirations of students, the instructor needs to be aware that people are greatly dissimilar in intellect, imagination, and interest. In every course, students will differ in aptitude, with some able to learn faster and more readily than others.[2] Any one student is a complex combination of strengths and weaknesses, curiosities, drives, and abilities.

●Conflicting Objectives

The desires of student and trainer are essentially parallel: the student wants to learn and the school wants to teach. It would be unrealistic, however, to ignore the fact that many training problems grow from a conflict between what students specifically want and what the training institution is prepared to provide. The student often sees the fulfillment of a role as an objective of learning. For example, the student who is training to be a policeman sees himself at the conclusion of training as an enforcer of the law who wears a uniform and carries a firearm. Because of his image of the law enforcement officer's role, the student may believe that training should emphasize procedures on how to make arrests and use a firearm. The objectives of training, however, might instead stress teaching a student to exercise great caution and restraint in the use of a firearm and the making of arrests. The practical demands of the learning situation require the instructor to address student expectations and at the same time achieve established learning objectives.

●Stress

A student who is prevented from reaching personal goals will experience inner stress. Beyond a certain level, stress is sure to erupt in a reaction of some type.

One common type of stress reaction is anger. Everyone gets angry occasionally. Anger is, in fact, a normal human emotion. When stress intensifies, anger gradually builds up to hostility, with a tendency to damage or destroy the person or object viewed as the source of stress. The teaching environment permits few direct outlets for anger. Consequently, anger is often expressed in indirect ways. An angry person, for example, may shout, curse, slam a door, or release his frustration in a number of relatively safe ways. Because of social conventions, a student's aggressiveness in the classroom is usually subtle. He may try to turn other students against the instructor, refuse to participate in classroom activities, or try to embarrass the instructor by challenging the accuracy of his information. When the instructor is not the object of aggression, a frustrated student may vent his hostility on another person or a neutral object. A physical assault by one student upon another or malicious damage to school property could be examples of stress reaction.

Another type of reaction is to give up. This occurs when an individual finds stress too difficult and admits defeat. His reaction may involve physical as well as psychological withdrawal. A student who chooses to withdraw might walk away from the teaching situation and never come back, or he might turn psychologically inward and ignore activities around him. Sometimes a student withdraws because he cannot meet academic standards. He may have failed to grasp fundamentals in the early stages of a course and has consequently fallen behind other students in the later and more difficult stages. The student may maintain an appearance of active participation even though his attention is negligible.

A student often escapes from a stressful situation by taking mental flight. He escapes temporarily by entering a fantasy world in which he achieves his goals. Daydreaming in class is normal—we have all engaged in it—but when fantasy exceeds reasonable bounds, learning is seriously impaired. Carried to an extreme, fantasizing substitutes the easily attained accomplishments of make believe for hard-earned, real-life endeavors.

A very common student reaction to stress is rationalization. When a student cannot accept the true reason for his behavior, he has a strong tendency to rationalize. The student thinks up logical, socially acceptable reasons for his behavior. With a little effort the student may be able to justify cutting class or not completing a study assignment. A student may become so adept at rationalizing that he comes to believe his own excuses. Moderate rationalization is normal, sometimes unavoidable, and can be tolerated in its milder forms.

In addition to helping a person justify unacceptable behavior, rationalization also aids in softening the disappointment connected with substandard performance.[3] Academic mediocrity is often rationalized on the basis of refusal to become involved in the competitive race for high marks. Although rationalization is an important adjustment mechanism in helping a student relieve stress, it exacts a price in terms of learning effectiveness.

Sometimes a person will convince himself that other people are responsible for his own shortcomings or misdeeds. This form of stress reaction is called "projection." It lets a person under stress direct frustration at others rather than at himself. Projection enables a person to blame someone or something for failures that are essentially his own responsibility. For example, a student who fails a course may claim that the instructor dislikes him or the examination was unfair. The student projects blame onto the instructor or the examination rather than onto himself. Such projections protect the individual's need for self-esteem.

A person acquires his individual reaction pattern the same way he develops habits. At first, stress reactions are conscious and deliberate. Over time, stress reactions form a pattern that becomes at least partially automatic. A reaction pattern can work to the advantage of the student by helping him to process routine stress and construct defenses against feelings of failure or unworthiness. However, the instructor should watch the behavior of students and identify stress reactions that interfere with learning.

THE EFFECTS OF GROUPS ON MOTIVATION

The goals of an individual will vary, depending upon the social systems within which he is behaving at any point in time. Most students operate within at least two social systems. There is the system of relations with fellow students, and there is the system of relations outside the training institution. To some extent, student motivation, and hence performance, is shaped by these two sets of social relationships.

●Informal Student Groups

Many students fulfill their social needs through membership in a small, informal group. In fact, it is likely that an individual student will belong to several informal groups.[4] One group might be established on the basis of friendships, another on the basis of shared common interests, and another as the result of students studying together.

The sum of an informal group is something more than the total of its parts. Members obtain satisfaction in being accepted by the group, and the group itself wields an influence over its members. In contrast with a formal organization, which is an organization on paper, the informal group is a living social organization, with all the intricacies and feelings associated with human relations.

A cohesive student group is likely to manifest a high degree of teamwork and thereby derive social satisfaction from learning together. A cohesive group usually has higher morale and lower classroom absenteeism than a group which lacks cohesion. The cohesiveness of a student group is a motivating ingredient for better learning performance. This, of course, holds true only if the norms of the group are essentially in line with learning goals. When group norms conflict with learning goals, poor student performance can be expected. A cohesive group will ostracize members who do not conform to group norms. It will reward those who do with approval and acceptance.

Thus, student performance levels are potentially changeable by changing the group norm in a direction desired by training management. Such a change, however, requires that the group be convinced that harder work is in its own interest. The instructor sees greater student effort as desirable—a means of achieving the institutional goals of high-quality students. The group, however, may see hard work as a disruption in its established habits and social life. To resolve this conflict and help the student group perceive its goals as being in line with institutional goals, the instructor will need to use a wide range of motivational techniques. (See Chapter 2.)

We often find that individual students interpret academic requirements as standards to be avoided wherever possible. When this type of perception constitutes a group norm, a student who wishes to be part of the group will resist the standards in exchange for social acceptance. But the student who sees academic excellence as a path to certain goals may choose to ignore the group norm, and as a consequence risk rejection by his fellow students.

●An Experiment in Group Pressure

Solomon Asch demonstrated through experiments that a cohesive work group can exert powerful pressures on individuals to conform to group norms. Asch assembled seventy-nine men in a classroom for what they were told would be an experiment in visual judgment. The subjects were shown two large white cards. The first card bore a single line. The second card bore three lines of varying lengths. One of the three lines on the second card was exactly the same length as the single line on the first card. The men in the experiment were told to select one of the three lines on the second card and match it against the single line on the first card. The differences in line lengths on the second card were rather substantial.

What was not known to one of the subjects was that all other members of the group were in collusion with the experimenter. All but one of the group were told beforehand to give incorrect answers in unanimity at certain intervals during the experiment. The single subject who was not a party to the plot was the real focal point of the experiment. He was placed in a position of doing one of two things: he could declare his judgment and thereby contradict the majority of the group, or he could agree with the majority thereby contradicting the evidence of his own eyes. Under group pressure the minority individual yielded to the majority's incorrect judgments in 36.8 percent of the selections.[5]

●Social Status outside the Training Institution

When academic excellence holds promises for social and economic advancement, the student for whom these goals are important will see hard work at studies as a path to success outside the school. But not all students are strongly motivated to increase their status position in the outside community. Instructors frequently assume that such a motivation does exist. This may reflect a projection of instructor aspirations onto students. For example, an instructor in the twilight of his years, long retired from the profession he now teaches, may strongly believe that training is a not-to-be-missed opportunity for getting ahead. He believes that students share his values and will work hard to achieve social goals that exist outside the training institution. He is often disappointed when the behavior of students does not conform to the expectation.

Furthermore, there are many goals outside the training institution which may be socially rewarding to the individual. Students frequently participate in social and fraternal organizations, churches, recreational programs, and similar activities. To the extent that the student receives extensive social rewards from such activities outside the training environment, he may have only slight interest in his studies. For such an individual, scholastic achievement may have no relationship to social goals.

CREATING A CLIMATE FOR LEARNING

To be successful, the instructor must use what he has learned about motivation—especially student needs and goals—to develop a climate for learning.

●Positive vs. Negative Motivation

Motivation can be positive or negative, and sometimes a combination of both. The traditional teacher-learner relationship is ready-made for negative motivation. A curse of the traditional style of teaching is its built-in propensity for authoritarian leadership. The authoritarian teacher generally restricts student participation and dominates the center stage of instructional activities. In a learning environment characterized by a teacher who is master and students who are subordinates, there is an inherent element of fear. Spurring people to action through fear is the basis of negative motivation. The fear of an instructor's criticisms, the fear of reprimand, the fear of a failing grade, the fear of academic probation, and the fear of expulsion are examples of negative incentives. Motivational techniques that employ negative incentives are founded on the premise that students will work toward training objectives not because they are persuaded of the value of the objectives but because they have no other choice.[6]

Positive motivation involves the establishment of mutually cooperative attitudes between instructor and students. There is an atmosphere of acceptance and approval of the training organization's objectives. There are many techniques for promoting positive motivation. A simple yet very effective technique is to keep students informed. When a student realizes the benefit or purpose of the instruction, he is more likely to increase his efforts to succeed and, in the process, to derive more enjoyment from his work. People feel insecure when they do not know what is expected of them. An instructor can reduce student insecurity by clarifying academic requirements and teaching methods. By giving clear and logical assignments, discussing individual and class progress, and by making advance notices of tests, the instructor meets student needs for security.

●**Challenge vs. Threat**

Creating a healthy climate for learning requires teaching techniques that will personally challenge each student. The goal is to open avenues for exploring new knowledge and to provide a chance for the student to grow intellectually. Challenge is enhanced when the instructor is able to construct learning situations that encourage students to work diligently at the business of learning. Care must be taken, however, to prevent challenge from being confused with "threat."

The challenge for learning provided by the instructor can sometimes be viewed by the student as threatening. The instructor who is insensitive to the potential impact of the learning challenge runs the risk of alienating his students. The difference between threat and challenge rests not so much in what the instructor believes he is doing but in what the students believe him to be doing. The instructor who pushes his students to extend the limits of their individual abilities believes that he is providing a challenge. His students on the other hand may see the situation as a threat. A probable result is that students will develop a defense against the threat, rather than respond to the challenge. The instructor should consequently recognize that a learning situation intended to challenge students may contain an element of threat to them. This is not to suggest that instructors should avoid instructional approaches that require hard work for students. The idea is to keep students busy at learning instead of defending themselves against threats, real or imagined.

●**Praise and Criticism**

To maintain satisfactory progress and enjoy the feeling of achievement, the instructor must establish a climate in which both praise and criticism are handled honestly and tactfully.

When a student excels, he expects to be recognized for it. Praise or credit from the instructor will not only reward a student but will provide him with an incentive to do even better. In the absence of encouragement, a student is liable to become frustrated and confused. When applied judiciously, praise will pay extra dividends in student achievement.

Although praise should be given for outstanding work, the instructor is also obligated to point out student mistakes. Whenever the quality of a student's effort is less than expected, the instructor must provide an explanation of why the work is deficient. A student cannot remedy his shortcomings if he does not know what they are. He needs constructive criticism to be able to correct his errors.

●**Innovation**

In attempting to create a climate conducive to learning, the instructor should be alert to new ideas. Sometimes he will need to innovate to meet the special needs of a particular class or lesson.

Innovative teaching methods more often than not simply involve minor adaptations and rearrangements of older, established methods. Rarely does a genuinely new teaching method appear on the scene. Even then, careful scrutiny usually reveals that it is nothing more than an older method renamed, or a recombination of something used before. Most so-called innovations are deeply rooted in past achievements.

The concept of innovation is hard to pin down. The word itself conjures up wide-ranging and conflicting ideas. Innovation is sometimes associated with words like creative, flexible, uninhibited, free-flowing, and so forth. In other cases, innovation is linked to eccentricity, radicalism, quackery, or nonconformity. Those who react negatively to innovation are likely to do so because the concept implies change. In some circumstances, opposition to change is based on fear that it will lead to human obsolescence.[7] At a minimum, a person can expect innovation to result in changes that affect status, position, esteem, and other aspects of a social nature.

Innovation is also stifled by habit. People and the organizations to which they belong operate through established routines. Attitudes and behavior are shaped by patterns of everyday living founded on habit. There is, of course, nothing sinister about habit. It prevents confusion and disorder. Within the patterns of human habits, the instructor can find chances to be innovative.

Natural human inertia is a restrictive factor. Many persons are willing to do something different only if they are required to do so. They seem to feel comfortable with the principle of physics that a body at rest remains at rest until subjected to an outside force. Simple inertia has been the downfall of many an innovative idea.

Perhaps the most powerful source of resistance to innovation is fear. An instructor may worry about being ridiculed for trying something different, or he may be concerned about losing status among his instructor peers. The potential innovator may fear being branded as an oddball or maverick. Above all, he dreads the thought of appearing foolish.

To be innovative, the instructor must overcome human opposition, most especially his own hesitancy to face the risks associated with originality. While it would be unwise for an instructor to pursue every new idea with unbridled enthusiasm, there is an ever-present need for him to apply imagination and fresh approaches in teaching.

NOTES

1. Maslow's hypothesis was advanced in an article entitled "A Theory of Human Motivation" which appeared in the *Psychological Review* 50, pp. 370-96, 1943.
2. *Principles and Techniques of Instruction* (Washington, D.C.: Department of the Air Force, 1974), p. 14-4.
3. Ibid., p. 14-3.

4. Conrad M. Arensberg, *Research in Industrial Human Relations* (New York: Harper and Row Publishers, Inc., 1957), pp. 144-45.

5. Solomon E. Asch, "Opinions and Social Pressure," *Scientific American* (November, 1955).

6. An interesting parallel to negative motivation is found in the "be strong" approach described by George Strauss and Leonard R. Sayles in *Personnel: The Human Problems of Management* (Englewood Cliffs, N.J.: Prentice-Hall, Inc., 1967) pp. 132-33.

7. Leon C. Megginson, *Human Resources: Cases and Concepts* (New York: Harcourt, Brace and World, Inc., 1968), p. 33.

14

THE INSTRUCTOR AS COUNSELOR

Counseling Methods • The Interview

A correlative function of teaching is to assist students in solving personal problems that detract from learning. Counseling can occur in almost any situation which brings the individual student and the instructor together for the purpose of helping the student to work out a problem. An instructor has a responsibility to guide each student in directions that will permit the student to devote sufficient attention and efforts to his studies.

Guidance should serve all students and should not be identified as a service intended only for problem students. If guidance is focused primarily upon students who are below academic standards, other students may be reluctant to seek help for fear of being identified as academically inferior.

A fundamental purpose of guidance is to help the individual student learn to deal with his own problems. This function of counseling places a heavy responsibility upon the instructor. The instructor should be able to help each student make intelligent decisions about his training program, social activities that are concurrent with training, and long-range job goals. To succeed, the counselor must be skillful in identifying student needs and in providing opportunities for the student to answer his own needs. Besides having a sincere desire to help the student, the instructor needs patience, confidence, judgment, and the ability to communicate on an interpersonal basis.

The instructor should avoid making decisions for a student. Providing too much assistance to a student is about as bad as not assisting at all. The overly helpful instructor is apt to develop in the student a sense of dependence rather than self-reliance.

The opportunities for an instructor to counsel students are frequent and varied. Perhaps the earliest opportunity occurs when a training program first begins. The new student is confronted with the requirements of becoming geographically oriented, meeting new people, and learning the rules under which the training institution operates. Often he is unsure of his ability to meet academic standards. Through the process of orientation, the instructor can counsel students about course requirements and school rules or regulations. The instructor can promote a sense of individual and collective belonging by arranging for students to meet one another. A well-planned and well-executed orientation will often prevent small initial problems from mushrooming into larger problems at a later time.

Throughout training the instructor is in a uniquely suitable position to evaluate each student's aptitude, interest, potential, and performance. Knowing something about an individual student is the key to providing helpful counsel to that student. If the instructor is to guide a student toward learning and career goals, he must have an understanding of the student as a person and must also possess practical and current information on matters relating to immediate and long-range job opportunities.

COUNSELING METHODS

The counseling session employs methods that differ from those used in the classroom. There are three general approaches to counseling—directive, nondirective, and co-analysis.

●Directive Counseling

The directive approach to counseling is instructor-centered. The instructor takes the initiative in the dialogue between instructor and student. Information flows from the instructor to the student, with the instructor choosing the ideas or subjects. The directive approach is designed to help a student understand what is expected of him and to help him eliminate or modify those deficiencies which obstruct learning. The directive approach, although instructor-centered, can only be successful if there is a sincere effort by the student to face and solve his problems.

●Nondirective Counseling

The nondirective approach to counseling is student-centered. The student is encouraged to talk, to "get his troubles off his chest," to clarify his own thinking, and in general to discover the solution to his problems by talking them out.[1] Through this process, the instructor encourages the student to assume the initiative in discovering solutions to his own problems and to move positively and constructively toward implementing those solutions. The nondirective approach can be successful in breaking down emotional blocks and releasing self-actuated motives for improvement.

●Co-analysis

The co-analysis approach falls somewhere between the extremes of directive and nondirective methods. This midway approach has the advantages of the directive and nondirective methods but, in addition, offers the instructor greater flexibility. Co-analysis is intended to produce a joint diagnosis of problems. The student and the instructor work together as a team to identify the student's problems and work out a program of solving them. This approach, of course, can only succeed if the student is willing to accept the instructor as a partner and sincerely wants to help himself. Empathy is an important quality in the instructor, who must be able to grasp how the student sees himself in his environment. Empathy is very often the key to the instructor's true understanding of the student and the student's understanding of himself.

THE INTERVIEW

Whatever general approach is used, a counseling session should be preceded by careful preparation.[2] The instructor should gather and study available data on the student, giving careful consideration to the student's abilities, aptitudes, and career desires. The instructor should commit to memory sufficient information so that during the interview there will be no distractions from referring to notes, records, or files. The presence of files or records and the taking of notes during an interview situation can inhibit the student.

The physical setting for the counseling interview should be relatively free from interruptions and out of general view. A student being counseled does not want to feel conspicuous. Privacy helps a student overcome his natural unwillingness to open up to the instructor.

Seating arrangements, lighting, room temperature, and the physical features of the interview room should make the student feel comfortable and at ease. Bright lights can promote a harsh atmosphere; dim lights can produce a sinister atmosphere. A room that is hot can be psychologically oppressive; one that is cold can detract from a warm and open counselor-student dialogue. Chairs placed too far apart can give the student a feeling of isolation, while chairs placed too closely together can make the student feel trapped. When the student has a timid personality, it might be useful to provide a chair that is larger or higher than that used by the instructor, thus giving the student a feeling of importance. But if the counseling session involves a disciplinary matter, it might be useful to seat the student in a chair smaller or lower than that of the instructor. And since a successful counseling session depends upon the undivided attention of the student, the student's chair should not face a window or outside area.

The initial phase of a counseling discussion is critical. It establishes the tone of the interview and influences the student's confidence in the instructor. Time spent showing interest in the student at the outset is likely to prove worthwhile later during the session. A few moments spent in establishing rapport with the student actually saves interviewing time in the long run.

Establishing rapport, however, is easier said than done. The counselor should not reveal his own attitudes or opinions at the opening of an interview. Doing so might cause the student to respond during the interview with information he believes the instructor wants to hear rather than what the student himself thinks. The purpose of the counseling is likely to be defeated by input of misleading and irrelevant information. A traditional way of establishing rapport is for the instructor to touch upon topics of common interest such as the student's achievements, strengths, hobbies, current events, and even his family matters. Such topics encourage the student to begin talking and help the instructor learn a little more about the person he is counseling.

Giving the student the chance to talk and to participate actively in the interview makes him feel that he is helping himself. In the early part of the interview, the interviewer should look for information that will help him diagnose the student's problem. By asking questions that require more than yes or no answers, the counselor can gain insights into the student's personality, attitudes, and reactions. The responses not only help identify or clarify problems but may also provide valuable clues to ways of leading the student to a solution of his own problems.

The student should be encouraged to freely express his thoughts in his own words with as few interruptions as possible. The instructor should talk only when the student is unable to continue. If the student becomes confused or lost in detail, a slight prompting can restore the student's flow of information. A helpful question is sometimes all that is needed to restore the conversation.

It is important that a student leave a counseling session feeling that some positive step has been taken toward a solution to his problem. Otherwise the session will have been completely wasted and probably prove counterproductive. Even if the student is only helped to realize the actual nature of his problem, this accomplishment itself represents progress. The instructor is sometimes unable to recommend solutions to certain problems because their resolution lies outside his area of competency. The instructor must recognize his own limitations and be prepared to turn to other persons or agencies. Problems that are psychiatric, financial, or religious demand specialized assistance. Referring students to highly specialized individuals or agencies for additional assistance is an acceptable and potentially beneficial procedure. It frees the instructor to concentrate on counseling to solve academic problems, and it keeps the instructor from becoming overly involved in problems beyond his scope and capabilities.

When the instructor refers a student to some outside source for assistance, he should follow up to be sure the student's problem is being addressed. A tactful display of interest assures the student that the instructor cares about him.

A record should be made of every counseling session. While it may not be desirable to take notes during the interview, it is important as quickly as possible following the interview to record its main points. A brief memorandum of the interview should include a description of problems discussed, courses of action proposed and agreed upon, and student decisions. Since confidentiality is an essential condition of successful interviewing, any records made of an interview should be limited to those persons having a need to know.

NOTES

1. Michael J. Jucius, *Personnel Management* (Homewood, Ill.: Richard D. Irwin, Inc., 1955), p. 170.
2. Ibid., p. 168.

15

THE INSTRUCTOR AS WRITER

Self-Appraisal • Preparing to Write • The Selection of Words • Paragraphs
• The Fog Index • Summary

An instructor really has no choice about whether or not he should write. Written communication is a part of teaching. Rather than trying to avoid it, an instructor with little talent for writing should search for ways to improve.[1]

SELF-APPRAISAL

Self-appraisal is the key to improvement. A cursory look at the products of writing, however, is not enough if the instructor wants to make a thorough self-appraisal. An instructor may struggle for years knowing that he does not write well, yet never know why. Although he recognizes writing as a personal shortcoming, he may never attempt to pinpoint and objectively analyze specific deficiencies. A first step is to identify problem areas. There are at least four important aspects of writing that deserve a careful look: organization, appropriateness, directness, and correctness.

●Organization

Clear, logical organization leads to clear, logical meaning. If the meaning is not clear, the writer has wasted both his time and that of the reader and may have even conveyed false or distorted meanings. If the idea does not stand out as clearly on the written page as it does in the writer's mind, the idea is not adequately expressed.

In organizing information, there are three principal considerations: coherence, unity, and emphasis. If an instructor organizes information with attention to all three elements, he can feel reasonably sure that his writing will be effective.

Coherence means that the writing moves with a natural flow from one idea to another. Each sentence contributes something to an idea and advances its meaning. Each paragraph is constructed according to a logical and planned arrangement. There is a perceptible progression of thought along a predetermined route.

Coherence can be likened to a series of visiting places along an established route, with the element of *unity* emerging as the route itself. Unity means that a single theme is stated early and repeated throughout. The writer stays with his theme, avoiding side roads which delay his arrival at the intended destination. Unity helps the reader travel without getting lost. It keeps the central message unmistakably clear from start to finish. Sentences and paragraphs may vary in length and purpose, but they are all unified in the sense that they work together toward a common goal.

The third element of good organization, *emphasis*, requires the writer to shift and sort his ideas before he commits them to paper. Some material may be relevant, while some material is less relevant or not relevant at all. Certain ideas may deserve prominence and others none. Some facts may be major and others minor. Such distinctions need to be made before writing begins. Information that does not support or contribute to the main message should be discarded. Relevant information needs to be organized so that important points stand out. The writer can do this in several ways:

- State directly that an idea is important;
- Provide emphasis through the use of italics, underlining, or the use of capital letters;
- Set the main idea physically apart from lesser ideas;
- Enhance an important idea through graphics;
- Devote more words to a major idea, explaining it in greater depth and detail and repeating it in a variety of ways;
- Examine the idea from several different perspectives so that it stands out by contrast over lesser ideas.

An instructor can be confident about his writing when he has limited his copy to key points that support a main theme, and when the theme moves along smoothly from sentence to sentence, paragraph to paragraph.

•Appropriateness

Appropriateness means that writing style should correspond to the topic. For instance, treating a serious topic flippantly is inappropriate. Frivolous language helps little to promote understanding of serious themes. The use of a joke to explain something serious might entertain the reader, but it is likely also to cause him to miss or forget the essential point. Humor can be effective, particularly in writing lesson plans, but when used inappropriately, it detracts from clear exposition of ideas.

Appropriateness also means that the material is suitable for the reader. How much a reader understands depends mainly on the reader's knowledge and background—not the writer's. A writer communicates effectively only when he selects words and combinations of ideas that have meaning to the reader. A common mistake is for an instructor to organize written teaching materials in terms that are perfectly clear to himself, but not at all clear to the students. Materials intended for use by students should be pitched at their presumed level or slightly below. (The reading skill of a target audience is usually lower rather than higher than what is predicted.)

The writer is free to use technical terms when the readers have the appropriate technical training; otherwise the language must be simple and nontechnical. Professional lingo, abbreviations, acronyms, and the like make reading difficult and hide the meaning.

●Directness

A reader can usually detect ideas that are presented superficially. He is quick to spot flowery language that is intended to disguise a lack of depth in the subject.

A reader can tell if an author is sincere. He is likely to give honest consideration to an idea presented with sincerity. Knowing this, the writer places his thoughts on paper as simply and as honestly as he can.

Directness is achieved with simple, uncomplicated sentences that can be easily read and quickly comprehended. It is not necessarily true that simple and short sentences make dull reading.

Word selection need not be restricted to a small vocabulary. The writer chooses exact words to express exact meanings. While it may be helpful to have a large vocabulary, it is far better for the writer to use a few precise words rather than an abundance of unclear words. In a letter to a friend, Mark Twain wrote, "I notice that you use plain, simple language, short words, and brief sentences. That is the way to write English."[2] Very good advice, indeed.

A simple way to achieve directness is to write in a conversational manner.[3] There is a built-in directness to oral communication. Without it, there would be breakdowns in the everyday, routine interactions of people. When a person wants a door kept shut, the spoken message is "Please keep the door closed." When the message is placed into writing, however, it might read, "It is respectfully requested that the door be maintained in the closed position." Written messages not only tend to be longer than oral ones, but they become indirect and impersonal as well. Written messages can be improved if they are written naturally and directly, much like spoken messages. When a person formulates his thoughts in writing as naturally as if he were speaking, he makes it easier for the reader to understand.

●Correctness

The correctness of writing relates to the accepted usage and standards of language. A writer's message may be well organized, appropriate, and direct, but if it contains many errors in usage the reader is apt to ignore it, concluding that it was prepared by an uneducated person. Even when ideas are sound and based on thorough topic knowledge, they are weakened by incorrect language.

The most common errors of usage occur in spelling, punctuation, capitalization, and the agreement of subjects and verbs. A writer who is reasonably competent in these areas will probably have little difficulty with other standards of correct usage. Learning the rules of language is like learning to type. A novice typist must consciously think what finger is used for a particular typing key. With practice, the typist becomes more proficient and needs less conscious effort to hit the right keys with the right fingers. Learning to follow language rules is similar. The novice writer must think about rules in order to comply with them. As his experience grows, he begins to apply the rules almost automatically. Just as the typist learns to type almost effortlessly, so the writer acquires a facility for writing without worrying too much about the rules.

PREPARING TO WRITE

To develop a more effective writing style, the following general suggestions can be invaluable to instructors.

●Know Your Purposes

Good writing rests upon the bedrock of preparation. Preparation involves thinking about your subject and determining the purpose for writing about it. Every piece of writing should have at least one worthwhile purpose or remain unwritten. Writing may be done to (1) direct, (2) inform, or (3) persuade. Writing that is directive usually emphasizes what is to be done; informative writing tells how to do it; and persuasive writing attempts to convince the reader why it should be done.

Purposes often overlap, as when the announcement of a change is accompanied by a reason for it. For example, if its purpose is to announce and gain acceptance of a change, the writing must state the change in terms that encourage understanding and agreement.

●Identify Main Ideas

Deciding what to leave out is nearly as important as deciding what to put in.[4] Information not important to the achievement of your purposes should be left out. Unessential ideas obscure and weaken. Preparing to write is mainly a process of defining, selecting, and discarding until only the primary message stands out, well supported by relevant ideas.

Is there a technique for identifying main ideas? There are several. One is the technique used in advertising contests which asks contestants to complete a sentence that begins "I like Humpty Dumpty Toothpaste because . . . . " The contestant simply supplies his "why" reasons for liking the product. Using this technique, an instructor of correctional science could, for example, attempt to persuade students of the value of work release programs by supplying reasons why such programs are needed. Other main ideas also surface by including "what" a work release program is, "how" it works, and "who" it affects.

It is important to distinguish between main ideas and supporting ideas. Main ideas are so vital to a writing purpose that the absence of one main idea places the others out of balance. There is an approximate equality among main ideas and, as a general rule, a writing will have not more than five. A writing in this sense means a lesson plan, a student handout, a reading assignment, or any training document equal to or smaller than a chapter in a book. The writer who finds he has more than five main ideas would do well to analyze his material to see if he has raised a lesser or supporting idea to the level of a main idea. The difference between a main idea and a supporting idea can be explained by examples. The main ideas in a writing intended to describe a truck would logically include engine, transmission, chassis, body, and cab. It would not be proper to treat the carburetor, muffler, or steering wheel as main ideas. They are supporting ideas. If the purpose is to describe a truck's performance, the main ideas might be speed, payload, and durability, with supporting ideas of range, comfort, and economy.

●Research the Topic

Research begins with an exhaustive examination of the writer's personal thoughts. Everything the writer knows or thinks he knows about the topic should be jotted down. This reveals gaps that will need to be filled in from other sources. It also guarantees that the final product will contain at least some original ideas of the writer and not just a rehash of old ideas. Organizing preliminary notes in the form of an outline helps the writer catalog the significant pros and cons of the subject. It also helps during the research phase to record on small file cards important facts or ideas together with references to the original sources.

●Write from an Outline

A working outline is more a sketch than a blueprint. It provides the writer with a visual picture and makes it easy to revise when better ideas or newer facts emerge. A paper of any type can be written more quickly and cogently when prepared from an outline. An outline need not be so detailed as to show an entry for every paragraph. It is quite common in writing from an outline to add, often spontaneously, points not covered in the outline.

When working from a long outline it can save time to draft each paragraph, double spaced, on a separate sheet of paper. Confining each paragraph to a single sheet of typing paper discourages long-winded paragraphs. This procedure also enables a writer to rearrange paragraphs in new combinations.

The general structure of a working outline might look like this:

I. Introduction.
   A. Statement of the paper's specific objective(s).
II. Body.
   A. Main idea.
      1. Supporting idea.
      2. Supporting idea.
         a. Lesser supporting idea.
   B. Main idea.
      1. Supporting idea.
         a. Lesser supporting idea.
         b. Lesser supporting idea.
   C. Main idea.
III. Conclusion.
   A. Summary of reasons that merit accomplishment of the objective(s).
   B. Recommendation, i.e., restatement of the objective(s).

(All outline entries which fall on the same dotted line are of relatively equal importance.)

●Review and Revise

When a first draft is completed the writer needs to review and revise. In addition to the routine search for violations of writing rules, the instructor evaluates his own objectivity in presenting his thoughts. Whether the purpose is to direct, inform, or persuade, the reader has every right to expect the writing to be honest. Anyone who writes a paper, particularly a paper that is intended to result in student learning, has spent time gathering facts and contemplating their meaning. Interpreting the facts is usually the most important part of the paper. The author has an obligation to his readers to clearly state what he believes is true. At the same time, he must fairly and honestly identify points that are controversial or unresolved.

THE SELECTION OF WORDS

The day-to-day language of education or training suffers from an overdose of many-syllabled words of obscure meaning. A large vocabulary which allows a writer to be precise in his choice of words is an important asset. It helps the reader to quickly grasp a writer's thoughts. But an extensive vocabulary becomes a detriment when a writer reaches for a big word when a simple word will do just as well.

Each trade or profession seems bent nowadays on coining a complex jargon known only to its members. Much of the trend toward technical language is intended to impress rather than express.[5] This trend is rooted in the foolish concept that complexity is a sign of wisdom. Exactly the opposite is true. Wisdom and simplicity go hand in hand. The wise mind is able to grasp a complex situation and then state it in simple, direct terms. Expressing complicated ideas in simple words is not easy. It calls for hard work and sophistication. To write well an instructor must pierce surface details, get to the heart of an idea, and express it in language that other people can easily understand.

Big words often result in obfuscation. To obfuscate is to cloud, confuse, or make unclear. The use of *obfuscate* is a good example of its definition. It is certain to occur when long, unfamiliar words are substituted for plain, purposeful words. The obfuscator will use *commence, initiate,* or *inaugurate* for *start* or *begin*; he will pick *accomplish, consummate,* or *effect* for *do*; and prefers *transmit, communicate,* or *forward* in place of *send.* The usual reason for the selection of big words is a writer's desire to impress. But few Americans today are fooled by fancy language.

●Verbs

Verbs are the electricity of language.[6] They provide vigor and directness. "The baserunner steals third base." That sentence has an active verb. "Third base is stolen by the baserunner." Something has gone out of the sentence. The spark of immediacy is missing.

Verbicide is the offense of killing an active verb by making it into a noun, which requires the use of a passive, weaker verb. A simple direct sentence such as "She decided to act" is converted to "Her decision was to act," or worse still, "The decision she arrived at was to take action." The idea gets smothered in extra words that are derived from active verbs. In successful writing, strong verbs account for about 10 percent of all words used. But in most writing for instructional purposes we find few active verbs. Consider this sentence taken from a handout for students for a course in personnel supervision: "The controversial ruling requiring mandatory arbitration of the employee grievances in question is being viewed with misgiving by management and labor alike." The absence of active verbs makes the handout hard to read.

The verb is the life of the sentence. Simple, direct verbs are often strangled with useless phrases. The best way to show this is through examples. Here are sentences that suffer from passive verbs. In each instance the active verb would make better reading.

PASSIVE: When an application of polish is made to the leather a color is imparted to it.

ACTIVE: Polishing the leather colors it.

PASSIVE: Teaching practices were based on the assumption that students were willing partners in the teaching-learning experience.

ACTIVE: Teachers assumed that students wanted to learn.

PASSIVE: Examination of her broken leg was conducted by the doctor.

ACTIVE: The doctor examined her broken leg.

Active verbs shorten sentences as well as bring them to life. When verbs are changed to gerunds or participles, the bounce is lost. Their suffocating presence in prose is easy to spot. The italicized words in the following statement are verbs smothered inside gerunds or participles:

The director stated yesterday that any *continuation* of expansion would be unlikely. The *opposition* of the Board to amalgamation was stressed in the annual *announcement*. Adding of new functions is not expected unless *enrollment* goes up.

Observe the word endings. They are *-tion, -sion, -ing,* and *-ment*. Others to be leery of are *-ant, -ent, -ance, -ence, -ancy,* and *-ency*. These endings—in the right instances—are very useful, but when poorly used they distract and obscure.

Punchy, active verbs provide zip. A lively writing style accounts for much of *Time* magazine's success. In the following example, a *Time* writer grabs the reader's attention through the skillful use of verbs:

In a gush of good will, the 95th Congress *convened* amid clinking glasses, receptions that *stumbled* on into the evening hours and cozy chatter about a new comradeship between Capitol Hill and the White House. Nearly 200 children *gamboled* about the House floor as all but one of the 435 Representatives *attended* the opening ceremonies, many bringing their families.

The event is described vividly. The reader can picture it in his mind. The verbs are direct.

●Adjectives

Although a warning must be made that adjectives can detract from writing which reports or informs, their use in the preceding example from *Time* is judicious and deserved. The nouns are tastefully flavored with a sprinkling of adjectives. "Clinking" and "cozy" give the reader a feel for the situation.

The argument against adjectives lies in the premise that readers prefer fact to opinion. When a report states that "the Mideast situation is extremely volatile" the writer is expressing an opinion. More convincing evidence of extreme volatilty would be the fact that Israeli and Egyptian tank forces were lining up on both sides of the Gaza Strip.

Similarly, exaggeration will turn readers off. Words that overstate stand out and become targets for dispute. A reader of the following announcement is entitled to be skeptical:

> Incalculable sums and strenuous effort have been expended to make this year's program hugely exciting and more beautiful than ever before.

Boosters like those appearing above should be used sparingly. Padding copy may be fine on Madison Avenue, but it has little acceptance in teaching, where truth and accuracy are the stock in trade.

●Crutch Words and Deadheads

Crutch words and deadheads are a drag to lively writing. Some writers develop a dependence on certain terms or phrases. A common crutch is *very*; it has been so overworked as to lose its meaning. Another is *such*. The uncaring writer uses such in place of *this, that,* and *these*. "The products of such writers suffer from such careless habits." A deadhead gets its name from an old railroad expression meaning a nonpaying passenger. A word that adds nothing to a sentence is like a passenger that takes up space but contributes nothing to the cost of the trip. Following is a list of deadheads. In parentheses are words that can be used in their place.

- at all times (always)
- at present (now)
- at any early date (soon)
- at your earliest convenience (when convenient)
- in compliance with your request (as you requested)
- in the near future (soon)
- in the event (if)
- in the amount of (for)
- in order to (to)
- in light of the fact that (as)
- afford an opportunity (permit)

There are many empty phrases that a writer can omit without the slightest loss. Included are *wish to take this opportunity, take steps, in the case of, appropriate, proper, wish to state, for the guidance of all concerned,* and *reference is made to.*

●Sentences

We speak in sentences and we write in sentences. Even though a good sentence depends upon right words in right places, the sentence as a unit is of greater importance to thought communication than single words. Plain words and short, simple sentences will help a writer avoid the pitfalls of poorly constructed sentences.

For the same reason that short words are preferred over big words, brief sentences are preferred over long ones—provided, of course, that the sentence idea is not sacrificed. Sentences that read like telegrams are just as hard to understand as extended, cluttered sentences. Brevity is desirable but not to the extent that the articles *a, an*, and *the* are left out. The best way to achieve brevity is to break complex ideas down into simpler ideas and then cover the simpler ideas in bite-sized sentences, taking care to avoid deadheads and crutch words.

Stating ideas immediately and directly encourages brevity. Unnecessary expressions get in the way and tend to place part of the sentence in the passive voice. Consider this example:

TOO LONG: It was the decision of the committee to recommend approval of the curriculum.

BETTER: The committee recommended approval of the curriculum.

Modifiers are potential targets for cutting unneeded words. A modifier is a phrase that, like an adjective, describes something. The italicized words in the following sentence constitute a modifier:

Mr. McIntyre, *who is chairman of the board,* will seek re-election.

In the above example, the modifier is one word longer than the rest of the sentence. With a little cutting it is shortened to:

Mr. McIntyre, board chairman, will seek re-election.

A drawn-out sentence is a likely place to eliminate useless words. The shortened version follows this extended sentence:

There is not enough time available for the average instructor to perform all those tasks that might be done and as a consequence it is necessary for the instructor to carefully select the minimally essential tasks, do them first, and then spend his remaining time on tasks that can be done but are not critically needed.

The average instructor lacks time to do everything that might be done. He must decide what tasks are essential and do them first. He can then spend his remaining time on tasks that are less critical.

With a little careful editing a fifty-six-word sentence is broken up into three short sentences having a total of thirty-five words.

Sentences that vary in length make reading easier. An occasional long sentence is usually not difficult to understand when it is preceded and followed by shorter sentences. A reasonable goal is to limit the average sentence in writing to twenty-one words or less.

If the writing is long or complicated, the average sentence length should be cut back to between seventeen and nineteen words. When counting words in sentences, colons, semi-colons, and dashes should be considered sentence endings.

It doesn't take a grammarian to recognize a bad sentence—it is a sentence that lacks clarity. Clarity is good evidence of good grammar. If a writer can avoid misunderstanding, the grammar will pretty much take care of itself. Murphy's law—the law that if something can go wrong, it will go wrong—is very much in force with respect to clarity of writing. It is not enough to write for understanding; one must write so that misunderstanding will not happen.

PARAGRAPHS

Because paragraphs exist to make reading easier, they work best when kept short. A paragraph ought to contain only as many sentences (ideas) as the mind is able to grasp in one grouping. The central concept should move in an unbroken chain from paragraph to paragraph. The chain is only as strong as its links. A paragraph containing eight or more sentences is probably too long. Popular books and magazines usually have three to five sentences per paragraph, while most textbooks or manuals have from four to six.

Readers often need help in bridging the gaps between sentences. One way to do this is to refer in one sentence to a previous sentence. A personal pronoun that refers back to another word helps tie ideas together. The italicized word in the following example is the personal pronoun:

Hard work is essential to good teaching. *It* implies dedication and purpose.

Transitions between sentences can also be made with words like *again, besides, similarly, likewise, for this reason, of course,* and *generally.* The transitional word is italicized:

Hard work is essential to good instruction. It implies dedication and purpose. *Frequently* we forget the sacrifices that good instructors make in the name of their profession.

The first sentence in a paragraph usually introduces the key idea. When it does, the first sentence is called the topic sentence because it alerts the reader to the paragraph's topic. Occasionally a writer will place his topic sentence at the very end of a paragraph. His psychology is to build the idea slowly and then ram it home with a strong, summarizing statement. In some paragraphs, especially long ones, the main idea is stated at both the beginning and the end. Having been introduced in an initial topic sentence, it is restated in different words in the final sentence. A sentence that repeats the key idea at the end is usually called a summary sentence.

Details develop and support the main idea expressed in a paragraph. Of the many kinds of details, four are commonly used—examples, facts, incidents, and reasons. Let's use a single topic sentence to state a paragraph's key idea and then follow it with examples of the four most common types of supporting details:

Support with example: Crime continues to be a major national problem. The president stated recently that crime reduction was a high priority goal of his administration.

Support with facts: Crime continues to be a major national problem. Data collected by the FBI reveals that crimes against persons are up 8.5 percent, and that crimes against property have increased by 22.3 percent.

Support with incidents: Crime continues to be a major national problem. Only last week a U.S. Senator was robbed and brutally beaten outside his home.

Support with reasons: Crime continues to be a major national problem. There is evidence suggesting the problem stems from the judicial system's failure to function effectively.

Note that the following paragraph contains a topic sentence, supporting details, transitional words, and a summary sentence:

Unity and clarity go hand in hand. Unity means sticking to main ideas and presenting them in a logical sequence. It involves balance and harmony among ideas within the same theme. Similarly, clarity requires an orderly arrangement of words, sentences, and paragraphs. When unity and clarity are present the reader is helped to understand the writer's message.

Note that the summary sentence reemphasizes the main thought introduced in the topic sentence, that supporting details are provided, and that the transitional words help all sentences flow and blend together.

THE FOG INDEX

Robert Gunning's *The Technique of Clear Writing* provides a yardstick for measuring readability.[7] Gunning developed a method to compute a value that will indicate what reading level is necessary for comprehension of any given written material. The value, or *fog index* as Gunning calls it, represents the number of years of schooling a reader must have to easily understand the writing evaluated by his method. The average high school graduate (twelve years of education) can read, with ease, written copy with a fog index of 12 or less. As the fog index goes up, so must the reader's ability to comprehend. When the index reaches 12, the writing moves out of the comprehension range of the great majority of readers. Most magazines are found at the low end of the fog index, with college textbooks and technical papers at the high end. The higher the index rises above 12, the smaller the reading audience becomes.

The index involves two variables: sentence length and word difficulty. It can be calculated in three simple steps.

Step One: Count the number of words in successive sentences. If the copy is long, extract several representative samples of sentences having a total word count of about 100. Divide the total number of words by the number of sentences. This gives the average sentence length.

Step Two: Count the number of words of three syllables or more per 100 words. Ignore words that are proper names; combinations of short easy words like watchmaker or bookkeeping; and words that are verb forms stretched to three syllables by adding -ed or -es. The number of words thus counted per 100 equals the percentage of difficult words in the piece.

Step Three: Add the average sentence length (Step One) to the percentage of difficult words (Step Two) and multiply the sum by .4.

The number derived, i.e., the index, correlates rather accurately with the number of years of schooling that a reader will require if he is to understand without difficulty. Let's compute the fog indexes of some types of writing. The first was taken from *True Secrets* magazine:

> I toyed with my food for a while, then sipped my coffee. Later, after my tray had been removed, I lay in the bed trying not to think. Then I heard the familiar rattle of carts going down the hallway, the high-pitched wail of hungry voices . . . and then quiet. Feeding time. I wrapped the pillow over my ears to block out the painful noises. For me there would be no small red face crying for its supper tonight, no soft warm bundle to snuggle against my cheek—only silence. Why me? Why my baby? I asked myself over and over.

Number of words:	101	
Number of sentences:	9	
Average sentence length:		11
Number of words:	101	
Number of hard words:	1	
Percentage of hard words:		1
Average sentence length plus percentage of hard words:		12
Multiplied by:		.4
Fog Index		4.8

Our second sample is from Edna Ferber's ever-popular *Show Boat*:[8]

> The two were very much in love. The others in the company sometimes teased them about this, but not often. Julie and Steve did not respond to this badinage gracefully. There existed between the two a relation that made the outsider al-

most uncomfortable. When they looked at each other, there vibrated between them a current that sent a little shiver through the beholder. Julie's eyes were deep-set and really black, and there was about them a curious indefinable quality. Magnolia liked to look into their soft and mournful depths. Her own eyes were dark, but not like Julie's. Perhaps it was the whites of Julie's eyes that were different.

Number of words:	109	
Number of sentences:	9	
Average sentence length:		12
Number of words:	109	
Number of hard words:	10	
Percentage of hard words:		10
Average sentence length plus percentage of hard words:		22
Multiplied by:		.4
Fog Index:		8.8

The final sample of writing was taken from John A. Seiler's *Systems Analysis in Organizational Behavior*,[9] a text for graduate students of business administration:

If, for example, the 1966 flare-up of congressional attention on safety devices and design-manufacture practices in the automobile industry is to achieve its goal of making automobile fatality statistics less appalling, it must comprehend the relationships among road conditions, social mores, dominant psychological states of drivers, and a host of other factors, in addition to the adequacy of the machine. It would be ironic, indeed, if, as a result of governmental investigation, auto companies significantly improved auto safety features, thereby creating an even greater confidence in the automobile than now exists—an increased confidence which, in turn, reinforced a false sense of security in the automobile, which, when combined with inadequate roads, desires for speed and thrill, and so forth, produced even greater carnage than is now the case.

Number of words:	129	
Number of sentences:	3	
Average sentence length:		43
Number of words:	129	
Number of hard words:	27	
Percentage of hard words:		21
Average sentence length plus percentage of hard words:		64
Multiplied by:		.4
Fog Index		25.6

These three samples support Gunning's observation that there is an approximate correlation between reading levels and the fog index. Persons with low reading skills are naturally attracted to written materials that are easy to read, i.e., materials that have low fog indexes. Gunning, of course was not the first to perceive this truth. For years successful pulp magazines have maintained very constant levels of sentence length and word complexity. Each magazine works hard to create its own brand of text to attract and hold a particular segment of the reading audience. *Reader's Digest* maintains a consistent average of 10 on the fog index. The editors of commercial copy know their readers well and see to it that reader interests are satisfied. Producers of copy intended for sale are compelled by the profit motive to write with the reader in mind. Instructors, and others who write not necessarily for profit, are chiefly motivated by good sense to adjust their writing style to reader interests and abilities.

SUMMARY

Clear writing does not come easily. It results from clear thinking, hard work, and attention to details. The instructor determined to enhance learning with the help of written materials will do well to observe these points:

- Be self-critical.
- Organize before beginning to write.
- Gear the writing to the topic and reader.
- Write directly.
- Observe standards of language.
- Identify main ideas.
- Research the topic.
- Prepare an outline.
- Select words carefully.
- Keep sentences brief and to the point.
- Construct paragraphs logically.
- Prefer the simple to the complex.

NOTES

1. Lieutenant Donald C. Lee of Florida Tech's police department looks at it this way: "So you hate to write? You've got two alternatives! 1. Learn how. 2. Go into another profession." From *Report Writing for the Professional Law Enforcement Officer* (Orlando: Florida Technological University, 1974).
2. Robert Gunning, *The Technique of Clear Writing* (New York: McGraw-Hill Book Co., 1968), p. 65.
3. Rudolf Flesch, *How to Write, Speak and Think More Effectively* (New York: Harper and Row Publishers, Inc., 1960), p. 167.
4. Dugan Laird, *Writing for Results* (Reading, Mass.: Addison-Wesley Publishing Co., 1978), p. 44.

5. Gunning, *Clear Writing*, p. 177.
6. Alec Ross and David Plant, *Writing Police Reports* (Schiller Park, Ill.: Motorola Teleprograms, Inc., 1977), p. 14.
7. Gunning, *Clear Writing*, p. 49.
8. Edna Ferber, *Show Boat* (Garden City, N.Y.: Doubleday and Co., Inc., 1926), p. 91.
9. John A. Seiler, *Systems Analysis in Organizational Behavior* (Homewood, Ill.: Richard D. Irwin, Inc., and the Dorsey Press, 1967), p. 3.

Glossary

Achievement unit. *See* Criterion unit.

Advance sheet. A handout that informs the student of a pre-class requirement such as reading a chapter.

Andragogy. A theory of teaching adults. It holds that teaching programs for adults should recognize that adult learners are self-directed, have life experiences that can serve as valuable resources for learning, have a readiness to learn, and have immediate uses for acquired learning.

Approach behavior. Action that signifies a favorable feeling or desire for an object, event, or activity; a behavior that brings one closer to or in more frequent contact with an object, event, or activity. Approach behavior is the opposite of avoidance behavior.

Aptitude. A person's capacity for performance in a particular field or in several related fields.

Artificial feedback. Feedback that is not a natural result of a task. A test score is an example of artificial feedback.

Attention gainer. The first of four subcomponents comprising the introduction section of a lesson plan. The attention gainer serves to capture the student's attention.

Attitude. Personal values that can be inferred from behavior.

Audience reaction team. A team of three to five audience members who are permitted during a panel discussion to ask questions of a panel member.

Audio-tutorial instruction. Recorded instruction used by the student individually and at his or her own pace.

Avoidance behavior. Actions that signify an unfavorable feeling or desire for an object, event, or activity; behavior that is aversive and unproductive. Avoidance behavior is the opposite of approach behavior.

Behavior. Observable actions.

Behavior modification. The changing of behavior through application of reinforcement and modeling principles.

Behavioral objective. A statement that describes precisely what student behavior is to be exhibited, the conditions under which behavior will be carried out, and the minimum standards of acceptable performance for the behavior. *See also* Student performance objective.

Binary choice item. A test item that offers the respondent two answers to choose from. A true-false question is a binary choice item.

Blanketboard. A training aid consisting of a blanket that supports fabric-gripping visuals.

Body. The second of three major components comprising a lesson plan. The body consists of supporting knowledge and the practical exercise.

Brainstorming. A teaching method in which groups of about five students each propose ideas or solutions to a stated problem. The rules of brainstorming encourage uninhibited expression of ideas which are later sorted out according to their usefulness in solving the problem.

Branched task. A student performance activity that requires a covert response (thinking) that precipitates overt behavior (action).

Branching technique. A programmed instruction technique in which large segments of information are presented to a student at one time. A student's responses to questions or problems cause him or her to move along branches that provide correction and reinforcement. Branching is also called intrinsic branching.

CAI. *See* Computer-assisted instruction.

Carrel. A study cubicle for use by one or a small number of students. A carrel is normally used for presentation of programmed audiovisual instruction.

Case study. A teaching method in which students analyze realistic cases involving problems or issues. The case study is used mainly to develop problem-solving and decision-making skills.

CCTV. Closed circuit television. An audiovisual training aid.

Classroom issue. A type of student handout. When distributed in connection with a practical exercise, it gives a situation (cue) requiring the student to do something (action) which is evaluated (feedback).

Closing statement. The last of three subcomponents in the review section of a lesson plan. It is intended to permit the instructor to make a final and convincing statement regarding materials covered.

Co-analysis. A method of counseling that blends the directive and nondirective counseling techniques.

Cognitive. A term descriptive of mental activity, especially awareness and judgment. Deciding what violation to cite on a traffic ticket is a cognitive act.

Competence level. The degree of performance proficiency.

Completion item. A type of fill-in test question in which the respondent is required to complete a statement by providing certain key words or terms.

Composite true-false item. A true-false question in which the respondent is required to provide a correction if he or she identifies an error in the premise.

Computer-assisted instruction (CAI). A method of instruction in which information is presented through a variety of media that are controlled or monitored by a computer.

Concept. A class of similar ideas that constitutes a larger and more general idea.

Concept inventory. A comprehensive listing of technical concepts used by workers in a job or occupational area.

Condition. A circumstance under which a student is required to perform the action (task) specified in a training objective. For example, a condition of night firing would require the student to fire at night.

Conference. A small group discussion of a problem or issue, with the instructor as the discussion leader.

Confirmation. A notice to the student of the correctness of his or her response. Confirmation is part of the feedback process. *See also* Feedback.

Consequence. A stimulus that follows a behavior; that which happens as a result of an action.

Constraint. A restriction that prevents or limits the attainment of desired course outcomes.

Control document. Any written material or device through which a course curriculum is put into practice. Lesson plans, tests, advance sheets, and practical exercise handbooks are examples of control documents.

Cost-effectiveness. A favorable comparison of economy to efficiency in accomplishing a specific goal or objective.

Course manager. The person responsible for managing a course. A course manager typically supervises course instructors and answers to a school director. He or she performs quality control functions by ensuring compliance with the course curriculum.

Course map. A diagram or flowchart showing the modules or units of instruction and the various relationships between them.

Cover sheet. An unnumbered outer page of a lesson plan providing certain administrative data.

Covert response. A nonvisible response which a student makes internally but which is neither recorded nor otherwise discernible. A covert response is a response in which the student "thinks" an answer.

Criterion. A statement of the degree of acceptable, expected, or desirable performance.

Criterion examination. A test used in programmed instruction to evaluate student achievement of objectives. *See also* Criterion-referenced test.

Criterion frame. *See* Prover frame.

Criterion-referenced instruction. Instruction in which prespecified performance criteria are achieved by each learner. The instruction is deemed completed when the learner has met the performance criteria (objectives). Criterion-referenced instruction is intended to result in mastery learning.

Criterion-referenced test. A test to determine if student behavior that is specified in a training objective has been demonstrated.

Criterion unit. A series of frames in a programmed module that relate to a training objective. A criterion unit contains teaching frames and a prover frame. A criterion unit is also called an achievement unit.

Criticalness or Criticality. The merit of a task being included in a training program; an indication of a need, based on an important job-related consideration, that training in a particular task is essential.

Critique. A formalized, structured criticism of student performance, usually held immediately after a practical exercise.

Cue. A signal to a student to do something. A question, a problem, or a hypothetical written situation are examples of cues.

Cue/Action/Feedback sequence. A basic principle of practical application in which students are required to do something (cue), they do it (action), and are then informed of their efforts (feedback).

Curriculum. A structured series of learning outcomes; a composite of statements that describe what is to be learned in a particular course or program; a document that specifies a training program's content, order, instructional methods and strategies, testing schemes, and similar elements.

Cut-away model. A training aid that replicates a job-related item or piece of equipment. A portion of the model is usually cut away to reveal its inner parts.

Decision-making. The process of formulating and selecting between or among options.

Derived content. Tasks of a job which have been found through job task analysis or some other objective method to be appropriate for inclusion in a training program. Job relevancy and criticality are usually important factors in selecting tasks for inclusion.

Diagnostic check. A check or inquiry intended to determine why a student or students have not been able to achieve a particular performance objective or objectives.

Directed conference. An instructor-controlled discussion of a problem or issue, by a small student group, with a fixed agenda that requires certain points or ideas to be addressed.

Directive counseling. A method of counseling in which the instructor directs the student's attention to a problem and its possible solution.

Discussion plan. An outline or agenda of teaching points intended to be covered during a small-group conference.

Distractor. A plausible but incorrect answer offered as one of four or five choices in a multiple-choice item.

Distributed instruction. A teaching method that spreads the same training over a longer period of time even though total teaching hours might remain the same. Distributed instruction is the opposite of mass instruction.

Duty. A large segment of closely related tasks. It is a part of a job.

Enabling objective. A performance objective which describes a skill or competence deemed essential within a larger or more complex competence. Also called a subordinate objective or enroute objective.

Enrichment. Supplementary or "nice to know" information which aids the student in progressing through a training course but is not considered critical to learning.

Enroute objective. *See* Enabling objective.

Entry-level skills. The skills brought to a training program by a learner which are over and above competencies specified as course prerequisites. Also, the skills expected to be possessed by a person performing a job at the entry level.

Enumeration item. A type of fill-in test question in which the respondent is required to name or list a number of homogeneous items.

Equivalency test. A test that measures skills and knowledge intended to be taught in a particular course of instruction. An equivalency test is usually arranged in modules that correspond with course training objectives. Students receive instruction only in those modules where testing has indicated a need.

Essay item. A test question in which the respondent gives the answer in the form of a written narrative.

Evaluation. The process of interpreting measured student proficiency.

Feedback. Information which results from an action. From feedback, inferences can be drawn about the correctness or incorrectness of the action. Feedback may be immediate, as when an instructor criticizes a student answer during classroom discussion, or feedback may be delayed, as when student evaluation questionnaires are reviewed upon completion of a course. *See also* Artificial feedback and Natural feedback.

Field demonstration. A teaching method in which a student, usually an on-the-job trainee, is shown a task or job function in the actual work environment.

Field test. A tryout of any training on a representative sample of the student target population to gather data on the probable effectiveness of instruction.

Field trip. A teaching method in which students observe procedures or on-the-job operations at a work location.

Fill-in item. A test question in which the respondent is required to supply one or more omitted key words or terms.

Flowchart. A graphic representation of the steps in a process or system. Flowcharts have many uses in training; for example, they are used to mark the sequence of student actions in practicing a task, to depict the order and interrelationships of instructional units, and to teach complex ideas.

Fog index. A method of measuring the readability of written material.

Formal evaluation. The process of interpreting measured student proficiency in order to assign grades or make some similar decision with respect to the passing or failing of a student.

Goal-analysis. A thought process through which a goal may be broken down, analyzed, and judged for its content and meaningfulness to a training program.

Group-pacing. A teaching procedure in which students progress together toward the same objectives.

Hands-on. A term that describes a student learning activity in which students directly apply skills or knowledge. A practical exercise is a hands-on activity.

Hardware. Audio, video, and film equipment and other physical equipment usually found in a learning center.

Identification item. A type of fill-in question in which the respondent is required to examine a pictorial representation or a three-dimensional object and name things or identify errors shown.

Independent learning. Learning which occurs outside of the training environment. It may be, but is not necessarily, learning attained from homework.

Individualized instruction. Instruction which takes into account each student's personal inventory of knowledge and skills.

Informal evaluation. The process of interpreting observed student proficiency for the purpose of correcting, guiding, or assisting students to learn.

Instruction. The process by which objectives are achieved, including the mechanics for achievement.

Instructional objectives. A statement of what is expected to result from instruction.

Instructional system. An integrated combination of resources and procedures designed to efficiently achieve established objectives.

Instructional unit. An organized arrangement of a single training subject within a curriculum.

Instructor-centered. A term descriptive of lecture or simpler training approaches that place the instructor at the focal point of teaching.

Instructor guide. A publication that provides the instructor or training manager with information regarding the proper use of certain instructional materials.

Intended learning outcome. A general statement which describes the learning a student is expected to have acquired by the end of a unit or course.

Intrinsic branching. *See* Branching technique.

Introduction. The first of three major components comprising a lesson plan. The introduction consists of the attention gainer, training objectives, lesson tie-in, and motivation.

Job. The composite of subtasks, tasks, functions, and duties actually performed by an individual in a work situation.

Job inventory. An instrument used for analyzing a job. It consists of items that identify and list the subtasks, tasks, functions, and duties that comprise a particular job.

Job performance aid (JPA). A simple written reference which assists a person to perform a particular job by reducing the amount of information the person must remember in order to successfully perform the job. A list of frequently called telephone numbers that is placed adjacent to a telephone is an example of a job performance aid.

Keystoning. Distortion of a projected image caused by an incorrect angle of the screen in relation to the projector.

Knowledge. Cognition of facts, concepts, rules, principles, and other forms of information.

Lead-up frame. *See* Teaching frame.

Learning. A change in the behavior of a person as a result of experience. The behavior that manifests learning can be cognitive, physical, or attitudinal.

Learning by doing. A process in which students acquire knowledge, skills, or attitudes by perfoming planned actions.

Learning center. A place specifically created to provide individualized instruction, which employs a variety of media to augment written materials and classroom teaching.

Learning objective. An instructional goal expressed in terms of measurable student performance.

Learning outcome. *See* Intended learning outcome.

Lecture. A teaching method that depends almost exclusively upon a one-way flow of communication from teacher to students.

Lesson plan. A guide for presenting instruction, written by an instructor. It includes an outline of teaching points plus a description of the teacher and student activities planned to occur within the time allotted for the lesson or instructional unit.

Lesson tie-in. The third of four subcomponents comprising the introduction section of a lesson plan. The lesson tie-in permits the instructor to describe the interrelatedness of a unit to earlier units and to units that will follow.

Linear technique. A programmed instruction technique in which small steps of information are presented with reinforcement following each step.

Listening team. From three to five audience members who record main issues discussed by a panel and summarize them at the conclusion of panel activities.

Lock-step instruction. The more traditional method of training in which students progress through a course at the same time and at the same pace. Lock-step instruction is the opposite of individualized instruction.

Magnetic strip. A poster board visual training aid that attaches magnetically to a metal surface.

Manipulative skill. A skill that supports a task and relies on a psychomotor action, such as to adjust squelch, draw a diagram, or use a baton.

Marginalia. Entries in the margin of a lesson plan that remind an instructor to do certain things. Examples of marginalia include questions to be asked, answers to be given, training aids to be displayed, comments to be made, handouts to be distributed, etc.

Master question bank (MQB). A bank of questions from which the various tests of a single course are constructed. The MQB approach is intended to allow tests to be easily modified.

Mastery learning. That which is demonstrated when a learner consistently performs a training objective in accordance with the prespecified performance criteria.

Matching item. A test question that usually consists of two columns of items. The respondent is required to correctly pair the items. One column might be terms and the second column definitions.

Media. A general term that describes a means of effecting or carrying out some part of the instructional process. Films, transparencies, mock-ups, tools, equipment, practical exercises, critiques, and closed circuit television are examples of media.

Mental skill. A skill that supports a task and relies on a mental or analytical process, such as to analyze a traffic-flow diagram or to compute speed from skid marks.

Mock-up. A model that imitates a real object.

Model. A frame of reference, real or abstract, that is intended to assist the learning process. A mock-up device is an example of a real model; a chemical formula is an example of an abstract model.

Modeling. Learning by imitation.

Module. A unit of instruction or a portion of a training course in which one or more smaller units of instruction are grouped. A module usually represents one or more training objectives in a common subject matter area.

Motivation. The urge to satisfy a need.

Motivation subcomponent. The fourth of four subcomponents comprising the introduction of a lesson plan. Motivation is intended to give the student an incentive for learning.

Multimedia approach. The coordinated use of several instructional media for presenting information. A multimedia approach is likely to use textbooks, workbooks, films, slides, television, and audiotape.

Multiple-track scheduling. A scheduling method which allows students of different aptitudes and backgrounds to arrive at overall course goals but by different routes.

Natural feedback. The evidence of the student's own senses as he or she performs a task. An image that comes into focus as the student adjusts the focus control of a camera is an example of natural feedback that informs the student regarding the correctness of an action.

Negative reinforcement. Reward of a performance by removal of an undesirable or unpleasant consequence.

Nondirected conference. An uninhibited discussion by a small student group of a well-defined problem or issue, with minimum control exercised by the instructor.

Nondirective counseling. A method of counseling in which the student is encouraged to discuss his problem and to find a solution to it.

Nonreferenced test. A test to determine a student's achievement in relation to other students. Curve grading is an example of nonreferenced measurement.

Objective. A written statement which describes an expected learning outcome. The term "objective" takes on different shades of meaning when other terms are added to it; for example, performance objective, student performance objective, training objective, enabling objective, behavioral objective, instructional objective, etc.

Occupational survey. A device for identifying the subtasks, tasks, functions, and duties which comprise one or more jobs.

Overlearning. An intended outcome achieved through extra practice of a task. It is used to aid retention of critical skills that tend to deteriorate.

Overt response. An oral, written, or manipulative act that is visible, and thereby recordable.

Panel. A teaching method in which three to nine selected persons discuss a problem or issue in the presence of a student audience.

Pass/Fail. An evaluation technique that establishes a minimum level of acceptable student performance. A student who performs at a level of competency below the minimum level has failed the evaluation. A student who performs at or above the minimum level has passed the evaluation. A student's score is unimportant except in respect to whether it falls above or below the pass/fail line.

PE. *See* Practical exercise.

Peer teaching. An instructional method in which a student who has successfully completed a portion of training instructs another student who is still learning that portion of training. As each student learns a particular skill, he or she is required to teach the next succeeding student the same skill before being allowed to progress to the next portion of training. This concept is sometimes referred to as "go/no-go" training.

Perception. The act of obtaining information from the physical environment through the human senses.

Performance. The carrying out of an act under given conditions to some predetermined standard of completeness and adequacy.

Performance measurement. The measurement of a student's performance of a task in accordance with established standards of excellence.

Performance objective. A written statement which describes an expected learning outcome in terms of student performance. This term is synonymous with student performance objective.

Performance-oriented training. A training method characterized by objectives which state precisely what the trainee must know and be able to do as the result of training. The term "performance-oriented" is derived from the fact that the objective of training is to prepare for on-the-job performance.

Positive reinforcement. Reward of performance by the application of a pleasing consequence for the performer (learner) with the intent of conditioning the learner to want to repeat the performance.

Post test. A test that is given upon completion of a course of instruction.

Practical exercise. An applied learning situation in which students perform or practice knowledge or skills.

Practical exercise subcomponent. The third and last subcomponent in the body section of a lesson plan. The practical exercise subcomponent describes an applied learning situation that is held as a part of the lesson.

Premise. The first part of a multiple-choice item. It usually takes the form of a question or an incomplete statement. Also called a stem.

Prerequisites. Competencies (skills and knowledge) that must be possessed by a student entering a course. In the absence of the prerequisites, a student is likely to fail. For example, minimum driving skill (as evidenced by a driving license) might be one of the prerequisites to a pursuit driving course.

Pretest. A test administered prior to entry into a course of instruction. The pretest is intended to identify the entering skills and knowledge possessed by a student. It can be used to identify instructional units that a student can bypass. *See also* Equivalency test.

Program of instruction (POI). A comprehensive document designed for use in course planning, organization, and operation. A POI reflects units of instruction within the course, training objectives, duration of instruction, description of units, instructional methods and media, support material, and other guidance information. A program of instruction is sometimes called a plan of instruction or a syllabus.

Programmed instruction. An instructional method in which training is presented in small, logically sequenced steps. Each student proceeds at his or her own pace, makes active responses to requirements posed by the instructional materials, and gains immediate feedback of progress.

Prover frame. The final frame in a series of frames called a criterion unit. The prover frame tests the student's ability to perform a specified task. Also called a criterion frame.

Psychomotor. A term descriptive of physical actions that proceed directly from mental activity. Directing traffic is a psychomotor function.

Punishment. A negative incentive to student learning.

Questioning technique. An instructional technique intended to stimulate student participation in classroom discussion.

Random access. A slide projector feature that permits automatic selection of slides in any sequence desired, regardless of placement order in the tray.

Rear screen projection. A method of projection that places the image on the back surface of a semitranslucent screen placed between the audience and the projector.

Recall principle. A principle of testing in which the respondent is required to supply an answer from knowledge possessed.

Recognition principle. A principle of testing in which the respondent is required to choose from among answers offered.

Reinforcement. The strengthening of a response by its repeated association with a stimulus. The stimulus is the reinforcer which may be pleasant (positive) or unpleasant (negative).

Relevant content. Content of a training program which includes student performance of tasks that are identical or closely similar to tasks performed in the work situation.

Resource person. A person available to the instructor to assist in a variety of ways, e.g., to role-play, demonstrate, set up or operate equipment, or monitor student performance.

Response. Any activity which is set off by a stimulus. Selecting which button to press, choosing from among several alternatives, giving an oral answer, making a diagram, and solving a complex problem are examples of responses.

Retain attention. The first of three subcomponents in the review section of a lesson plan. It is intended, following the conduct of a practical exercise, to recapture class attention.

Review. The third of three main components of a lesson plan. It represents the final portion of instruction on a particular subject. The review consists of retain attention, summary, and closing statement subcomponents.

Reward. A positive incentive to student learning.

Scope. A brief statement of key topics covered within one instructional unit.

Scrambled book. A programmed text with pages that are numbered in the usual way but which are not read consecutively.

Selection item. A type of test question in which the respondent selects an answer from offered choices. A selection item is based on the principle of recognition.

Self-paced instruction. A teaching method which allows students to progress through an instructional program at their own rate.

Sentence form (or narrative form). A writing style used in preparation of a lesson plan. Each key teaching point and supporting point is described in complete sentences so that its meanings and interrelationships are made clear.

Simulation. A teaching technique in which real-life job characteristics are imitated.

Situational item. A test question in which the respondent is required to analyze a situation and formulate a response in a manner specified in the question.

Skill. A human performance activity that involves psychomotor dexterity. A skill often requires knowledge or cognition for proper execution.

SME. *See* Subject matter expert.

Software. Slides, films, tapes, and similar items used with hardware in a learning center.

SPO. *See* Student performance objective.

Standard. A criterion for evaluating student performance of the action (task) specified in a training objective. An example of a standard would be "with 70 percent accuracy."

Stem. See Premise.

Stimulus. The signal or cue to which a response is made.

Student centered. A term descriptive of training approaches that cause students to be the focal point of instruction. Such approaches emphasize what the student has acquired through training rather than what the instructor has taught.

Student-centered instruction. An instructional approach in which students are active participants.

Student handout. Any material given to the student to keep for study or future reference. Classroom issues and summary sheets are types of student handouts.

Student performance objective (SPO). A statement consisting of conditions, an action, and standards, in that order. The conditions are circumstances under which an action must be performed; the action is a statement of the task specified in the training objective(s); and the standards are the criteria for satisfactory performance.

Subject matter expert or specialist (SME). A person who has a thorough knowledge of instructional content and material. The SME is usually an experienced practitioner who also knows the theoretical aspects of his subject.

Subordinate objective. *See* Enabling objective.

Sub-subtask. A supporting knowledge or skill. Also called a teaching point.

Subtask. A part of a task.

Summary. The second of three subcomponents in the review section of a lesson plan. The summary provides a recapitulation of key teaching points, particularly as they relate to specified training objectives.

Summary sentence. A sentence that summarizes the key idea in the last sentence of a paragraph.

Summary sheet. A student handout normally distributed to students during the review portion of a lesson presentation. It summarizes the main points of an instructional unit.

Supply item. A type of test question in which the respondent provides an answer from knowledge possessed. A supply item is based on the principle of recall.

Supporting knowledge. The second of three subcomponents comprising the body section of a lesson plan. The supporting knowledge subcomponent comprises that body of information which must be understood by a student for him or her to perform tasks specified by training objectives.

Supporting skill. A skill that supports the performance of a job-related task. The skill might be manipulative in nature, such as skill in firing a revolver, or mental in nature, such as skill in interpreting body language.

Symposium. A panel method of teaching in which the audience has an opportunity in advance of the session to study the issue and to prepare questions that challenge panelists to defend their views.

Systems engineering. A methodical process for planning and developing instructional programs to teach the skills, knowledge, and attitudes essential for successful job performance.

Target population. The students or persons for whom instructional materials are designed.

Task. A discrete unit of work performed by one person, with a definite beginning and a definite end.

Task analysis. A process of describing job tasks in terms of human performance requirements for the purpose of designing an instructional system that will meet operational needs.

Task inventory. A listing of all tasks comprised in a job.

Task inventory questionnaire (TIQ). A task list with one or more questions asked concerning each task. A TIQ is used in task analysis.

Teaching frame. A frame containing information to be learned by a student receiving programmed instruction. Information presented in teaching frames is tested by a prover frame. Teaching frames are also called lead-up frames.

Teaching machine. Any of several devices used in programmed instruction. Continuous active student response to information provided by a teaching machine gives the student practice and testing of knowledge presented in the program.

Teaching point. A key piece of knowledge or skill that supports the performance of a task.

Teaching points outline. An outline of key ideas planned to be covered in the teaching of a subject. A teaching points outline can be a part of a lesson plan but is not a plan in itself.

Team teaching. A teaching method in which two or more instructors share the responsibility for teaching one or more subjects. The method might involve instructors as rotating speakers, panelists, evaluators, monitors, or coaches.

Terminal objective. An objective which describes a skill or competence representing a final outcome of a course. Enabling objectives might be sub-elements of a terminal objective since, by definition, they are parts of a larger or more complex objective.

Topic sentence. A sentence that introduces the key idea in the first part of a paragraph.

Training aid. Any item that assists in teaching or learning.

Training objective. A training objective specifies student performance behavior that must be exhibited for it to be said that training has been successful.

Training objective(s) subcomponent. The second of four subcomponents in the introduction of a lesson plan.

Transfer of learning. The application of acquired knowledge to real-life situations.

True-false item. A test question consisting of a premise followed by two choices, usually true/false or yes/no.

Validation. The process of evaluating and revising instructional material so that intended learning outcomes are attained.

Venetian blind. A type of training aid consisting of strips in a ladder arrangement. Each strip has a very brief written message. Strips can be covered or uncovered one at a time.

Verbicide. Making an active verb into a noun, which requires the use of a passive, weaker verb.

Index